# That Ever Loyal Island

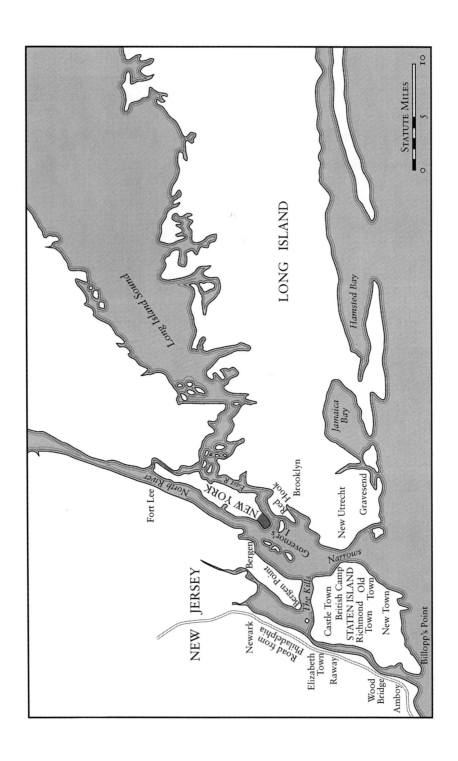

STATUTE MILES

NEW JERSEY

NEW YORK

LONG ISLAND

Long Island Sound

North River

Fort Lee

Bergen

Bergen Point

Road from Philadelphia

Newark

Elizabeth Town

Raway

Wood Bridge

Amboy

Billopp's Point

The Kills

Castle Town

British Camp

STATEN ISLAND

Richmond Old Town Town

New Town

Narrows

New Utrecht

Gravesend

Governor's I.

Red Hook

Brooklyn

East R.

Jamaica Bay

Hamsted Bay

# That Ever Loyal Island

*Staten Island and the
American Revolution*

Phillip Papas

NEW YORK UNIVERSITY PRESS
*New York and London*

NEW YORK UNIVERSITY PRESS
New York and London
www.nyupress.org

© 2007 by New York University

First published in paperback in 2009.

Library of Congress Cataloging-in-Publication Data
Papas, Phillip.
That ever loyal island : Staten Island and the American Revolution /
Phillip Papas.
p. cm.
Includes bibliographical references and index.
ISBN-13: 978-0-8147-6766-5 (pbk. : alk. paper)
ISBN-10: 0-8147-6766-4 (pbk. : alk. paper)
ISBN-13: 978-0-8147-6724-5 (cloth : alk. paper)
ISBN-10: 0-8147-6724-9 (cloth : alk. paper)
1. Staten Island (New York, N.Y.)—History, Military—18th century.
2. Staten Island (New York, N.Y.)—Social conditions— 18th cen-
tury. 3. New York (N.Y.)—History—Revolution, 1775–1783—
Campaigns. 4. United States—History—Revolution, 1775–1783—
Campaigns. 5. New York (N.Y.)—History—Revolution,
1775–1783—Social aspects. 6. United States—History—
Revolution, 1775–1783—Social aspects. I. Title.
F127.S7P37     2007
974.7'02—dc22          2006036581

New York University Press books are printed on acid-free paper,
and their binding materials are chosen for strength and durability.

Manufactured in the United States of America

c   10 9 8 7 6 5 4 3 2 1
p   10 9 8 7 6 5 4 3 2 1

*To my parents Nicholas and Elisabeth Papas
and to my brother Peter*

# Contents

# Acknowledgments

This book could not have been completed without the encouragement and valuable assistance of family, friends, and colleagues. I am especially thankful to Professor Carol Berkin, my dissertation adviser at the City University of New York Graduate Center, who has influenced much of my thinking about Colonial and Revolutionary America. Her patient guidance, valuable advice, and constructive criticism helped me clarify my arguments, reexamine my assumptions, and improve the quality of my work. Professor Berkin guided this study while it was still a dissertation, and her steadfast support always inspired me and lifted my spirits. To her I owe an enormous debt of gratitude.

In addition, my thanks go to the members of my dissertation committee, Professors Eli Faber, Jacob Judd, and Jonathan D. Sassi, for their comments and insightful critique of the study.

Thank you, too, to my colleagues Angelo Angelis, Laura Chmielewski, Kathy Feeley, Cindy Lobel, Julie Miller, Mark Sgambettera, and Iris Towers. They read drafts of chapters, listened to my ideas, and offered many excellent suggestions that sharpened my arguments and improved my grammar. Their friendship, generosity, and scholarly camaraderie will always be treasured.

I want to thank everyone at New York University Press and especially my editor Deborah Gershenowitz for her advice and enthusiastic support of this book. She deserves special praise for shepherding the project and for her work to make the manuscript better. I also want to thank the reviewers at New York University Press, especially Robert M. Calhoon, for their constructive comments. Their suggestions have helped me tell more effectively the story of Staten Island in the American Revolution.

I want to take this opportunity as well to thank the many archivists, librarians, curators, and genealogists who promptly responded to my questions and aided my search for materials. I wish to thank especially the staffs of the Staten Island Historical Society; the Staten Island Institute of Arts and Sciences; the New York Historical Society; the New Brunswick (Canada) Museum and Archives; the Harriet Irving Library at the University of New Brunswick in Fredericton, New Brunswick, Canada; the New York Public Library, especially its New Dorp, Richmond Town, and St. George branches on Staten Island; the Saint John Public Library in Saint John, New Brunswick, Canada; the Mina Rees Library at the CUNY Graduate Center; the Kenneth C. Mackay Library at Union County College; and the College of Staten Island Library. A thank-you also goes to the staff and board of directors of the Conference House Association for their efforts to preserve the history of the Billopp manor house. Special thanks to Katherine Hilder of the Harriet Irving Library at the University of New Brunswick; to Patricia M. Salmon, curator of history at the Staten Island Institute of Arts and Sciences; and Elisabeth Sommer, the former director of research and interpretation at the Staten Island Historical Society. Thanks also to Hugh Powell, a volunteer researcher at the Staten Island Historical Society, for his conversation and for sharing with me his extensive knowledge of Staten Island's history, and to Dr. John R. Dungan for providing me with the genealogical information about the Dungan and Charlton families.

I was especially fortunate to work with Carlotta DeFillo, the librarian at the Staten Island Historical Society. Her kindness, diligent assistance, accommodating nature, cheerful enthusiasm, and shared admiration for Staten Island's past always made my visits to the society's library and its archives a great joy. Her remarkable patience as I meticulously went through each collection in the archives will always be fondly remembered and appreciated.

A blanket thank-you must go to all the teachers in my life. I could not have reached this moment without their knowledge, support, inspiration, caring words of advice, and enthusiasm for teaching. Thank you to Professors Hans L. Trefousse, Ari Hoogenboom, and Barbara Welter for believing in me.

Thanks to the local historians of Staten Island who came before me. Their work built a solid foundation for all future research into the island's past.

Thank you to my late friend Anthony Schifando, who was the caretaker of the Conference House where I worked for several years as a docent, for his support and encouragement. I will never forget the conversations that we had and the laughter that we shared. He will always be in my thoughts and prayers.

Finally, I want to express my deepest gratitude to my parents Nicholas and Elisabeth Papas and my brother Peter. My parents have always stressed to my brother and me the importance of education. They not only gave us moral and emotional support but also instilled in us a tireless work ethic and dogged determinism. They never allowed me to give up on the pursuit of my dreams. Words alone cannot express my admiration for them. They have given me more than one could imagine. And to my brother Peter, his friendship, advice, and support I appreciate and cherish more than he knows. It is to them that I dedicate this book with all the love in my heart.

Driven by social military history

not successful.

Not organized

No propaganda

Local

*Revisionist –*
*Revising the old ideology*
*Case Study*

# Introduction

*How Loyalism develops*
*Chronological + Building Forward.*

*90%*

In 1775, Alexander McDonald of Staten Island, New York, was deeply disturbed by the "unhappy State of America."[1] Although he initially had been content to leave the debates over colonial rights to others, McDonald could no longer remain silent as, in his words, "madness prevails all over America" and "King & Country [are] reviled & their Laws treated with Contempt."[2] For McDonald, the moment was extraordinary because the American colonists were "Commencing Rebellion."[3] By 1775, the colonists' protests against British imperial policy had escalated, leading some Americans, like McDonald, who valued their bond with Britain, to do what they could to defend "the Authority of the Parent State."[4]

Many of Alexander McDonald's neighbors on Staten Island shared his views of the imperial crisis. In fact, almost 99 percent of Staten Islanders remained loyal to the Crown by defying the colonial resistance movement and refusing to support American independence. Loyalism was thus a communal experience both unique and important to Staten Island. This book analyzes how such factors as the island's expanding commercial agrarian economy, the deferential structure of its society and political culture, its history as a British military staging area during the French and Indian War (1754–1763), the methods used by the Whigs[a] to enforce con-

[a] The term Whig refers to the earlier supporters of a limited monarchy and guarantees of political and religious liberties in Britain. To Whig propagandists, colonists who refused to cooperate with the colonial resistance movement and resisted the measures taken by the Continental Congress were enemies of American liberty. The Whigs labeled these Americans Tories, after the traditional supporters of the authority of the church and the monarchy in Britain. American Tories believed that the political impasse between the colonies and Britain could and should be peacefully reconciled. They felt that colonial grievances could be redressed within the existing framework of government and by means of negotiation. As the American Revolution progressed, the terms Patriot and Loyalist were used to denote the differences between the two opposing viewpoints.

I

*Self-interested choice*

formity to the colonial resistance movement, and the creation of an Anglican culture hearth contributed to the Staten Islanders' decision to remain loyal. These factors set the scene for understanding Loyalism on
Staten Island in reference to local considerations and its residents' lived
history.

Using Staten Island as a case study, I explore several issues pertaining
to the American Revolution and Loyalism. The first is that Loyalism was
a logical and self-interested choice that was equally as progressive as the
Whig cause. Second, the Loyalists were a potential source of support for
Britain and a counterweight to the colonial resistance movement. Finally,
the effect of the war on the populations of Staten Island and adjacent
communities in New Jersey shows that the northern theater of the American Revolution was more than a singular contest between conventional
armies, that it was a vicious civil war pitting family members and neighbors against one another. This study's emphasis on these issues places it in
the revisionist historiography of the American Revolution and Loyalism.

Loyalism in American historiography is first found in the highly na-
tionalistic, patriotic literature that followed the American Revolution,
which either ignored or treated the Loyalists as the villains of the revolutionary conflict.[5] The noteworthy exception is Lorenzo Sabine's *Biographical Sketches of Loyalists of the American Revolution*, which is
sympathetic to Loyalist aspirations.[6] Then, during the first two decades
of the twentieth century, scholars who had abandoned the intense na-
tionalism of the previous century rescued the Loyalists from historical
purgatory. Many of these scholars—most notably Moses C. Tyler, Claude
H. Van Tyne, and Alexander C. Flick—examined the Loyalists from the
dual lenses of intellectual and institutional history. Whereas Tyler assessed the Loyalists' arguments against revolution and for empire, Flick
and Van Tyne explored the legal and political dynamics of the Loyalists'
relationship to royal officials and the newly formed state governments.[7]
In particular, Flick's *Loyalism in New York during the American Revolution* (1901) brought attention to state laws and committees designed to
control and to punish Loyalists and subsequently influenced numerous
state studies of the subject.[8]

With the emergence of the Progressive school of historiography following the 1909 publication of Carl L. Becker's *History of Political Parties in the Province of New York, 1760–1776*, scholars developed a social
profile of Loyalism. Because Progressive scholars viewed class struggle as
the most important characteristic of early American politics, their studies

*Was not reactionary*

At First dismissed

Why

Who they were

often depicted the Loyalists as wealthy white males: merchants, large landowners, professionals, royal officials, and Anglican clergy. Progressive scholars saw these men opposing American independence because their social position depended directly on the British government. They also argued that the Loyalists feared a successful war for independence because it would disrupt the social and political hierarchy and lead to major class antagonisms in American society. Historians later challenged the Progressives' social profile of Loyalism, insisting that the Loyalists comprised a heterogeneous group that included not only wealthy white males but also white male yeoman farmers, skilled artisans, journeymen, apprentices, day laborers, shopkeepers, schoolteachers, free and enslaved African Americans, Native Americans, and their wives and families.

mixed

One of those scholars challenging the Progressive paradigm was Leonard W. Labaree. In his *Conservatism in Early American History* (1948), he argued that regardless of their social position, the core of the Loyalists' experience was a shared fundamental caution and fatalistic pessimism: "Loyalism in the Revolutionary period, while it had for many men an economic basis, cannot be explained wholly on materialistic grounds, nor can the Loyalists be fully classified into economic groups." Instead, Loyalism "was not only a consequence of social or economic position; it was quite as much the result of an attitude of mind." For Labaree, the "Tory Mind," which refused to accept a future without guarantees and feared that colonial resistance and American independence would lead to social upheaval, was shaped by an individual's circumstances, regardless of his political ideology or social class standing. Thus, he urged historians to look beyond the narrow constraints of ideology and social class to "factors of personality, of individual conditioning, of subconscious motivation, and of sheer human inertia" when discussing the Loyalists' response to the American Revolution.[9]

Attitude of mind

William H. Nelson's *The American Tory* (1961) also remains an important work in the field of Loyalist studies. Nelson maintained that the Whig leadership's ability to formulate a clear argument favoring independence and republicanism provided the energy necessary to drive the American Revolution. The Whigs' success was the result of a "commonness of purpose" that was seriously lacking among the Loyalists. Unlike the Whigs, Loyalist leaders never created the propaganda or the effective communications network to disseminate their ideas and shape public opinion. Thus, the Loyalists never coalesced into a coherent movement but instead were fragmented both socioeconomically and regionally. Nelson contended that the Loyalists were motivated to oppose revolution and independence by various disparate factors stemming from concerns about self-preservation, personal animosities, and political and social rivalries.[10] Other scholars, notably Robert M. Calhoon, agreed with Nelson, finding no direct connection between ideology and the Loyalists' motivation. In *The Loyalists in Revolutionary America, 1760–1781* (1973), Calhoon wrote, "Loyalist beliefs and pretences never coalesced into a common, vital persuasion with its own logic and momentum," adding that the events of the American Revolution "moved too rapidly for them, constantly cutting the ground of their arguments . . . and frustrating their belated and often clumsy attempts to rally their adherents to action."[11] Like Nelson, Calhoon saw a myriad of factors in shaping Loyalist motivations and actions.

In contrast, Ann G. Condon and Janice Potter refuted the Nelson–Calhoon thesis, contending that regardless of social class or region, the Loyalists' shared ideology promoted a strong commitment to the supremacy of Parliament, affection for the empire, and a fear that revolution would destroy political and social stability and cause anarchy to descend on America.[12] In *The Liberty We Seek: Loyalist Ideology in Colonial New York and Massachusetts* (1983), Janice Potter argued that the Loyalists' rejection of American independence and republicanism and their support for British imperial rule "merits definition as an ideology because it was a comprehensive, logical, and consistent alternative to Patriot proposals."[13]

In the late 1960s and early 1970s, scholars made an effort to produce a more comprehensive and balanced history of the American Revolution. In his 1974 biography of the Massachusetts royal governor Thomas Hutchinson, Bernard Bailyn stressed the need "to see the Revolutionary movement from the other side around."[14] The studies of Loyalism that were produced during this period relied solely on the experiences of the social elite and depicted Loyalists as tragic figures caught in a vortex of events that they could not control. Although these studies focused on the Loyalist elite, they also described the dilemma faced by many Americans who chose to remain loyal.[15]

The mid-1980s witnessed a resurgence of state studies reevaluating the methods and interpretations employed by Alexander C. Flick and others at the turn of the twentieth century. These studies synthesized the earlier institutional history with the approaches pioneered by Labaree, Nelson, and Calhoon. Although they did not ignore the various state laws and committees designed to curtail and punish Loyalist behavior, studies by Rick J. Ashton, Robert S. Lambert, Anne M. Ousterhut, Philip Ranlet, and Dennis P. Ryan concentrated on the Loyalists' personal thoughts and individual actions and motivations.[16]

More recently, the focus of Loyalist studies has shifted to the local level, to explain the Loyalists' motivation and behavior from the perspective of the economic, political, and social relationships forged over time by the residents of a particular community. Beyond its importance to the study of Loyalism, the localist paradigm looks at the American Revolution as a civil war. With only a few exceptions, historians of the American Revolution have not paid much attention to the local dynamics of the war in the north,[17] instead applying the localist paradigm mainly to southern communities.[18] Moreover, historians have treated the extreme episodes of partisan warfare in the war's northern theater as tangential to the conventional combat operations of the two main adversaries. But in many northern communities, partisan warfare carried out by Whig and Loyalist guerrilla bands was the norm, not the exception.[19]

My study of Loyalism and the American Revolution on Staten Island, New York, addresses many of these issues. It draws on the insights of those historians who have examined the local Loyalist experience and on the recognition that the American Revolution was both a civil war and a war for independence. This study applies these insights to northern communities, thereby extending the notion of the American Revolution as a civil war outside the south.

Chapter 1 discusses the island's physical and cultural landscape, including several variables that affected the settlement and development of Staten Island into a society of prosperous yeoman farmers inclined to favor political moderation over radicalism. It challenges the problematic assumption made by local historians that Staten Islanders lived in economic isolation. The island's geographic proximity to the urban markets of New York City and New Jersey and its network of roads and ferries linked Staten Island to the transatlantic market economy and exposed Staten Islanders to manufactured goods that they did not produce for themselves. The chapter points out that the island's physical landscape helped produce a pattern of mixed farming that utilized slaves, indentured servants, and wage laborers that contributed to the development of Staten Island into a prosperous community of commercial agricultural production. Moreover, the island's dense hardwood forests, offshore fisheries, and oyster and clam beds provided residents with an extra source of food and income, and its long jagged shoreline helped produce a cottage industry of clandestine trade. Staten Island's physical landscape and its location at the entrance to New York Harbor also contributed to its economic prosperity and its value as a strategic military site.

Even though it was ethnically and religiously pluralistic, Staten Island was principally Anglican. Chapter 1 also tracks its success in cultivating a shared sense of English identity and bringing Anglican uniformity to the island. In this way, chapter 1 offers a historical account of Staten Island's transformation into a hearth of Anglican culture and shows its political significance to the island. Both the Crown's sovereignty as well as English religious and cultural institutions were securely extended to Staten Island.

Chapter 2 examines the methods that Staten Islanders used to avoid participating in the colonial resistance movement against British imperial policy. The community's strong sense of social and political deference had conditioned most of its residents to defer judgment on political issues to a small group of prominent men who favored reconciliation over resistance. The chapter also describes the political measures that the Whigs undertook to coerce Staten Islanders into conforming to the colonial resistance movement. These measures convinced Staten Islanders that the Whigs posed a greater threat to their community's political and social stability, its material prosperity, and the islanders' individual liberties than did the British government.

Chapter 3 outlines the Whigs' plans for the military campaign of 1776 in the region around New York City and its failure to defend Staten Island against a British landing. It demonstrates that the Whig military commanders were acutely aware of the local political culture in situating and organizing their forces. Chapter 3 also points out that the measures imposed by the Whig military authorities for the effective governance of the island placed additional strain on the relationship between Staten Islanders and the Whigs.

Chapter 4 explores Staten Island's pivotal role in Britain's plans for the military campaign of 1776. The chapter recounts the events leading up to the decision by General William Howe, the commander in chief of the British army in America, to secure Staten Island as a prelude to military operations against New York City and examines Staten Island's strategic and logistical advantages to the British. The chapter also discusses the island's history as a military staging area during the French and Indian War (1754–1763) and points out that this experience fostered amicable relations between Staten Islanders and British military personnel. In the summer of 1776, Staten Island's Loyalists welcomed the British military as liberators, and this chapter looks at the logistical problems faced by the British and the actions that they took to secure supplies, firewood, and livestock from the island's residents. In addition to giving the British logistical support, Staten Islanders gave them information about the movement of Whig troops in the region and the strength of their defenses. They also readily joined the British army. Indeed, by late August 1776, Staten Island had been transformed into a British fortress, a military force moving into a specific social environment. General Howe had amassed 32,000 soldiers and sailors, including Loyalist refugees and Hessian mercenaries, and more than 450 warships on the island.

Chapter 5 is a historical account of the events that shaped Staten Islanders' wartime experiences. Staten Island remained under British occupation for seven and a half years, longer than any other community in America. Although a large part of the regular British army had left after August 1776, the British still used the island as a military staging area for operations in the middle colonies, a hospital, and a base for Loyalist refugees and the provincial regiments that they joined. Thus, the fact that the regular British army had moved on from Staten Island did not mean that the war had moved on as well. In addition, the American Revolution brought new challenges: plundering, kidnapping, physical violence, murder, rape, economic stress, and partisan warfare. Staten Islanders were terrorized daily by bands of Whig and Loyalist partisans and abused by disillusioned and poorly disciplined British regulars and their Hessian allies. The realities of the war and the British army's failure to protect them eventually led many Staten Islanders to question their initial political loyalty to Britain.

Staten Island was a community on the periphery of the British Empire and accordingly was constantly subjected to the unanticipated force of imperial decisions regarding war and peace. Just as the Anglican culture governed the island in the 1760s, political and military realities held sway in the late 1770s and early 1780s.

Even though the experiences of Staten Island's Loyalists were replicated in other areas of America, Staten Island presents a unique case. Historians have explained the origins of the strong Loyalist sentiments in some communities of New York's Hudson River valley as arising from conflicts between landless, oppressed tenants who yearned to own property and the wealthy landlords who denied them that opportunity or, as in the case of the North Carolina Regulators, from economic and political animosities between backcountry farmers and the tidewater planter elite. But Loyalism on Staten Island was rooted in the community's experience of social stability. This had been brought about by decades of political and social deference by a population composed of middle-class property owners long settled on their lands, the tremendous influence of the Anglican Church in the community, and the development of transatlantic commercial ties threatened by colonial boycotts and a war for independence. In essence, the communal experience of Staten Island Loyalism sets it apart from other communities that have been studied.

The implications of Loyalism and the American Revolution on Staten Island extend beyond the confines of community-based studies. They remind us of the importance of the local environment where ordinary Americans lived and enable us to view similarities in vastly different regions. This study also allows us to ask questions about New York's political culture during the American Revolution and the city's complex socioeconomic and political relationship with its neighboring communities. The threat posed by Staten Island's Loyalists to the security of New York and New Jersey introduces an investigation into the relationship between the Whig governments of these two states. In addition, this study of Loyalism and the American Revolution on Staten Island may prompt new questions about military-civilian relations in areas occupied by either the British or the Continental army. It could also give historians a new perspective on the northern theater of the American Revolution as a civil war. Finally, it enables a better understanding of the revolutionary struggle and an appreciation of individuals' and communities' difficult choices when confronted by the events of the American Revolution.

Argument: Staten Island being unique

# 1

*(handwritten: ① Prime Farm Land Wheat ② Osters)*

## The Crossroads of the Middle Colonies

### *The People, Society, and Environment of Staten Island*

*(handwritten: NY - Polyglot - diverse ✳ Sandy Bottom Slaves / Free Black man)*

On October 30, 1748, Peter Kalm, a protégé of the Swedish botanist Carolus Linnaeus, boarded "a wretched half rotten ferry" at Elizabethtown, New Jersey,[a] that took him across the Arthur Kill.[b] "As soon as we had got over the river, we were upon Staten Island," he wrote in his travel journal, adding, "this is the beginning of the province of New York." As he crossed the island, Kalm was fascinated by its physical and cultural landscape. "The prospect of the country here is extremely pleasing," he commented. "It offers more cultivated fields" than anywhere else, and its topography is broken at places by "hills and valleys." Although Kalm often had been optimistic about other places he visited, in this particular case it was true. He also noticed that "most of the people settled here were Dutchmen, or such as came hither whilst the Dutch were yet in possession of this place, but at present they were scattered among the English and other European inhabitants." Staten Islanders "spoke English for the greatest part," Kalm noted, and established prosperous farms located close to one another. Kalm ended his trip to the island the next day by boarding another ferry "to cross the water, in order, to come to the town of New York."[1]

Staten Island is located about ten miles southwest of Manhattan at the confluence of the Hudson, Passaic, and Raritan rivers. Roughly 13.9 by 7.3 miles at its maximum dimensions, the island measures 57.1 square

[a] Present-day Elizabeth, New Jersey.

[b] Or Staten Island Sound.

9

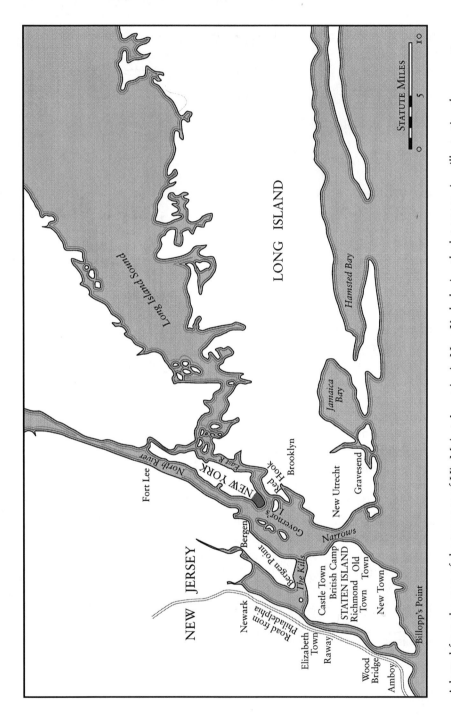

Adapted from the map of the progress of His Majesty's armies in New York during the late campaign, illustrating the accounts published in the London Gazette, ca. 1776. Courtesy of the Staten Island Historical Society.

miles, or about 36,600 acres. The island's eastern shore borders upper New York Bay, and its western shore runs along the Arthur Kill, a waterway that separates Staten Island from New Jersey at distances of often less than five hundred feet. The Kill van Kull and Newark Bay separate the island's northern shore from New Jersey's Bayonne peninsula, and its southern shore runs along the Atlantic from lower New York Bay to Raritan Bay. The Narrows, a body of water one mile wide that is located at the entrance to New York Harbor, separates Staten Island from the western end of Long Island. Two ridges of hills rise up from the island's landscape, the taller of which is more than four hundred feet and runs six miles from the eastern shore to the center of the island,[c] with the smaller ridge extending southwest from the Narrows and rising to more than 170 feet. Staten Island's extensive shoreline is broken by numerous coves and inlets, shallow bays, and tidal marshes. The island's topographic features—its proximity to New York City, New Jersey, and Long Island, its location at the entrance to New York Harbor, and its extensive shoreline—not only give Staten Island important regional and economic advantages but also provide a valuable strategic military site.

Today, the dense development of suburban townhouses and malls makes it difficult to imagine the physical landscape and the natural abundance that Peter Kalm encountered on Staten Island more than two centuries ago. The many creeks, streams, and brooks that once flowed through the island, gave its residents access to regional marketplaces, and were ideal "for fishing and catching oysters and for being near salt meadows" are now only distant memories replaced by paved streets, storm sewers, and landfill.[2] Staten Islanders also once used the flow of these waterways to power their mills and dug rudimentary channels to divert the fresh water to their fields. Along the shores of Staten Island's waterways, tidal marshes, and bays grew thick fields of tall salt grass that settlers valued as an important source of hay to fatten their livestock. Moreover, the island's fisheries were so plentiful that a fisherman's average daily catch was fifty to one hundred pounds. "The haul of fish on the sand banks of Staten Island and the Raritan Bay is most remarkable," observed Captain Philipp Waldeck, the chaplain of the Third Waldeck Regiment of Hessian Troops stationed on the island during the American Revolution.[3] In addition to fishing, residents harvested oysters, clams, and crabs from the

---

[c] At 410 feet above sea level, Todt Hill on Staten Island is the highest point along the eastern coastline south of Massachusetts.

Kill van Kull, Arthur Kill, and Raritan Bay. Fish, oysters, crabs, and clams were an extra source of food and popular with consumers in New York City and the market towns of New Jersey.[4]

Staten Island's most important internal water system was the Fresh Kills and its tributaries. The Fresh Kills, which has become synonymous with the landfill that occupied its space during the twentieth century, was a broad tidal marsh interspersed with islands[d] and small peninsulas. It opened to the Arthur Kill and was fed by the Richmond Creek and the Main Creek. Both creeks meandered through the Fresh Kills marsh and were navigable for more than a mile, giving residents who lived in the interior an outlet to the Arthur Kill and a good source of salt grass.[5] Sales advertisements for farms located near the Fresh Kills and its tributaries highlighted the waterway's ability to accommodate vessels of up to fifty tons. Peter Kalm described the value to residents of the Fresh Kills marsh with its salt grass: "The country was low on both sides . . . and consisted of meadows. But there was no other hay to be got, than such as commonly grows on [these] swampy grounds."[6]

Many of Staten Island's internal waterways were irrigated by a collection of natural springs fed by numerous underground sources. These springs supplied clean water to residents, who hauled it in pails and barrels to their farms. The most famous Staten Island natural spring was the Watering Place. Located on the eastern shore near the Narrows, the Watering Place was an important source of good drinking water for the crews of ships sailing from the port of New York out to sea, ensuring that they would stop at the island. As one visitor wrote, "The eastern part [of Staten Island] . . . is the usual place where ships, ready for sea, stop to take in water . . . previous to their departure."[7] The Watering Place on Staten Island also was attractive to the British military, which established a major staging area there in 1761 during the French and Indian War (1754–1763).

Until the American Revolution, Staten Island was "as well timbered as any part of America,"[8] covered by a dense hardwood forest of predominantly red and white oaks, firs, cedars, and hickories as well as chestnuts, walnuts, locusts, and white ash. As Daniel Denton observed in a brief promotional tract in 1670 designed to encourage English settlement in areas of the former New Netherland, Staten Island's "excellent good land" facilitated the growth of "black walnut and locust as . . . in Vir-

[d] Or hummocks.

ginia, with mighty tall, straight timber."[9] Two Dutch travelers, Jasper Danckaerts and Peter Sluyter, found "nothing but woods" as they walked across the island in 1679. With some exaggeration, they recalled that they "could see nothing except a little of the sky through the thick branches of the trees above our heads."[10] Staten Islanders made good use of the forest for building, heating, and fencing materials and other products such as barrels. They also sold cordwood to consumers in New York City and Perth Amboy, New Jersey.[11] In addition, the island's proximity to several commercial centers, combined with the richness of its woodlands, supported the development of shipbuilding. By 1770, two residents, Joshua Mersereau and Richard Lawrence, had established competing shipyards along the Kill van Kull that built small boats for coastal fishing and local transport.[12]

Although the sea and the forest provided sources of income to Staten Island's residents, it was farming that sustained their livelihoods. Staten Island's "climate and soil are without exception, the loveliest, the healthiest, and the most agreeable on the face of the globe," reported a visitor, adding that "a person, were he so disposed, could easily lay here the foundations of a great fortune for his progeny should he invest a reasonable sum in land."[13] By the time of the American Revolution, less than 5 percent of Staten Island's white male residents were non-land-owning tenants.[14] Instead, the island was a community of middle-class yeomen and their families who owned farms ranging in size from eighty to 275 acres. The one exception was Bentley Manor, the 1,600-acre south shore estate owned by the wealthy and politically powerful Billopp family.[15]

Only part of each farm was devoted to cultivation; the rest was valuable woodlands, untilled pasture, and salt grass. Wheat was the main crop and a major component of their trade networks. After wheat, Staten Island's principal crops were rye, barley, Indian corn, and buckwheat. Staten Islanders also grew small amounts of tobacco and flax, the latter of which, when spun, produced linen for bedding and clothing. Large orchards of apples, cherries, peaches, and pears were found wherever there were houses. On his journey through Staten Island in 1748, Peter Kalm noticed that "near every farmhouse was an orchard with apple trees and cherry trees" and that these orchards "stood . . . round corn fields." The fields that he observed were "excellently situated, and either sown with wheat or rye."[16] In addition, vegetables were grown in island gardens, as well as grapes, berries, melons, and nuts. Residents grew oats and clover to feed to the livestock and horses that they "raised [in] immense quantities."[17] They raised cattle, sheep, and hogs for sale at local urban markets and also for their meat, milk, cheese, and butter to consume and to sell. Horses and oxen hauled wagons and pulled plows. Poultry provided Staten Islanders with meat and eggs, and bees were kept for honey, beeswax, and pollination.

Staten Island's preindustrial economy was apparent in the residents' reliance on household production for many of their basic needs. Indeed, their survival and economic success depended on the contributions of individual family members and white indentured servants, African American slaves, and hired laborers. Artisans did not comprise an important or separate class on Staten Island. Instead, many items were crafted at home by farmers, as demonstrated by the tools for specialized crafts frequently appearing in their estate inventories and wills. Wives and daughters helped the male family members by spinning wool and flax, butchering animals, milking cows, maintaining gardens, and preparing and preserving food.

Although they relied on household production for many of their basic needs, Staten Island's farmers were not self-sufficient yeomen. Instead, they participated to a greater or lesser extent in the eighteenth century's transatlantic market economy through local networks of barter and exchange, cash transactions and bills of credit, and the purchase of slaves. Two major settlements were located on the island: Richmond (in the center of the island) and Decker's Ferry[e] (on the Kill van Kull), both serving as transportation and commercial hubs. Here merchants and shopkeepers bought and sold a variety of goods and offered the island's farmers basic commercial services.

The success of Staten Island's commerce depended on these local merchants and shopkeepers as well as the mills that processed its raw materials into marketable commodities, the roads that linked its settlements and farms, and the ferries that connected the island to the surrounding region. In fact, the best and quickest routes between New York City and Philadelphia, the colonies' two largest commercial centers, were by ferry from New York City to Staten Island and then across the island to ferries that transported people and livestock as well as freight wagons and stagecoaches to numerous landings in Bergen Point,[f] Elizabethtown, Woodbridge, and Perth Amboy, New Jersey. From these landings, roads led

[e] Present-day Port Richmond.

[f] Present-day Bayonne, New Jersey.

through New Brunswick and Princeton to Trenton, on the eastern bank of the Delaware River. Then at Trenton, passengers and cargo were transferred to ferries bound for Philadelphia.[18]

Both eighteenth-century American towns and cities and farmers needed the other to prosper, as exemplified by Staten Island's connection with the surrounding towns and cities. But this connection was not exclusively with New York City. Unlike the farmers in Westchester County and in Kings and Queens counties on Long Island who relied solely on the New York market, Staten Islanders had the option of also sending their commodities to urban markets in New Jersey. As a result, Staten Island's grains, flour, fruits and vegetables, fish, livestock, flaxseed, cordwood, and lumber were sold in the markets of Elizabethtown, which was New Jersey's largest municipality, in Perth Amboy, one of the colony's twin capitals[g] and a port of some consequence, and in Woodbridge, a crossroads town of artisan shops and small farms founded by Quakers and lying adjacent to Perth Amboy. The bulk of goods brought back to Staten Island from New York City or the markets located in New Jersey met its residents' needs: housewares, food items, furniture, cloth, and garments from different parts of the transatlantic world. Indeed, the appearance of these items in Staten Island's homes shatters the perception of it as an isolated community dominated by subsistence agriculture. Instead, Staten Islanders actively participated in the consumer revolution of the eighteenth century, comprising a community sophisticated and wealthy enough to provide a market for these items.[19]

Clandestine channels also offered a way to obtain consumer goods and money. Staten Island was a smuggler's haven, as were the larger ports of Philadelphia, New York, and Boston, as well as several smaller seaboard communities. Ships involved in illicit trade would duck into the island's coves, inlets, bays, and coastal tidal marshes to elude customs officials. With help from the residents, smugglers offloaded the goods and hid them on the island until it was safe for them to be shipped to remote sections of eastern New Jersey and from there secretly transported to New York City. One resident recalled that "much of the tea, gin, china, and sundry dry-goods" found in Staten Island homes were obtained by these means.[20]

---

[g] Before New Jersey became a royal colony, it had been two distinct proprietary colonies: East Jersey and the Quaker-dominated West Jersey. In 1702, East and West Jersey were united as a single royal colony and agreed that the assembly would meet alternately at the two old capitals: Perth Amboy in East Jersey and Burlington in West Jersey.

In the eighteenth century, despite their participation—through legal or illegal channels—in the transatlantic market economy, Staten Islanders still depended on the community for their daily subsistence. A complex web of interconnections and mutual exchange among the island's residents provided economic security, strengthened bonds among neighbors, and encouraged cooperation that enabled the community to function. For several Staten Islanders, this interconnectedness came in the form of family networks. In this sense, the island resembled New York's Hudson River valley, New Jersey's Hackensack valley, and Virginia's more distant Chesapeake region.

The gradual settlement of Staten Island created a community of interrelated families that established ties of kinship, merged and controlled assets, and reinforced their social position. Marital ties gave some Staten Island families, like the Billopps, useful contacts with the social and political elite of New York and New Jersey. The Billopps were related by marriage to the Seamans of Staten Island, the Willets of New York City, and the Farmar, Leonard, Nickleson, and Skinner families of New Jersey who belonged to a small circle of Anglican merchants and landowners known as the "Perth Amboy Group."[21] Networks of personal connections increased the wealth of families like the Billopps and the Seamans, solidified their social status, and brought them the patronage necessary to construct an intricate web of local political deference. Many Staten Islanders depended on these families for social, economic, and political guidance, and they "pretty much governed the Island."[22]

Among those governing the island, none was more influential than Christopher Billopp, the proprietor of Bentley Manor. He lived in a fine manor house[h] built by his great-grandfather and namesake in 1680 on a bluff overlooking Raritan Bay and Perth Amboy. His grandfather Thomas Farmar had served in numerous public offices, including that of sheriff of New York City (1717), chief justice of New Jersey (1728–1729) and member of the New Jersey Assembly (1708–1743). He also helped raise money to build an Anglican church, St. Andrew's, on Staten Island. Christopher Billopp's father was Thomas Farmar Billopp, who had been a justice of the peace, and his father-in-law Benjamin Seaman was the island's surrogate judge.[23] Both Christopher Billopp and Benjamin Seaman

[h] Today the house is known as the Conference House for the peace conference held there on September 11, 1776, between British Admiral Richard Lord Howe and delegates of the Continental Congress John Adams, Benjamin Franklin, and Edward Rutledge. It is the central feature of Conference House Park in the Tottenville section of Staten Island.

The Old Billopp House, at Bentley, west end of Staten Island. Print after a drawing by Alfred DeGroot, originally published in *New Pictorial and Illustrated Family Magazine* 7 (1846): 107. The manor house of Staten Island's leading family is also known today as the Conference House. Note Perth Amboy, New Jersey, in the distance. Courtesy of the Staten Island Historical Society.

Portrait of Lieutenant Colonel Christopher Billopp ca. 1820. From Ira K. Morris, *Morris's Memorial History of Staten Island, New York*, 2 vols. (New York: Memorial Publishing Company, 1898–1900), vol. 1, 119. Courtesy of the Staten Island Historical Society.

served in the New York Assembly and were leading figures in the Anglican Church. Wealthy and imbued with strong political and religious convictions, Billopp played a prominent role in the activities on Staten Island before and during the American Revolution.

Europeans had settled on Staten Island for more than a century before the American Revolution. As early as 1661 Staten Islanders began forming a community when Peter Stuyvesant, the Dutch governor of New Netherland, and his council gave permission to a group of Dutch, French, and Walloon[i] settlers "to look up a convenient place on Staten Island and lay it out for a village."[24] This village, Oude Dorp, became the first permanent European settlement on the island. After Stuyvesant surrendered New Netherland to an English naval expedition in 1664, an influx of English, Irish, and Scots joined the Dutch, French, and Walloons who already had settled on Staten Island. Many settlers brought white indentured servants or African American slaves to the island. By 1706, Staten Island's population had reached 1,066. The Indians, chiefly members of the Hackensack, Raritan, and Tappan tribes of the Lene Lenape, were gone, leaving a population that was 87 percent European (Dutch, English, French, Walloon, Irish, and Scottish) and 13 percent African, giving the island an ethnic cross section of many colonial populations.[25] Compared with the rest of the colony of New York, which grew at a rate of 3.2 percent during the first half of the eighteenth century, Staten Island's population increased by only 1.9 percent.[26] At this rate, the island's population reached 2,154 by 1749 and stood at 2,847 on the eve of the American Revolution.[27]

The ethnic diversity of Staten Island was mirrored by its religious pluralism, creating a major source of conflict. Even though Staten Islanders belonged to a variety of Protestant sects—Anglican, Dutch Reformed, Presbyterian, and Moravian—beginning in 1713 the Anglicans began a concerted effort to create a uniform culture. Although Anglicanism had been established on the island in 1693 and a church, St. Andrew's, was built in the village of Richmond, the parish was not formally recognized until 1713 when Queen Anne granted it a charter.[28] The charter confirmed the Reverend Aeneas Mackenzie, a man "of good Learning and of an admirable temper," as its minister.[29] Mackenzie's main mission

[i] The Walloons were from southern Belgium and spoke a dialect of French. In New Netherland, Dutch authorities often grouped them together with the Huguenots.

was to strengthen the church's position in a community as ethnically diverse as Staten Island, and to a great extent he succeeded. He asked the Society for the Propagation of the Gospel in Foreign Parts, otherwise known as the SPG, to send him prayer books in Dutch and in English. "The few [prayer books] I had have gained some of them already to a juster Opinion of our Form of Worship," he wrote in his first report to the SPG in November 1705. He also argued that the lack of an English school on the island placed the church at a disadvantage, "for the children have no education, but what they have from their parents' language and principles." Mackenzie predicted that "numerous and regular congregations" would form "in a few years time" once SPG-supported English schools opened.[30]

By 1709, two SPG-supported English schools had opened on Staten Island, enrolling both Anglican and non-Anglican children, boys and girls, white and black, enslaved and free.[31] Although they taught the children reading, writing, arithmetic, spelling, and psalmody, their main objective was religious indoctrination. Instruction in the Bible and the Book of Common Prayer comprised the core of the curriculum.[32] The SPG-sponsored education program was a huge success on the island. "The French [and] some of the Dutch," Mackenzie commented, "allow their Children to be taught the Church Catechism."[33] Without an affordable alternative, many Staten Island parents enrolled their children in the SPG-supported schools, even though doing so meant exposing them to Anglican doctrine.

Anglican education efforts extended to the island's slaves. All the Anglican ministers who followed Mackenzie at St. Andrew's parish worked with SPG schoolmasters to educate and convert those slaves brought to the church by their masters. The efforts to baptize and convert slaves were consistent with the Anglican promotion of societal stability and conformity.

Slavery was a common and visible institution on Staten Island because the island's economy relied considerably on slave labor. Indeed, slavery's importance to the economic and social fabric of Staten Island was reflected in the steady growth of the slave population from 1698 to 1790, which coincided with the development of commercial agriculture in the colonies and the expansion of the transatlantic slave trade during the eighteenth century.[34] Slaves made up between 10 and 23 percent of the island's population.[35] Ordinary white Staten Islanders owned from one to three slaves, and the more affluent owned between five and ten, figures similar to those for New York City and the rural counties of eastern New

Jersey.[36] One visitor was surprised by the many slaves on Staten Island. The residents "have many blacks, which they call Negroes," he observed. "These are slaves and are bought and sold like cattle."[37]

The effort to Anglicize and bring a religious uniformity to Staten Island showed first among its Huguenot residents. A small number of these French Calvinists were among the first Europeans to settle permanently on the island in the 1660s, but the main Huguenot migration occurred after the Catholic King Louis XIV revoked the tolerant Edict of Nantes in 1689 that had guaranteed them limited freedom of worship in France.[38] The Anglicanization of the Huguenots was aided by two factors: a high rate of intermarriage with Anglicans and the conciliatory stance toward Anglicanism of their minister, the Reverend David de Bonrepos, who established close working relationships with leading Anglicans and encouraged Huguenot parents to enroll their children in SPG-supported schools.[39] In 1734, a majority of Huguenots voted to join St. Andrew's parish. "We now are most of us joined and united to the English congregation," the elders of the French congregation informed the SPG.[40] Indeed, by the American Revolution, French surnames outnumbered those of English origin in the list of communicants for St. Andrew's parish.[41]

Unlike the Huguenots, many Dutch Staten Islanders clung to the Reformed Church and joined with the island's small Presbyterian congregation in refusing to conform to Anglicanism. These Dutch dissenters built a church in the village of Decker's Ferry, hired the Reverend Cornelius Van Santvoord, an acquaintance of the evangelical Reverend Theodore J. Frelinghuysen of New Jersey's Raritan valley, and welcomed the small number of Huguenots who joined the congregation either through intermarriage or because they had become disgusted by the Reverend Bonrepos's Anglican sympathies.[42]

During the 1720s, Frelinghuysen had held several revivals throughout New Jersey and on Staten Island. He preached on issues concerning morality and personal "conversion" and urged the creation of an American-based church.[43] In fact, his revivals were a harbinger of a religious movement, called the Great Awakening, that swept across America between the 1730s and 1745.[44] Itinerant preachers and laypersons known as "Awakeners" visited different communities, delivering fiery sermons that charged the spiritual energies of many Americans. George Whitefield, an Anglican minister from Britain and perhaps the most charismatic of the Awakeners, visited Staten Island on two occasions in 1740.[45] Similar revivals were led on the island by the Presbyterians

Gilbert Tennent of New Brunswick, New Jersey, and John Cross of Basking Ridge, New Jersey.[46]

The large audiences that Whitefield, Tennent, and Cross attracted became a major concern for local Anglican officials, who feared that these Awakeners might undermine their efforts to Anglicize the island. In 1742, the Reverend Jonathan Arnold, the minister of St. Andrew's parish, informed the SPG that "the followers of Mr. Whitefield and Tennent have been numerous and for a while zealous."[47] Arnold charged that Whitefield and other Awakeners were spreading "erroneous Doctrines" and "sowing Discord" and warned that they sought to undermine "the Order of Men" and "to dissolve the Hyerarchy of the Church of England . . . [to] confound the Establishment, and [to] pull down the Bishops and Clergy."[48]

For many ordinary Americans, the Awakeners' appeal was their methods and their message. The Awakeners criticized the established clergy in America as being too intellectual and tradition bound, and instead, they emphasized the individual's responsibility of directing his or her own spiritual affairs. They preached that regardless of age, gender, race, or class, each person was responsible for his or her own salvation and for spreading "God's truth." The Awakeners' message led to the development of a kindred democratic spirit among ordinary Americans and to the spread of populist antiestablishment ideas. The Awakening also loosened the established clergy's grip on religion and empowered ordinary Americans to challenge political and religious authority and defy assigned societal roles.[49]

Although the Awakeners' message and religious frenzy inspired many Americans, they also angered and alienated others, which led to divisions within congregations between warring factions of revivalists and traditionalists. In Dutch Reformed congregations the schism was between the Coetus (revivalists) and Conferentie (traditionalists) factions. Among Presbyterians the division was between the New Sides (revivalists) and the Old Sides (traditionalists).[50] In 1742 Rev. Jonathan Arnold of St. Andrew's parish addressed the Awakening's divisive impact on Staten Island's Dutch Reformed and Presbyterian congregations: "The followers of Mr. Whitefield and Tennent are much divided among themselves," and "their . . . irregular doctrines and practices" have confounded the growth and influence of the dissenter congregations on the island. He therefore was pleased that many of the disgruntled members of these congregations found refuge at St. Andrew's.[51] In 1743, Arnold informed the SPG that the number of Anglicans on Staten Island was increasing at the expense of the dissenters, and a year later he reported that "many of the Dutch" were leaving their congregation to protest the influence of the Awakeners and joining St. Andrew's.[52]

Thus, unlike many communities in Virginia where the appeal of New Side Presbyterianism and the rise of the Baptists during the Awakening coalesced into a populist movement that broke local Anglican social and political monopolies, on Staten Island the Awakeners weakened the dissenting congregations and inadvertently strengthened the community's Anglicanization.

By the 1760s, Anglicans were firmly in control of the island's religious and political affairs. Competition for political offices escalated from parity among the different religious groups to complete domination by Anglicans. Of the six Staten Islanders who served in the New York Assembly between 1750 and 1775, five were Anglicans, and one, Henry Holland, a supporter of the Conferentie in the Dutch Reformed congregation, was elected in 1761 with the full support of the Reverend Richard Charlton of St. Andrew's parish.[53] "Mr. Holland has pleased to declare to some Gentlemen in N. [New] York," wrote Charlton to his friend James Duane, "that if I had not assisted him he would have failed in his former Election." Charlton admitted that he had influenced "more votes than I chuse to mention."[54] A grateful Holland thanked Charlton and the congregants of St. Andrew's for their "successful exertions" on his behalf by donating a bell and two silver collection plates to the parish.[55]

Rev. Richard Charlton had come to St. Andrew's in 1747 from Trinity Church in New York City and immediately became an esteemed and respected member of the Staten Island community. He possessed an unquestioned "Attachment to the Constitution, in Church and State" and was closely acquainted with Rev. Thomas Bradbury Chandler of Elizabethtown, New Jersey, who was the leader of a group of Anglican ministers calling for the appointment of a bishop for America. Charlton was one of the group's more vocal members. From his pulpit at St. Andrew's, Charlton preached the importance of deferring to God, the monarchy, and one's social "betters" as a means of maintaining social order, and he called on his parishioners to support the appointment of an American bishop.[56]

Charlton's advocacy of an American bishop and his guidance of the continued expansion of Anglicanism on Staten Island heightened the dissenters' animosities toward the Anglican Church. So as to more effec-

tively challenge the Anglican monopoly on the island's political and social authority, the dissenters united their congregations[57] under the aus-
pices of the Reverend William Jackson, who was a member of the Coetus
and widely respected as a preacher. His emotional, politically charged sermons electrified audiences and earned him a reputation as an orator "second only to Whitefield."[58] To the dismay of Staten Island's Anglicans, in
1769 Jackson oversaw the construction of the United Reformed Church
in the village of Richmond, which joined the earlier church at Decker's
Ferry as the island's main dissenter churches. By the early 1770s, the new
unified dissenter congregation had built a small meetinghouse to serve its
members living on the island's south shore. Although Jackson occasionally led Sunday services in the new houses of worship, their congregants
were often served by local laypersons or Presbyterian ministers who traveled to the island from New Jersey.[59]

Most historians accept that the structure of the established and dissenter churches influenced their politics. That is, unlike the episcopal
structure of the Anglican Church, which relied on the political authority
of the Crown and on bishops in London for the ordination, confirmation,
discipline, and assignment of clergy, the dissenters' churches were less au-
thoritarian, often giving congregations to the care of a layperson if an ordained minister could not be obtained. Moreover, the dissenter ministers
were trained and ordained by American-based ecclesiastical bodies. According to Patricia U. Bonomi,

> Dissenters feared Anglican expansion in part because churches and min-
> isters were carriers of a national as well as a religious culture, that is, the
> Church of England, like its German, Scottish, and Dutch counterparts,
> not only preserved transatlantic patterns of language and custom but in-
> culcated attitudes toward government and authority—by no means al-
> ways congenial—through the agency of worship rituals, ecclesiastical
> forms, and church schools.[60]

Thus the dissenters equated episcopacy with the rigorous promotion of
civil and religious conformity, which in Britain in the seventeenth century
had led to a series of persecutions.

The Anglicans' political control of Staten Island was supported by
local Moravians. By the American Revolution, intermarriage and migration had resulted in the creation of a multiethnic Moravian community
led by the Reverend Hector Gambold. Although the Moravians were the-

ologically similar to the dissenters, the episcopal structure of their church and their cordial relations with Anglicans brought scorn from dissenting ministers and laypersons. This antagonism was then played out politically on Staten Island, as Moravians often voted for Anglican candidates over candidates affiliated with the dissenter congregations.[61]

By the 1760s, in their attempt to break the Anglican grip on Staten Island and revive their languishing congregation, the dissenters conflated local religious issues with the widening political division between Britain and the colonies that followed the end of the French and Indian War in 1763. They argued that the Anglican Church was a monolithic obstacle to political and social advancement not only in the community but also throughout America. The dissenters expanded on this politically by arguing that Parliament's taxation of the colonies to help pay for the war— the Stamp Act (1765), the Townshend Duties (1768), and the Tea Act (1773)—was misguided and tyrannical. In his sermons, Rev. Jackson simultaneously denounced the British government and the Anglican clergy as immoral tyrants seeking to undermine political and religious freedom in America. He also told his listeners that resistance to British civil and religious policies was righteous and justified.[62]

Anglicans answered these charges by portraying the dissenters as a small group of fanatics who were trying to satisfy their personal ambitions at the expense of the social order. An Anglican schoolmaster recalled that a "great uneasiness" came upon Staten Island which was "mostly Occasioned by the Decenters."[63] In 1776, a British officer overheard several Staten Islanders complain about the "mischief [that] the Republican principles of the Dissenters [and] the Ambition of their few intoxicated Leaders" had brought to the island.[64] Another officer was told that the conflict between Britain and the colonies was caused by dissenting ministers, who "hoped to have a great advantage from it, for if the English government were abolished, then the Episcopal Church could no longer impose its parish system on the local community churches."[65] Rev. Charlton of St. Andrew's parish on Staten Island likened the dissenter attacks to "a virus . . . that may be productive of a Gangrene."[66]

The dissenter attacks against the Anglican Church's political and social role in the empire exacerbated the island residents' concerns about the escalating protests against British policies imposed throughout America between 1763 and 1775. One Staten Islander described the protestors as "Merciless, cruel, ignorant, and misled Rabble."[67] Another island resident blamed the violence on "the people in the cities . . . who had not enough to do and wanted to be great lords and get rich quickly, especially the merchants [and] lawyers [who] . . . roused the rabble" against Britain.[68] "All America had broken out in open Violence and Rebellion," remembered Alexander McDonald, and everyday "the People [grew] more violent and Insolent."[69]

Despite these tensions, Staten Island, a small, prosperous agricultural community on the fringes of the British Empire, had no major quarrels with Britain. Rather, its problems tended to be local, not imperial. Whereas vocal and sometimes violent protests against British policies inflamed many American communities between 1763 and 1775, Staten Islanders generally pursued a course of restraint and moderation and were reluctant to upset the status quo. Indeed, the island's relative silence during the tumultuous years following the French and Indian War was remarkable and can be explained by a combination of factors: the success of Anglicanization on the island and the influence of powerful local Anglican leaders; a prosperous local economy that bred contentment with the imperial system among residents; and the absence of a large, radicalized artisan class comprising the rank-and-file of such organizations as the Sons of Liberty that formed the backbone of the colonial protests in many American communities. Just how content Staten Islanders felt about their position in the British Empire and how reluctant they were to join the colonial protest movement became clear in 1774 and 1775.

# 2

## "An Unfriendly Disposition Towards the Liberties of America"

### Staten Islanders and the Colonial Resistance Movement

In the spring of 1774, Parliament took radical steps to punish the inhabitants of Massachusetts for carrying out the so-called Boston Tea Party in the previous December. Many colonists were outraged. Local committees of correspondence—which had first appeared in 1765/1766 during the protests over the Stamp Act and later helped enforce the boycott against the Townshend duties—now coordinated the response to what colonists were calling the "coercive acts." In May, the colonists called for a "continental congress," and by late July, twelve colonies had selected delegations to the congress, scheduled to meet in Philadelphia in early September. On July 28, members of New York's committee of correspondence chose John Alsop, James Duane, John Jay, Philip Livingston, and Isaac Low to represent the city and county of New York at this First Continental Congress.[1] The next day, the committee requested that the residents of the other New York counties hold meetings for the same purpose. The committee suggested that participants at the county meetings either choose a delegation of their own or approve the city's slate of delegates.[2]

On September 2, three days before the congress opened, James Duane informed Peter Van Schaack of Albany County that the leading residents of Kings County had selected Simon Boerum to represent them and that "there will be a meeting in Queen's." But Duane had received no word at all from Richmond County on Staten Island.[3] On September 19, New York's committee of correspondence repeated its request to the island, only for it to be ignored again.[4] Consequently, Staten Island was the only county in New York that did not send delegates to the First Continental Congress.

The delegates who met in Philadelphia demonstrated their support for the Massachusetts residents who bore the brunt of Britain's wrath, calling on all colonists to withhold payment of British taxes and to prepare for a possible war against the mother country. They also unanimously adopted a nonimportation, nonexportation, and nonconsumption agreement known as the Continental Association, which local committees of observation (or inspection) were to enforce. These committees used a variety of coercive tactics, such as social ostracism, economic sanctions, violence, and intimidation, to enforce the boycott. According to historian Ray Raphael, because the association crossed regional and class boundaries, it became "the voice, and force, of revolutionary America."[5] The association was used as a tool to identify colonists who opposed colonial resistance to British policy, and the local committees were valuable weapons for suppressing dissent.

Staten Islanders were less than enthusiastic about the congress's measures, especially the association and its system of enforcement. Like many other New York agrarians, Staten Islanders opposed the association not only because it closed the transatlantic market to their products and threatened to cut off their access to desirable British manufactured goods and specie but also because cutting off imports meant higher prices for domestic products. Staten Islanders flatly refused to abide by the association's provisions, and they never established a local system of enforcement. In fact, they did the opposite, using the island's topography and their years of experience aiding and abetting smugglers to elude the committees of observation in New York and New Jersey.

The association's first test in New York came in early February 1775 when the *James*, a merchant vessel, arrived from Glasgow, Scotland. The local committee of observation immediately ordered the ship to leave the port of New York without offloading its cargo. Complying with the committee's demand, the ship's captain then sailed the ship into New York Bay. But the *James* returned the next week, sparking waves of protests in the city which eventually forced the *James* to leave the port of New York again with its cargo onboard.[6]

Even though the *James* had left the port of New York, rumors immediately circulated that it had stopped somewhere along Staten Island's shoreline and that with the assistance of several residents, the captain had offloaded part of its cargo. It also was said that a large group of Staten Islanders had attempted to prevent the *James* from returning to Europe.[7] Because of the island's historical connection to smuggling, these rumors were credible.

Staten Island was also linked to another controversial scheme to elude the association. On February 17, 1775, New York's committee of observation prevented the *Beulah*, a merchant ship carrying European goods, from entering the port area, and thus it was forced to anchor off Sandy Hook, New Jersey. The *Beulah*'s owners, John and Robert Murray of New York City, tried in vain to convince the committee of observation to allow the vessel to enter the port area. Frustrated, they decided to circumvent the association by secretly unloading a portion of the ship's cargo at Staten Island. From there, they intended to transport the goods to Elizabethtown, New Jersey. The Elizabethtown committee of observation, however, learned of their plans and promptly investigated the matter.[8]

On March 10, the chairman of the Elizabethtown committee, Jonathan Hampton, reported the investigation's findings to the committee in New York City. "It appears," he wrote, "that a Boat belonging to this Town did, last Monday morning, sail from New-York to Sandy Hook." Hampton added that "on Tuesday evening she returned here [Elizabethtown] . . . and we believe it was the Boat seen to be hovering about the *Beulah*." The investigators discovered that this boat belonged to Elizabethtown merchant Isaac Woodruff but was leased to another resident of the town, Samuel Lee. It was Lee who used the boat to transport John Murray and part of the *Beulah*'s cargo to a landing area on Staten Island. Hampton told the New York committee he was certain there would be "more important discoveries on Staten-Island, where we think the Goods were undoubtedly landed, at the East Ends, or in the Kills."[9]

The *Beulah* affair ended on March 13. Samuel Lee confessed that Isaac Woodruff had no knowledge of the plan to transfer a portion of the ship's cargo to Staten Island but that he, John Murray, Ichabod Barnet, John Graham, and Samuel Reed had offloaded the goods at Staten Island and waited for the opportune moment to ship them to Barnet's store in Elizabethtown.[10] That same day, John Murray made a corroborating confession to the New York committee of observation.[11]

Some New Jersey Whigs responded to incidents like this with violence. On February 8, 1775, Staten Islander James Johnson was transporting oysters to the market in Elizabethtown when he was attacked by an angry mob "for no other crime than because some people of that ever loyal Island [Staten Island] were supposed to have been ready to assist in land-ing some goods from . . . the Scotch ship [*James*]," reported the March 2 edition of *Rivington's Royal Gazette*.[12] The mob, composed of ordinary residents of Elizabethtown, beat Johnson and dragged him and his small boat to the Liberty pole and gallows located in front of the town's cour-thouse. Finally, Whigs John Blanchard, Elias Boudinot, and Jonathan Hampton, three of Elizabethtown's leading citizens, intervened on John-son's behalf, disbursing the crowd and later condemning the attack.[13]

These men's response to the violence against James Johnson reflected a broader trend among middle-class leaders of the colonial resistance movement. Even though they promoted violence in order to enforce con-formity at the local level, they had difficulty keeping it in check. Conse-quently, the movement's leaders were often torn between initiating demonstrations by ordinary people against British policy and controlling the violent impulses that those demonstrations often unleashed. For these men, Parliament's abuse of power and the defense of traditional English rights were the main issues of the conflict; they had no interest in de-stroying property or encouraging physical violence and social upheaval.[14] The response by Blanchard, Boudinot, and Hampton to the attack against Johnson's person and property illustrates this problem. These three men may or may not have directly instigated the crowd's actions, but once they became too violent, they interceded to bring them under control.[15]

Besides the violence used against individual Staten Islanders to enforce conformity, the island also had to endure economic sanctions from sev-eral committees of observation in New Jersey. On February 13, 1775, the committee of observation in Elizabethtown declared that Staten Islanders possessed "an unfriendly disposition towards the Liberties of America" and condemned them for their failure "to join . . . [the] association pro-posed by the Continental Congress." The committee thereupon banned "all trade, commerce, dealings, and intercourse" with the island until its residents agreed to join the association.[16] A week later, the committee of observation in Woodbridge, New Jersey, did the same.[17] In Dover, New Jersey, Staten Islander Peter Waglom was condemned as a "publick enemy" for attempting to sell a quantity of India tea to the townspeople, in violation of the association's rules. The town's committee of observa-tion then demanded that its residents refrain from purchasing items from him or any other Staten Islander.[18]

The rigorous enforcement of the association's rules by New York and New Jersey Whigs hurt Staten Islanders and led to resentment of the colonial resistance movement. Gradually, Staten Islanders learned how to balance their fear of economic sanctions against their loyalist feelings by evading the association and supporting colonial resistance only when necessary.

In January 1775, the New York Assembly convened to discuss the actions taken by the First Continental Congress, and two political factions squared off. The De Lancey faction, led by James De Lancey of New York and Joseph De Lancey, Frederick Philipse, and Isaac Wilkins of Westchester County, argued that imperial issues should be handled by the legally constituted assemblies in each colony. But the Livingston faction, led by the Albany County triumvirate of Peter R. Livingston, Abraham Ten Broeck, and Philip Schuyler, contended that all of the colonial assemblies should fully support the decisions of the First Continental Congress. The Livingston faction also called for the colony of New York to participate in the upcoming Second Continental Congress, which was set to meet in May 1775.[19]

Staten Island's assemblymen, Christopher Billopp and Benjamin Seaman, supported the De Lancey position. Billopp "opposed every measure . . . in favor of the Congress," recalled one acquaintance, and he "took a great deal of pains to prevent the County [Richmond County] he represented from joining their Measures."[20] Benjamin Seaman consistently demonstrated his "attachment to the British by a steady opposition to the Measures of the Congress," according to Ambrose Serle, the civilian secretary to British Admiral Richard Lord Howe during the American Revolution.[21] Billopp and Seaman insisted that the congress was an illegal governing body that had usurped the constitutionality of the colonial assemblies, and so they voted to repudiate its measures. They also rejected a motion thanking New York's delegates for their participation in the congress and its "Merchants and Inhabitants . . . for their firm adherence to the association." Finally, both men opposed sending a delegation to the Second Continental Congress.[22]

Their actions set the stage for the events of early March 1775, when New York's committee of observation proposed organizing a "provincial convention" to select delegates to the Second Continental Congress. Each county was expected to choose deputies to the Provincial Convention.[23] A meeting was scheduled for April 11 on Staten Island. At the meeting, Christopher Billopp and Benjamin Seaman succeeded in persuading those in attendance not to choose deputies to the convention.[24] Rev. Richard Charlton of the Anglican St. Andrew's parish on Staten Island praised them for standing up to the "few Republican malevolent Spirits" who sought to destroy social stability in order to further their own interests.[25]

After mid-April, Staten Island's refusal to support the Provincial Convention and other revolutionary organizations became more serious. The Provincial Convention opened in New York on April 20 and chose twelve delegates to represent the colony of New York at the Second Continental Congress and then adjourned on April 22. But the next day news arrived from Massachusetts that on April 19 an armed conflict between colonists and British regulars had taken place near the towns of Lexington and Concord.[26]

The military confrontations at Lexington and Concord inflamed the colonists, and in New York, the Sons of Liberty led a series of protests.[27] The agitation lasted for a week, turning the city into "one continued scene of riot, tumult, and confusion."[28] Armed mobs roaming New York's streets forced Lieutenant Governor Cadwallader Colden, who had temporarily assumed executive duties while Governor William Tryon was in Britain, into a precarious situation. With only one hundred troops at his disposal and a local militia composed of men sympathetic to the protestors, the use of force to disperse the mobs and protect the citizens and their property was not an option. In effect, royal authority in the colony of New York had become "entirely prostrated."[29]

Like other colonists, Staten Islanders were stunned by the armed confrontations in Massachusetts and the protests that followed. In May 1775, Christopher Billopp, Benjamin Seaman, and twelve other New York assemblymen drafted a message to General Thomas Gage, the commander in chief of British military forces in America, in which they expressed alarm at "the late melancholy transactions in the Province of Massachusetts-Bay, ending in actual bloodshed." They warned that an escalation of violence would lead to "an unnatural civil war" and demanded that Gage "immediately order a cessation to further hostilities."[30] For Staten Islander Alexander McDonald, it seemed as if "the Spirit of Rebellion & treason [were] blasing every where . . . [as] the People [were] constantly exercising themselves to Arms."[31] He warned that "the affairs of America are far from being settled" but hoped for "a Mode of reconciliation between Great Britain & her Colonies Consistent with the dignity and Grandeur of Great Britain as well as the interest & happiness of America."[32] Rev. Charlton of St. Andrew's parish wished for "a Speedy suppression to insulting Mobs, and a restoration of Loyalty and obedience to our Parent State."[33]

But the Staten Islanders were disappointed. By late April 1775, New York's committee of observation had taken charge of the unsettled political situation. It urged each county in the colony of New York to select delegates to the Provincial Congress, which would function as the de facto government of the colony. In addition, the committee issued the General Association, to which the signers pledged to support the Continental and Provincial Congresses.[34] On May 1, Staten Island freeholders met in Richmond to choose delegates to the first New York Provincial Congress, scheduled to meet on May 22. Benjamin Seaman presided over the meeting, in which five moderate-to-conservative community leaders were unanimously chosen to represent the island: Richard Conner, a native of Ireland and a leader in Staten Island's Moravian community; Aaron Cortelyou, another leader in the Moravian community and the father-in-law of Benjamin Seaman's son Richard; John Journeay, an Anglican acquaintance of both Christopher Billopp and Benjamin Seaman; Richard Lawrence, the owner of one of the island's two shipyards; and Paul Micheau Jr., the county clerk and a close acquaintance of Christopher Billopp's and the husband of Benjamin Seaman's daughter Mary.[35] These five men were united in their support for reconciliation.

The island's decision to send a delegation to the Provincial Congress was motivated by a sense of self-preservation in the face of pressure to respond to the New York committee's call for delegates. Although Staten Islanders were shocked by the outbreak of armed hostilities, they never gave the faintest hint that they sympathized with the plight of Massachusetts. "This Island till the last week generally opposed the choosing a committee, or having any Thing to do with the [Provincial] Congress," noted the Reverend Hector Gambold of the Moravian congregation, "but when they saw that . . . Force was daily expected to compel them to submit . . . they unanimously chose One, viz. Mr. Arthur [Aaron] Cortelyou, Richard Conner & 3 more."[36] The collapse of royal authority had left Staten Islanders with few, if any, options to stem the tide of revolution in the colony of New York. Therefore, with no other alternatives, they were forced to accept the Provincial Congress as the governing body for the colony.[37]

Frustrated by events, the Staten Island delegates tried to thwart every measure that strengthened the colonial protest movement, casting the only votes against a motion by Isaac Low of New York City that demanded "implicit obedience . . . be paid to every recommendation of the Continental Congress." On June 2, the island's delegation supported a resolution calling for the appointment of a committee to draft a plan for reconciliation based on constitutional principles.[38] Despite the Staten Island delegates' strong support, however, the resolution failed to pass the congress.

This disappointment did not end the island delegates' efforts to undermine the Provincial Congress. In early June, they supported the creation of a committee to assist British military officials who were investigating the theft of arms and ammunition from the royal storehouse located in the Turtle Bay section of Manhattan. Then, on June 20, the Staten Island delegation rejected a plan to spend £2,000 to manufacture gunpowder. They also opposed transferring the royal cannon at Fort George in lower Manhattan[a] to fortifications being constructed on the bluffs overlooking the Hudson River, and they objected to granting the congress the authority to nominate and appoint "any Field-Officer or Officers" and to keep its deliberations secret.[39]

But their efforts proved futile. The Whig majority pushed ahead with their plans to use the Provincial Congress to promote resistance to British policy and to enforce conformity, and they succeeded in enacting a measure that required all provincial congressmen to sign an oath to uphold the General Association issued in April. The residents of each county also were directed to organize committees of safety to enforce both the General Association and the measures of the Continental and Provincial congresses on the local level. These committees were instructed to turn over, by July 15, a list of any residents who refused to sign the General Association. If they did not so by this date, the counties would risk economic sanctions.[40]

This tactic succeeded on Staten Island. The threat of economic coercion from the Provincial Congress, combined with the ongoing boycott of the island by the Elizabethtown and Woodbridge committees of observation in New Jersey, forced Staten Islanders to select a committee of safety and to sign the General Association. They could not afford to further jeopardize their local economy. But the men chosen for the Richmond County committee of safety did not include any who held pronounced Whig views. The members of the committee were George Barnes, Joseph Christopher, Daniel Corsen, Moses Dupuy, Christian Jacobson, David Latourette, Lambert Merrill, Peter Mersereau, Henry Perine, John Poillon, and John Tyson. All were well known in the community and from re-

[a] Present-day Battery Park.

The Christopher House, home of Joseph Christopher, where the Richmond County committee of safety frequently met. Photo ca. 1938. Courtesy of the Staten Island Historical Society.

spected families. Except for Jacobson, who was a leading member of the island's Moravian community, and Christopher, who was a member of the Dutch Reformed Church, all were Anglicans. The committee chose Jacobson as its chairman. One Staten Islander recalled that residents had no choice but to choose a committee of safety and "to Sign an association with [the] Rebels."[41] Once this was done, the committees of observation in Elizabethtown and Woodbridge, New Jersey, lifted their five-month old bans on trade with the island.[42]

Although the New York Provincial Congress had to deal with the threat to its authority posed by the recalcitrant Staten Islanders, a more ominous threat lay in New York Harbor. By late May 1775, two British warships—the *Asia* and the *Kingfisher*—had been deployed to the port area. The presence of these two warships, hovering off the coast of lower Manhattan, frightened the residents of New York City, who feared an impending British invasion.[43]

The Provincial Congress understood the seriousness of the situation. To prevent violence, it continued to allow the sale of provisions to the warships by authorized suppliers, who were required to file regular reports with the congress so that the provisions would not be given to the British army in Boston. This army was desperate for supplies, since the countryside around Boston was firmly controlled by Whigs who had cut off the flow of local supplies into the city. The logistical problems grew even worse for the British when Whigs outside Massachusetts tried to prevent supplies from reaching Boston.[44]

Nonetheless, despite the best efforts of New York's Whigs, the British in Boston managed to obtain supplies from New York City and the surrounding communities. In early August 1775, General George Washington, the commander in chief of the Continental army, notified the New York Provincial Congress that "a vessel cleared lately out of New York, for St. Croix, with fresh provisions and other articles, has . . . gone into Boston, instead of pursuing her voyage to the West-Indies."[45] The congress responded by prohibiting the exportation of "Cattle, Sheep, Poultry, or Live Stock of any kind, except Horses." In September, it announced that any persons who attempted "to furnish the Ministerial Army or Navy with Provisions or other necessaries" would be arrested and tried and, if found guilty, disarmed and fined "double the value of the Provisions or other necessaries so furnished." Violators who could not pay the fine would be imprisoned, and repeat offenders would be banished from the colony of New York.[46]

Staten Islanders were not deterred and continued to sell produce and livestock to the British warships.[47] Even though the island's residents did not need this additional market, given the steady and proven opportunities to sell their goods in New York City and the market towns of New Jersey, they defiantly smuggled produce and livestock to the warships with the understanding that it would be sent to the British army in Boston. "I take this opportunity," a New York City resident notified the Provincial Congress, "that there is a set of . . . people on Staten Island, who, for the sake of a little gain . . . sell their . . . hogs, sheep, geese, ducks, and fowls, to go on board the ship that lies now in the North River,[b] to go to Boston," adding that Staten Islanders were "determined to continue thus in letting them [the British] have such stock as they want, as far as they are able to supply them, and will spare no pains to provide for them."[48]

The New York committee of safety urged the Staten Island committee to investigate these allegations, that residents were overtly aiding the British military. But the Staten Island committee was so slow to act that the New York committee launched its own investigation, which found that a New York merchant, John Wetherhead, and an unnamed British officer had apparently purchased large quantities of livestock and produce from Staten Islanders. Wetherhead then fled to the *Asia* in New York Harbor to escape from the colonial protestors' "perpetual Insults and Menaces." On September 17, 1775, he admitted that he and a British officer had "purchased some stock from two or three persons." But he did not reveal their identities or whether the livestock had been sent to Boston. But he hinted sarcastically that the Staten Islanders who had sold their livestock to the British had also saved New York City from destruction. With no further information, the investigation was dropped.[49]

Tensions between Staten Islanders and New York's Whigs did not vanish with the end of this investigation. In early October, the Provincial Congress called for the election of delegates to the Second Provincial Congress, set to meet on November 14. Charlotte, Cumberland, Gloucester, Tryon, and Queens counties eventually held elections, and all but one, Queens, sent delegates. But Richmond (Staten Island), frustrated in its attempt to undermine the Whigs in the first congress, refused to hold an election.[50] The Provincial Congress demanded an explanation.[51] On December 1, Paul Micheau Jr., who had served in the first congress, replied

[b] Hudson River.

that "a meeting of the [Richmond County] Committee was called . . . and not a majority appearing, those that did appear concluded they were not empowered to act."[52] The island's flippant attitude infuriated the congress. By refusing to hold an election and brazenly continuing to trade with the British warships in the harbor, Staten Islanders not only were materially supporting the British presence in the area but also were undermining the colonies' efforts to form a unified front against British imperial policy.

On December 2, the Provincial Congress sent a sternly worded letter to Staten Island's committee of safety, ordering it to hold an election immediately. The congress warned that any delay or refusal to carry out this order would result in dire consequences for the island. "Rest assured, gentlemen," the letter read, "that the neighboring Colonies will not remain inactive Spectators, if you show a disposition to depart from the Continental Union."[53] In essence, the Whigs were now threatening Staten Island with military intervention if it did not conform.

The Staten Islanders' response to this threat was as follows: After two weeks, they voted overwhelmingly against sending delegates to the Second Provincial Congress. They had sent delegates to the first congress, expecting it to work for reconciliation. But instead, their delegates were ignored like recalcitrant children, and all efforts at reconciliation were pushed aside in favor of measures that could have led the colony of New York into war against Britain. By the middle of December, Staten Islanders believed that reconciliation was no longer possible, and their vote reflected their unwillingness to participate in a government that they felt was leading the colony of New York to armed rebellion and possibly independence.[54]

The Provincial Congress acted swiftly and decisively. On December 21, 1775, it announced that Staten Island was "guilty of a breach of the General Association and of an open contempt of the authority of this Congress." The Staten Island committee of safety was ordered to make "a list of the names of . . . the delinquents against the common cause" and to forward that list to the congress within fifteen days. Residents whose names appeared on the list would be "entirely put out of the protection of this Congress . . . [and] all friendly and commercial intercourse between the said persons . . . and other inhabitants of this Colony . . . shall be totally *interdicted*" until further notice.[55] But the fifteen-day deadline passed without a list from Staten Island. On January 12, 1776, Christian Jacobson, the chairman of the island's committee of safety, testified before the New York committee that "a majority of the Inhabitants of Richmond County [Staten Island] were not averse, but friendly to the measures of the Congress."[56] Richard Lawrence, another Staten Island community leader, confided to a member of the New York committee that Staten Islanders "would very speedily elect Deputies to represent them in Provincial Congress." Lawrence later conveyed this information to the full committee and also testified that Staten Islanders were more than willing to hold an election for delegates to the Second Provincial Congress.[57] What had led to this change of heart? By the middle of January the threat of another boycott of the island had forced its residents to submit to the Provincial Congress's demands.

New York's committee of safety remained skeptical. Although they reported what they had heard from Jacobson and Lawrence to the Second Provincial Congress, the congress then launched another investigation of the island's questionable support of colonial resistance. This time, it presented an ultimatum. If Staten Islanders had not held elections for delegates to the congress and the outstanding list of delinquent residents had not been forwarded to New York's committee by January 22, trade with the island would be banned.[58] This ultimatum succeeded. On January 19, two community leaders, Adrian Bancker, a moderate Whig and the brother of New York City merchant and congressman Evert Bancker, and Richard Lawrence, who had served in the first congress, were elected.[59] By late February, both men had taken their seats at the congress and actively participated in its sessions.[60]

Without this second ultimatum, the island's residents would never have sent delegates to the congress. The decision to hold elections was based solely on the threat of economic sanctions; it did not reflect a sudden upsurge of radicalism on the island. Instead, the results of the elections for the New York Assembly in February of 1776 were more indicative of Staten Island's political culture.

In January, while on board a British merchant vessel in New York Harbor, Governor William Tryon called on the freeholders in each county to elect members to a new assembly, scheduled to meet in the middle of February.[61] Tryon and other New York Loyalists were attempting to revive the colonial assembly in an effort to counter the Provincial Congress's actions. "I have much reason to suspect that the tories have it in contemplation to steal a march upon us, if they can, in respect of a New Assembly," observed Alexander Hamilton, who anticipated such a maneuver as early as December 1775, adding that the motives for it at this time are probably these: It is hoped that the attention of the people being engaged with their new institutions, Congresses, Committees and the like; they will think the assembly of little importance, and will not exert themselves as they ought to do, whereby the tories may . . . elect their own creatures [or] at least it is expected the people may be thrown into divisions and ferments, injurious to present measures.[62]

Tryon truly believed that a new assembly would undermine New York's Whigs and revive royal government in the colony.[63] But he grossly underestimated the Whigs' strength in the colony of New York.

On Election Day, the Whigs rallied their supporters and won twenty-four of the twenty-eight seats in the new assembly. Of the four Loyalists elected, Christopher Billopp and Benjamin Seaman were from Staten Island.[64] In fact, the island was the only community to elect an all-Loyalist delegation to the new assembly.[65] Faced with an assembly dominated by Whigs, Tryon prorogued it, and the New York Assembly never met again.[66]

By the end of 1775, the British military forces in Boston were eager to strike New England. But beginning a military campaign into the New England countryside from Boston posed major risks, as the British had little or no support outside the city. For this reason, British military strategists decided to use another battle plan. They would place a stranglehold on the New Englanders by using their powerful navy to blockade the coast from Newport, Rhode Island, to Halifax, Nova Scotia; march an army from Canada into northern New York; and use a coordinated sea and land assault to capture New York City. And with their naval superiority, the British could control the lower Hudson River valley. They also assumed that logistical and military assistance would be available from the Loyalists living in the communities in the surrounding area. By controlling New York City and the Hudson River valley, the British could isolate New England and geographically divide the colonies. If successfully implemented, British military officials believed that this plan could swiftly bring the rebellion to an end.[67]

To properly defend New York, the Whigs had to develop a plan to control the communities around the city where the Loyalists were numerous, and Staten Island was clearly one of those communities. In addition, the harbor island's location and its residents' Loyalist sympathies made it potentially troublesome. So beginning in February 1776, Whig troops were deployed to Staten Island to secure its livestock and control its residents' activities. But this action only added to the Staten Islanders' resentment of the Whigs, who had ignored their delegates' efforts for reconciliation in the Provincial Congress and imposed economic sanctions on the island. For Staten Islanders, the Whigs were the oppressors, not the defenders, of the political liberty portrayed in their propaganda. As the military campaign of 1776 approached, the Whigs sought more aggressively to control Loyalist activities and to limit dissent in the New York region. But the methods they used to achieve these goals only further angered and alienated Staten Islanders.

# 3

# "As the Tempest Approaches"
## Staten Island and the Whig Defense of New York City

As 1776 began, the Continental forces commanded by General George Washington were effectively besieging Boston and the ten thousand British troops stationed there. But persistent rumors circulating throughout the Continental lines that the British were planning to evacuate Boston and to make New York City their next target caused Washington great consternation. Although Boston may have been the ideological soul of the colonial protest movement against British imperial policy, New York City was its strategic heart. Washington and other Whig military leaders well knew that if New York City fell to the British, it could have dire consequences for the war effort. By capturing New York City, occupying the St. Lawrence River valley, and using their navy to control communications and move troops freely along the Lake Champlain–Hudson River corridor, the British could drive a wedge between the colonies, squeeze New England into submission, and end the rebellion. Correctly assessing the situation, Washington wrote to John Hancock, the president of the Continental Congress, asking "to have some of the Jersey Troops thrown into New York, to prevent an evil, which may be almost irremediable, should it happen: I mean the landing of [British] Troops at that place, or upon Long Island near it."[1] But time was of the essence, and Washington could not wait for Hancock's reply. Instead, he ordered General Charles Lee, his most experienced staff officer, to go to New York City to oversee its defense. Lee arrived in New York on February 4. Defending the city would test his military expertise.

New York City's physical geography and the Loyalist-dominated areas surrounding it created strategic burdens unlike those in Boston, where the Whigs eventually scored their first victory. There, the Continental army

43

bottled up the British by fortifying and blockading the many heights and roads surrounding the city. But more important, the British found little or no support from the surrounding countryside. Lee recognized immediately that New York did not have the same advantage.

The numerous islands and waterways dominating New York's geography favored the British navy. "What to do with this city . . . puzzles me," Lee confessed to Washington. "It is so encircled with deep navigable water," he continued, "that whoever commands the sea must command the town."[2] The British navy's ability to control the Hudson and East rivers that bordered Manhattan would easily allow an amphibious assault on the city. Although Lee predicted that the Whigs could not hold New York against a sustained British attack, he was confident that the city could be fortified in such a way as to inflict heavy casualties on the enemy.[3] Accordingly, he devised a defensive scheme that included fortifications within the city and at key water approaches such as on Brooklyn Heights in western Long Island, at Paulus Hook in New Jersey,[a] and at Horn's Hook in northeastern Manhattan, which overlooks "Hell Gate," a treacherous body of water connecting the Long Island Sound to the East River.

A crucial part of Lee's plan was posting artillery on Brooklyn Heights, which commanded the city and the East River. "This," he wrote to Washington, "is the capital object; for should the enemy take possession of New York, when Long Island is in our hands, they will find it almost impossible to subsist."[4] In Lee's estimation, Brooklyn Heights was the key defensive position in the New York region. There, he warned the New York Provincial Congress, "an enemy is perhaps more dangerous than in any other spot of America."[5] If the British were to take possession of Brooklyn Heights, it would mean a reversal of the situation in Boston, where the Whigs controlled the high ground overlooking the city. Lee's plan to construct fortifications at Paulus Hook was designed to frustrate the British navy's ability to navigate the Hudson River, and the fortifications at Horn's Hook would protect against a British approach from Long Island Sound.

But in this plan, Staten Island, whose residents had demonstrated a disdain for colonial resistance and were widely known for their Loyalist sentiments, would be left undefended. The strategic value of the island should have been obvious. If the British secured it, they would effectively

---

[a] Present-day Jersey City, New Jersey.

most important

control the entrance to New York Harbor and, perhaps just as important, easily procure the provisions—wood, fresh drinking water, produce, and livestock—necessary to sustain the army during a military campaign against New York City.

Lee's choice not to fortify Staten Island and, by extension, the Narrows is problematic given his larger strategy. Even contemporaries viewed protection of the Narrows as important to New York's defense. Colonel William Douglas, who was posted with the Sixth Connecticut Regiment on Long Island, recognized that it would be impossible to defend the city "unless we . . . fortify the narrows."[6] The Continental Congress hoped that Lee would consider "the practicability of obstructing or . . . of fortifying . . . [the Narrows] so as to prevent the entrance of the enemy."[7] Artillery placed along the shorelines of Staten Island and Long Island, and especially on Staten Island's heights, would be in a position to fire on the British fleet as it sailed through the Narrows into upper New York Bay. The batteries might not prevent the British from landing in those areas, but they would make it costly; which would be in keeping with Lee's overall strategy. In addition, a sandbar that extended from Sandy Hook, New Jersey, to Coney Island would force British ships to carefully navigate the channel between lower New York Bay and the Atlantic Ocean, slowing their progress and leaving them vulnerable to crossfire from Continental riflemen and artillery posted on opposite sides of the Narrows.[8] But Lee kept to his original plan, fortifying only Brooklyn Heights, Manhattan, and the approaches to the Hudson and East rivers.

Problem

This did not mean that Lee had not thought about the island strategically. He did recommend to the New York committee of safety that Staten Island's livestock be protected from falling into British hands,[9] and the New York committee asked the New Jersey Provincial Congress for help in carrying out Lee's recommendation. The New Jersey Whig government was asked to guard the livestock "on the Island till we have opportunity to determine on the expediency of removing it."[10] This decision was prompted by the arrival in New York of three British warships on their way from Boston to Charleston, South Carolina. The warships carried General Sir Henry Clinton and several hundred British troops. News of Clinton's arrival brought panic to the city, as residents feared that invasion was imminent. But Clinton's arrival was strategic. He reconnoitered the area, met with Governor William Tryon, who was still on board a British vessel in the harbor, and obtained valuable intelligence about the strength of New York's defenses.[11]

The New York committee of safety, however, was unsure of Clinton's true intentions and wrote to the Provincial Congress of New Jersey that Clinton's arrival signaled that "some lodgment of troops was intended to be made in or near this city." The situation was made more urgent on February 11 when Colonel Abraham Lott of the New York militia reported to the New York committee that he had obtained information from a person near the Kill van Kull that the three British warships were planning to "commit depredations on the stock" on Staten Island.[12]

The New Jersey Whig government immediately responded to the New York committee's request. Colonel Nathaniel Heard of Woodbridge, New Jersey, who commanded seven hundred men from Essex, Middlesex, and Sussex counties, was dispatched to Staten Island.[13] Meanwhile, the Elizabethtown committee of observation and General William Livingston of the New Jersey militia, who later served as the first governor of the state of New Jersey, deployed troops to support Heard, to protect the island's livestock, and to gather intelligence.[14]

On February 12, Staten Islanders were surprised by the sight of New Jersey militia patrolling the island. Colonel Heard arrived four days later from a successful expedition to Queens County on Long Island, where he had disarmed and arrested several Loyalists.[15] He deployed his troops along Staten Island's shoreline and at key intersections and ferry landings. The crisis dissipated when the three British warships carrying General Clinton and his troops sailed out of the New York area.[16] But the island's vulnerability to a British landing and the Loyalist sympathies of numerous residents remained problems needing attention.

Staten Islanders resented the presence of New Jersey troops on the island. They also were incensed that the New York Provincial Congress had not notified them of its plans. The island's provincial congressmen-elect, Adrian Bancker and Richard Lawrence, claimed that the presence of the New Jersey troops would further weaken the Whigs' cause on Staten Island.[17] The congress responded that it had received several reports indicating that Clinton was planning to send landing parties to the island to carry off livestock and other provisions and that the New Jersey troops were intended for no other purpose than to protect the livestock.[18]

Meanwhile, Colonel Heard grew impatient with the island residents' blatant disregard for the Whig cause, who peppered his men with insults and threats.[19] He therefore decided to take action and arrested four Staten Islanders: Minah Burger, Richard Conner, Isaac Decker, and Abraham Harris. Heard accused Decker, a ferry and tavern proprietor, of providing supplies to General Clinton, of publicly opposing the Provincial Congress, and of helping Cortlandt Skinner, a New Jersey Loyalist who had simultaneously held the offices of attorney general and speaker of the assembly, elude capture by Whig authorities. Harris allegedly drank "damnation to Independency" and had recruited thirty men in Egg Harbor, New Jersey, for the British army. The charges of Loyalist behavior against Minah Burger, a farmer, and the former provincial congressman Richard Conner, were vague at best.[20] Instead of turning them over to Staten Island's committee of safety, Colonel Heard sent the four detainees to Elizabethtown, where he believed the men were more likely to be convicted. There, Robert Ogden, the chairman of the committee of observation, ordered the men placed in the town's jail to await trial.[21]

The Staten Island committee protested the arrests. In what seemed to be an obvious attempt at appeasement, the New York Provincial Congress responded to their concerns by issuing a formal protest to the Elizabethtown committee of observation. The congress informed the Elizabethtown committee that under New York law, the men had to be turned over to "the County Committee of the County in which such delinquents reside."[22]

Ogden reluctantly remanded the four men to the custody of the Staten Island committee. He also delivered to the Staten Island committee all the evidence he had obtained from Colonel Heard against the defendants. The trial, which was held on March 7, was a farce. Some of the witnesses failed to testify, and others suddenly claimed that they had not seen or heard anything in connection to the charges. One witness who testified against the men complained that the Staten Island committee allowed him to endure "insufferable abuse." He was called "an informer, cut-throat, dirty rascal, dirty dog, liar" and threatened with physical harm.[23] Consequently, the charges against the four defendants were dropped, and they were released. New York Whigs condemned the Staten Island committee's handling of the trial as "improper and ineffectual."[24]

These events are reminiscent of the failed British investigation into the burning of the *Gaspee*, a royal revenue cutter that had run aground near Pawtucket, Rhode Island, in June 1772 as it patrolled for smugglers. Although the British were able to identify the persons responsible for attacking the ship, the lack of witnesses willing to testify against them doomed the investigation. In the case of the four accused Staten Island Loyalists, however, it was the Whigs who could not mount a successful prosecution because of the lack of witnesses.

Colonel Heard's actions further angered Staten Island residents and stiffened their Loyalist sympathies. Alexander McDonald complained that Heard's actions demonstrated the lengths to which the Whigs would go to force people to "abide by the Laws of Congress." He hoped that the events on Staten Island "will Serve to open the peoples Eyes to show them what Slaves they will be, if ever they had the misfortune, to come under the Yoke of such tyrants."[25] The already strained relationship between Staten Islanders and the Whigs worsened in the coming months.

Meanwhile, General Lee's plans for defending New York City were moving forward when he was reassigned to command the Continental army's newly created Southern Department. On March 7, he departed for Charleston, South Carolina.[26] Lee was replaced in New York by General William Alexander of New Jersey, who was known to contemporaries as "Lord Stirling" because of his claim to a Scottish peerage.[27]

On his way to Charleston, Lee stopped in Philadelphia to update congress's Board of War on the situation in New York and to warn them of the danger that Staten Island might pose to New York's defense.[28] Interestingly, Lee's *Report on the Defence of New York* admitted that any plans to defend the city would be fruitless if precautions were not taken to secure Staten Island. Referring to the island's residents, Lee reported that "the bonds they have given [to the British] are too ridiculous to be mentioned, the Association they have signed they consider as forced upon them and, consequently, null." He concluded that Staten Islanders "should without loss of time, be disarmed, and their arms delivered to some regiment already raised, but unfurnished with muskets." If this measure was not successful, he suggested that congress "secure their children as hostages."[29]

Neither congress nor Lord Stirling acted on Lee's drastic recommendation to hold Staten Island's children hostage to discourage their parents' Loyalist sympathies. Despite a reputation for heavy drinking, Stirling was viewed by his contemporaries as an able military commander. He had surveyed his predecessor's plans for New York City's defense and recognized that the dearth of troops, skilled engineers, arms, gunpowder, and artillery would delay the completion of fortifications and thereby the defense of numerous areas.[30] A similar observation may have also influenced Lee's decision to seek an alternative solution for Staten Island.

Stirling wrote numerous dispatches to his military superiors, to the Continental Congress, and to the Whig governments in the region pleading for more troops. "It will require at least eight thousand men to put

Portrait of American General William Alexander (Lord Stirling). From Ira K. Morris, *Morris's Memorial History of Staten Island, New York*, 2 vols. (New York: Memorial Publishing Company, 1898–1900), vol. 1, 232. Stirling succeeded General Charles Lee in March 1776 as commander of Continental forces in New York City. Stirling worried that Staten Island was the greatest weakness in the Whigs' plans for the defense of the New York City region and urged its fortification. Courtesy of the Staten Island Historical Society.

*8000 men were needed*

this place in any posture of defense by the month of May," he wrote to General Philip Schuyler, who was in command of the Continental army's Middle Department.[31] Stirling also had difficulty convincing the Whig governments of New York and New Jersey to assign more militia to the city's defense. "As the Tempest approaches and threatens to burst upon Them," wrote John Hancock, "I flatter myself the Convention of New York will strain every Nerve in speedily raising and arming the four Battalions, ordered to be raised there for the Defence of their Colony."[32]

While his military superiors and the local civil authorities mulled over his requests, Stirling proceeded with New York's defenses. He was especially concerned with the slow progress on the fortifications on Brooklyn Heights and accordingly ordered that all the able-bodied male residents of New York City and Kings County on Long Island,—whether free persons, indentured servants, or slaves—report with their spades, pickaxes, and hoes for fatigue duty on Brooklyn Heights.[33] The joint military-civilian effort was extended to include Fort Washington on the upper wide side of Manhattan and Fort Lee[b] on the New Jersey Palisades. Both forts overlooked the Hudson River and would force British vessels to run a gauntlet of artillery and small-arms fire to successfully navigate the river. If necessary, they could also be used as fallback positions by Continental troops posted in New York City. By late March, Stirling was able to report that significant progress had been made on the fortifications on Brooklyn Heights and along the Hudson River.[34]

But the Loyalist problem remained and would continue to threaten as reports surfaced of the imminent British invasion. Stirling had earlier worked closely with Lee to try to control Loyalist activities in the New York region. They also tried, unsuccessfully, to convince the New York Provincial Congress to repeal its policy permitting the limited provisioning of the British vessels in the harbor.[35] Both men correctly assumed that in addition to supplies, the British were obtaining valuable military intelligence. On March 8, Stirling informed the congress that he viewed the fear of a potential British blockade or bombardment of the city as keeping it from repealing its policy toward provisioning the British ships in the harbor. But he also pointed out that it was important to prevent valuable intelligence about the deployment of troops and the progress made on fortifications from reaching the enemy. The congress agreed to a compromise that would allow officially authorized boats and crews to deliver

[b] Fort Lee was also known as Fort Constitution.

*# ② Quest— did the congress allow—*

a limited amount of supplies to the British ships. Crew members were not to board the vessels, nor were the owners of the provision boats to hire extra crew without official approval from the military authorities.[36]

Although it was relatively easy to monitor the flow of supplies and information from New York, controlling the activities of the Loyalists in the countryside surrounding the city was not. Especially troublesome were the Loyalists on Staten Island. "The enemies to American liberty are busy on Staten-Island . . . and some dangerous movements are now going on among them," Stirling wrote to New York's committee of safety.[37] He was determined to end these dangerous movements.

Stirling believed that the best way to prevent Staten Islanders from making contact with the British ships was to enlist the aid of the New Jersey Whigs. He wrote to Samuel Tucker, the president of the Provincial Congress of New Jersey, asking him to halt "all communication . . . between any part of the Province of New-Jersey and Staten Island, on the one part, and the Men-of-War which now are, or hereafter may be, within Sandy Hook, or any ship or vessel that has any connection with them." He suggested that Tucker deploy four hundred New Jersey militia men on the island's heights and near the Watering Place, where they would be able to prevent the British from receiving wood and fresh water, keep watch over the Atlantic Ocean for the arrival of the British fleet, and guard the Kills.[38]

Although the New Jersey Whig government stopped all shipping from its ports to the British warships, it did not send troops to Staten Island. Because of the low number of enlistments, not enough troops were available for duty on the island. Frustrated, Stirling could only read daily reports of Staten Islanders making contact with the British vessels in the harbor.[39]

Meanwhile, the Continental siege of Boston tightened as Washington ordered that artillery captured from the British forts at Ticonderoga and Crown Point in New York be moved to Dorchester Heights, overlooking the city. Here the artillery made Boston untenable for the British. General William Howe, who had replaced General Thomas Gage as the British military commander in chief in America, initially planned to dislodge the Continentals from Dorchester Heights. This must have been a difficult decision for the man who the previous summer commanded the devastating assault on Breed's Hill in what is popularly referred to as the "Battle of Bunker Hill," resulting in more than one thousand British casualties. But with provisions in short supply, many of his men ill after enduring a cold

Portrait of General William Howe, the commander in chief of British forces in
North America from 1775 to 1778. From Ira K. Morris, *Morris's Memorial
History of Staten Island, New York,* 2 vols. (New York: Memorial Publishing
Company, 1898–1900), vol. 1, 207. Courtesy of the Staten Island Historical
Society.

and bitter winter, and the Pyrrhic victory at the Battle of Bunker Hill still haunting him, Howe decided to abandon Boston, believing that evacuating the city would afford the best chance to keep the army intact to fight another day.[40]   *Blunder*

Preparations for the evacuation of Boston began immediately. In their haste to abandon the city, however, the British left behind several field-pieces, wagons, horses, and a large cache of small arms, gunpowder, and flint. On March 17, the last British vessel sailed out of Boston Harbor, leaving the city and the abandoned supplies to the Continental army.[41] When and where in America would the British army appear next?

Although Washington was convinced that his opponent would immediately descend on New York City, the British were actually bound for Halifax, Nova Scotia. The need to defend New York was more urgent now than ever before. "We should secure New York and prevent the Enemy from possessing it," Washington advised John Hancock, adding that "New York is of such importance; prudence and policy require, that every precaution that can be devised, should be adopted to frustrate the designs which the Enemy may have of obtaining possession of it."[42] He counseled Stirling that while the British military's plans were not definitely known, "supposing New York to be an Object of much importance & to be in their view, I must recommend your most strenuous and active exertions in preparing to prevent any designs or Attempts they may have against it." Washington also informed Stirling that as soon as Boston was fully secured and the British fleet had sailed from its immediate vicinity, he would be sending a detachment of riflemen and five battalions to reinforce New York City.[43] Until then, Stirling should continue to work on New York's defenses, for "the fate of America depends upon this campaign," Washington exclaimed, "and the success of this campaign will a good deal depend upon your exerting yourselves with vigour upon this occasion."[44]   *Fate of America*

As rumors of a British descent on New York City increased each day after Boston was evacuated, securing Staten Island took on more importance for Stirling and the Whig governments of New York and New Jersey. On one occasion, Stirling received intelligence that the Staten Islander John James Boyd had made "expressions injurious to the country, and in favour of Ministerial tyranny." He ordered Captain John Warner of the New York militia to collect any evidence against Boyd that he could find and to turn it over to the civil authorities in New York.[45] But after reviewing the evidence, the New York Provincial Congress dismissed the case, concluding that Boyd was "so unimportant and insignificant a person in the community, as not to deserve the expense or trouble of apprehending him without further testimony of some overt acts inimical to the American Colonies." Nonetheless, Whig military and civil authorities continued to closely monitor the Staten Islanders' activities.[46]

The Whigs also were still concerned about the exposure of Staten Island's livestock to British landing parties. On March 27, New York's committee of safety urged the Staten Island committee to arrange to have the livestock moved to New Jersey if necessary. It also warned that its failure to prepare such a plan would result in the livestock's being removed by New Jersey troops.[47]

On March 20, General William Thompson of Pennsylvania arrived in New York City and, because of his senior rank, replaced Stirling as commander. Although Stirling returned to New Jersey to help plan its defenses, he remained a strong advocate for securing Staten Island, which was as important to the security of New Jersey as it was to that of New York.[48] He wrote to General Livingston of the New Jersey militia that it was "highly Necessary to possess some Commanding height on Staten Island; the Men employed in these works will be in the most proper places to Guard the province."[49]

Unfortunately for the Whigs, Stirling's plans for securing Staten Island did not progress. General William Heath, who had assumed command in New York City from Thompson after the latter was transferred to the Canadian theater, reiterated to the New Jersey Whigs the importance of fortifying the island. He wrote to General Livingston that the defense of New York and New Jersey "in a very great Measure depends upon our being well possessed of Staten Island."[50] On April 1, Stirling warned Washington, who was still in Boston, that the island remained the region's greatest weakness. Staten Island was open to a British invasion, and he wrote that "I should be glad we were possessed of it that we could prevent . . . any lodgment in it." Stirling also sought Washington's permission to take charge of the defenses there.[51]

On April 3, General Israel Putnam of Connecticut arrived from Boston with more reinforcements and took command of New York's defenses. Putnam, who was a veteran of the French and Indian War, immediately occupied Nutten Island[c] in New York Harbor and ordered the construction of fortifications on Staten Island.[52]

[c] Present-day Governors Island.

As the frequency of reports of a British invasion increased, Putnam and the other Whig military leaders in the region became even more anxious to fortify Staten Island and sent three companies of Virginia and Maryland riflemen to the island. There they would receive their orders from Stirling, who was in New Jersey. To prevent the British from supplying their vessels with fresh water from Staten Island's springs, Stirling posted several riflemen on the east shore near the Watering Place. Riflemen were also positioned at other key locations along the island's shoreline, at important crossroads, and on the heights overlooking the Narrows. "The Rifle Men are all over Staten Island," reported Andrew Elliot, the former collector of the port of New York, to Governor William Tryon, "by the best accounts I can get there is about 1100."[53] One Staten Islander recalled that the troops were "billeted among the farmers on the North shore . . . [and others] were stationed at the Narrows."[54]

On April 6, Putnam received intelligence that two British vessels—the *Savage* and the *James*—had anchored off Staten Island's north shore. He believed that this maneuver signaled the British forces' imminent invasion of New York City. The island's history of collaborating with the British and the high state of alert in and around New York added to Putnam's concerns, so he immediately ordered Captain Hugh Stephenson, who commanded a company of Virginia riflemen already on Staten Island, to step up patrols of the island's shoreline in search of Loyalist collaborators.[55]

On the morning of April 7, the two British vessels slowly maneuvered under a thick cover of fog closer to Staten Island's shoreline. They eventually moored near the Watering Place and sent two landing parties ashore. While the British troops filled casks with drinking water to take back to their ships, Captain Stephenson marched his troops to the Watering Place hoping to surprise them. But a Staten Islander warned the landing parties of his approach, and they quickly retreated to their ships. Despite a barrage of cannon and musket fire from the British warships, Stephenson and his men pressed the attack and were able to capture ten prisoners.[56]

Although brief and of little strategic importance, the skirmish at the Watering Place marked the beginning of a new phase in the war for New York. After he received reports of the skirmish, Putnam wrote to John Hancock that "Hostilities are now commenced in this Province."[57] On April 8, Putnam ordered an immediate end to all communication with the British warships in the harbor. He also announced that supplies would no

*Great point Provincial Congress*

longer be allowed to be delivered to the British vessels and that any persons who "have been on board, or near any of the ships, or going on board, will be considered enemies, and treated accordingly."[58] But Putnam's actions did not receive the full support of the New York Provincial Congress, which still did not want to risk a British blockade or bombardment of the city. *Why*

In addition to their orders to fortify Staten Island, the riflemen also were to disarm and arrest residents suspected of Loyalist behavior. "More Tories have Been sent for and brought before the Captain," wrote one Virginia rifleman.[59] On April 7, Continental troops arrested Darby Doyle, a ferry operator who lived near the Watering Place. Was Doyle the person who warned the British landing parties of the approach of Captain Stephenson and his riflemen before the skirmish at the Watering Place? The Whigs certainly thought so and sent him to New York City for questioning by military authorities.[60] The Staten Island committee of safety, however, protested Doyle's arrest on the grounds that it could not "approve of such conduct in taking him out of County."[61] After he was questioned by the Whig military authorities in New York, Doyle was released. He returned to the island and lived under the watchful eye of the Whig military authorities.

Before he left Staten Island for Halifax, Nova Scotia, where he joined the Royal Highland Regiment, Alexander McDonald had become a major target of Whig acrimony because he refused to "offer such violence to my honour and Conscience . . . and [join] in a Cause of which I always entertained a bad Opinion."[62] He told a close confidant that several Whigs had threatened to "skin me alive."[63] On one occasion, McDonald's wife Susannah and their children were harassed by Continental soldiers "with more than Savage rudeness." She suffered "a vast many insults & abuses As far as words & Language & Quartering the Villains in her house could do." Yet, Susannah "behaved with an Uncommon degree of Courage & even went so far as when they cursed the King she cursed the Congress to their faces."[64] Similar incidents were repeated throughout the island. Tensions between residents and Continental troops intensified as reports mounted that the British invasion of New York City was imminent.

On April 12, Putnam ordered Stirling to deploy a brigade of New Jersey Continentals to reinforce the riflemen on Staten Island. In an attempt to diffuse tensions and avoid the type of reception given to Colonel Heard and his men in February, Stirling asked the New York Provincial Congress to inform the Staten Islanders that troops would be quartered in their homes "until the season of the year will admit of their being encamped." He also asked the congress to reassure the Staten Islanders that he would do his best "to render the residence of the troops among them as little burdensome as possible" and that he would make sure that they were compensated fairly and promptly for the use of their homes, supplies, and labor.[65]

The New York Whigs requested that Staten Island's committee of safety "prepare empty Farm-houses . . . and where those cannot be had, that they prepare quarters and places . . . in Dwelling-houses" for Stirling's New Jersey troops.[66] On April 16, Christian Jacobson, the chairman of the Staten Island committee, responded to this request. "Nothing on our part shall be neglected in quartering the troops under the command of Lord Stirling," and he noted that the Staten Island committee had agreed "to exert our influence with the inhabitants, to give them all possible assistance." Finally, Jacobson took the opportunity to remind the Whigs that if they wanted the full cooperation of the island's residents, they should respect both persons and property and keep their promises to fairly and promptly compensate them.[67]

The Staten Island committee used its influence and Whig promises of fair and prompt compensation to obtain quarters, provisions, and labor for the New Jersey troops. By early May, however, Staten Islanders had not been compensated. In addition, several residents complained that their fields and gardens had been "over-run and eaten up by the Rebels."[68] The duplicity of these actions outraged Staten Islanders. They now distrusted the Whigs more than ever before.

Meanwhile, elections were held in April for delegates to the Third New York Provincial Congress. On April 22, Staten Islanders elected Richard Conner, Aaron Cortelyou, John Journeay, and Paul Micheau Jr. to the congress, all four of whom had served in the first Provincial Congress, where they strongly supported reconciliation. Now Staten Island's slate of delegates voted against supporting independence and the creation of a new government for America. They also opposed a law calling for the arrest of persons who held a military or civil commission under the king or who were reputed to be enemies to the cause of American liberty. These persons were to be tried by a special committee within the congress.[69] Thus, as Continental troops occupied the island and the New York Whigs were moving closer to independence, Staten Island's delegates to the Third Provincial Congress continued to support reconciliation.

Washington arrived in New York City on April 12 and immediately assumed command of its defenses. Like Lee, he quickly realized the difficulty of preparing the New York region as a favorable theater of war against an enemy with a superior navy.[70] Washington even considered abandoning New York, but the Continental Congress wanted the city defended. So Washington, who understood the politics of warfare better than did any other officer in the Continental army, did his best to accommodate the congress's wishes.[71]

Expecting the British invasion to begin at any moment, Washington tried to expand the defenses originally designed by Lee. But the Continental army in the New York region was in pitiful shape because of frequent desertions, few reenlistments, and the failure of local Whig governments to fill militia quotas. It also lacked artillery, small arms and ammunition, and an officer corps with substantial battlefield experience. Overcrowded, unsanitary living conditions and a shortage of fresh supplies overwhelmed Washington's troops, draining their physical strength. Malnutrition and scurvy permeated the ranks, and desperate, undisciplined, and bored soldiers stole from residents.[72] Private Joseph Plumb Martin of Milford, Connecticut, recalled that the men "imagined that it was no injury to supply themselves when they thought they could do so with impunity."[73] In addition, news of the ill-fated invasion of Canada led by General Richard Montgomery and Colonel Benedict Arnold tempered the excitement of victory that Washington's men brought with them from Boston.

But their commander in chief was undeterred. He continued to move forward with New York's defenses, pressing his weary soldiers and subordinate officers to focus on the work at hand. In his general orders, Washington inspired them to sustain the cause, not to shrink from the challenge at this crucial moment in the history of their country.

> The time is now near at hand which must probably determine, whether Americans are to be, Freemen, or Slaves; whether they are to have any property they can call their own; whether their Houses, and Farms, are to be pillaged and destroyed, and they consigned to a State of Wretchedness from which no human efforts will probably deliver them.

He closed his message by impressing on his officers and troops that

> the fate of unborn Millions will now depend, under God, on the Courage and Conduct of this army—Our cruel and unrelenting Enemy

leaves us no choice but a brave resistance, or the most abject submission; this is all we can expect—We have therefore to resolve to conquer or die: Our own Country's Honour, all call upon us for a vigorous and manly exertion, and if we now shamefully fail, we shall become infamous to the whole world.[74]

Work was soon completed on Fort Lee on the New Jersey Palisades, on Fort Washington on the upper west side of Manhattan, and on Fort Independence at Kings Bridge at the southern end of Westchester County,[d] designed to protect the Hudson and Harlem river crossings. Washington also ordered chains, *chevaux de fries*, and sunken ships placed at key locations along the Hudson River to hamper its navigation. He pressed the Whig governments in New York and New Jersey to prepare plans to be able to call militia into service quickly in case of an emergency; he ordered his officers to have their men practice marksmanship and decamping at a moment's notice; and he reinforced the Continental positions on Brooklyn Heights.[75] Finally, Washington directed Generals Nathanael Greene, John Sullivan, and Stirling to establish signal stations on the "Heights and Head Lands at the entrance of the Harbour." The system used a series of flags and fires "to convey the first notice of the approach of an Enemy's fleet." Signal stations were eventually located on the Highlands of the Navesink River near Sandy Hook, New Jersey, and on the heights of Staten Island overlooking the Narrows.[e][76]

By early July, Washington was able to write to John Hancock, "I have the pleasure to inform you, that an agreeable spirit and willingness for Action seem to animate and pervade the whole of our Troops."[77] But the local Loyalists still posed a danger, which was revealed by the failure of conspirators, under the direction of Governor William Tryon and the mayor of New York David Matthews, to kidnap Washington, murder his staff officers, destroy the King's Bridge connecting northern Manhattan to the southern end of Westchester County, promote mass desertions from the Continental army, and secretly recruit a large Loyalist regiment.[f]

Washington was fully aware of the seriousness of the Loyalist problem in the New York region. Therefore, for New York to be thoroughly secured, Loyalist actions and movements in and around the city had to be

---

[d] Located in what is today the borough of the Bronx.

[e] The signal was located on a hill in present-day Fort Wadsworth National Historic Park.

[f] This conspiracy is alternately referred to as the "Hickey Conspiracy" or "Tryon's Plot."

No communication again

controlled. Accordingly, Washington suggested that New York's committee of safety issue a resolution banning all trade and communication with
the British vessels in the harbor. He promised that the military would fully
cooperate in enforcing this resolution and issued a proclamation to that
effect. The New York committee promptly announced that persons
caught communicating with or supplying the British would be "dealt with
in the severest Manner as Enemies to the Rights and Liberties of the
united North American Colonies." That the New York committee supported such a measure with British warships still in the port area is testa-
ment to Washington's political skill and astuteness.[78]

On May 4, Staten Islander Peter Poillon was apprehended by a Whig
patrol after he was seen leaving the British warship *Asia*, anchored in the
Narrows. He was charged with supplying the British "in violation of &
contrary to the regulations which have been adopted for preventing such
practices."[79] On May 8, Poillon appeared before New York's committee
of safety and explained that he had departed from his house "with a considerable sum of Money to discharge a debt he owed to a person in King's
County and with some articles of provisions, intended for the New-York
market." He testified that although he kept close to shore, the *Asia* fired
at his boat, causing him to give up his provisions. Poillon claimed that the
New York committee's ban on trade with the British ships and Washington's proclamation were never publicly made known on Staten Island.
The New York committee thereupon acquitted Poillon, but not before ordering him "to endeavour to prevent any other inhabitant of Richmond
County from attempting to come, with any Provisions, within reach of
the guns of the said Ships, or of any other Ministerial Ship or Vessel" by
doing his best "to make the Regulations adopted with respect to the said
Ships pubickly known in Richmond County."[80]

The failure of the Staten Island committee of safety to notify residents
of the ban on trade with the British vessels and its questionable handling
of residents suspected of Loyalist behavior once again raised suspicions
as to where its sympathies lay. On May 6, Dr. Thomas Frost, the Richmond County sheriff, was accused of sending information to the British.
Frost denied the allegation. When the Staten Island committee called
William Dunn, Frost's principle accuser, to testify, he refused, explaining
that he "did not choose to trust" the committee. He also argued that
Frost should be sent to Whig-occupied Perth Amboy to be tried. Dunn,
like Colonel Heard earlier in February, rightfully believed that obtaining
convictions against residents accused of Loyalist behavior was impossible

on Staten Island. Although Dunn finally acquiesced and gave his testimony, the Staten Island committee felt that it was not enough to bring Frost to trial and immediately released him.[81]

Washington, too, had serious doubts about the political loyalty of Staten Island's committee of safety, as seen in his effort to remove the island's livestock. The exposure of Staten Island's livestock remained a crucial concern for the Whigs. Thus, in an attempt to deprive the British of provisions, Washington worked out a new plan that made the New York Provincial Congress responsible for removing the livestock and horses from the island.[82] The congress cooperated with this new plan by ordering Staten Island's committee to work with the Elizabethtown committee of observation to have all the livestock, except those animals deemed "indispensably necessary," taken to New Jersey.[83] But Washington did not trust the Staten Island committee to carry out the congress's order. Instead, he directed Captain Ephraim Manning of the Third Connecticut Regiment, which was already posted on Staten Island, to immediately "drive the Stock off, without waiting for the assistance or direction of the Committee there, lest their slow mode of transacting business might produce too much delay."[84]

Despite his political expertise, Washington still was unable to untangle New York politics. The Staten Island committee delayed carrying out the congress's order, and the residents refused to cooperate, instead hiding their animals in the island's forests. "Our infamous brethren of Staten Island, instead of assisting the troops in removing the stock," reported General John Morin Scott of the New York militia, "they drove them into hiding places."[85] Governor Jonathan Trumbull of Connecticut remarked that Staten Islanders were "mostly Tory's" who when "ordered to send off their stock . . . found means to delay & delay."[86] In this way, defiant Staten Islanders undermined Washington's plan to remove the livestock and demonstrated the weakness of the Whig position on the island.

During the first half of 1776, the Whigs did everything they could to defend the New York region against a British invasion. But their efforts only further alienated Staten Islanders, who were firmly attached to the British government and waited patiently for its assistance.[87] While for most Americans the British military represented the scourge of imperial tyranny, to Staten Islanders it was the cure for what ailed them: Whig oppression in the name of liberty. The cure eventually came in the form of 450 of His Majesty's warships and 32,000 soldiers and sailors.

# 4

## "Our Inveterate Enemies"

*Staten Islanders and the Arrival of the
British Fleet at New York*

On the morning of June 29, 1776, as a thin haze rose off New York Bay, Continental lookouts posted on the rooftops of lower Manhattan gazed across the water toward the Narrows, just as they had done routinely for several months. But this morning was different: the men glimpsed three white flags waving lazily on the heights of Staten Island, indicating that the British fleet from Halifax, Nova Scotia, had been sighted off Sandy Hook, New Jersey. This was the moment for which the Whigs had been preparing since March. But for the Staten Islanders, it was the moment when the British military had finally arrived to rescue them from the clutches of Whig tyranny.

Following its hasty evacuation of Boston in March, the British army had had major logistical problems. Although he was eager to proceed to New York, General William Howe knew that capturing the city would be impossible without fresh provisions, adequate supplies, and healthy soldiers. He decided therefore to retreat to Halifax where he could regroup his forces, obtain local supplies, and await the arrival of a fleet and reinforcements from Europe, commanded by his brother Admiral Richard Lord Howe. The British thus remained in Halifax throughout the spring of 1776, delaying their move to New York by three months. Nonetheless, they continued monitoring the Whigs' progress on New York's defenses, and General Howe worked on a strategy for the upcoming military campaign season.

With Boston now lost, New York City became the key objective of British military plans for 1776. By the end of 1775, British military officials in America and London had decided on a plan to isolate New England by capturing New York City and gaining control of the Lake

Champlain–Hudson River corridor. Their strategy called for a naval blockade of the New England coast from Newport, Rhode Island, to Halifax, Nova Scotia, and the landing of an army commanded by General Howe at New York. After the city was secured, Howe's army would proceed north along the Hudson River and eventually meet up with an army marching southward from Canada, led by General Sir Guy Carleton. Then the combined armies would march eastward to subdue New England. As part of this plan, Howe intended to lure Washington into a decisive battle for New York City, thus crushing in one stroke his protagonist's inexperienced and overmatched army and the rebellion. The British commander in chief was confident that this strategy was "the most effectual means to terminate this Expensive war."[1]

By early June 1776, several transports and supply vessels had arrived in Halifax from Europe. Although this was not his brother's fleet, General Howe believed that he now possessed enough supplies and transports to begin the campaign against New York.[2] He therefore sailed ahead of the fleet and arrived in New York on June 25. The next day Howe met with Governor William Tryon and several Long Island Loyalists, who notified him of the condition and extent of the Continental fortifications on Brooklyn Heights and in Gravesend on Long Island.[3] Although the Whigs were firmly entrenched in these positions, Howe's informants advised him to strike at them immediately, confident that the world's finest professionally trained army could easily rout Washington's citizen-soldiers and secure Long Island as a preliminary step to capturing New York City.[4]

The British fleet's arrival in Sandy Hook was a stunning sight. Viewing it from the second-floor window of a building in lower Manhattan, Marylander Daniel McCurtain described New York Bay as "a wood of pine trees trimmed. . . . I could not believe my eyes . . . the whole bay was as full of shipping as ever it could be, I declare that I thought all of London was afloat."[5] One Staten Island resident described the lower bay as a cedar swamp.[6] The pro-Whig *New-York Journal* reported that the arrival of the British fleet was reminiscent of the apocalyptical "swarm of Locusts, escaped from the bottomless pit."[7] By dawn on June 30, more than 130 British warships had entered lower New York Bay in a display that was a portent of things to come.[8]

On July 1, Howe prepared his troops for landing at Gravesend on Long Island. The fleet hoisted sail, entered Gravesend Bay, and anchored for the evening opposite the Long Island town of Utrecht. Washington regarded Howe as a predictable, unimaginative strategist and was convinced that he would attack the Continental fortifications on Brooklyn Heights in a replay of the events of Bunker Hill. By capturing Brooklyn Heights, Howe could relegate Washington to the same fate as befell the British army in Boston after the Continentals had posted artillery on Dorchester Heights. In order to prevent this happening, Washington decided to reinforce Brooklyn Heights by, perhaps dangerously, dividing his army. Although some regiments remained on Manhattan to defend New York City, he sent most of his forces to Brooklyn Heights. By so doing, for the first time in the war Washington demonstrated a lack of tactical skill. The Continental troops on Manhattan and Long Island were now separated by the easily navigated East River, from which the British army and navy could surround and cut off the men on Brooklyn Heights. Facing a tactical war for the first time, Washington quickly learned that New York was not Boston and that Howe was not as predictable as he had assumed.

As Washington predicted, Howe intended to land his forces at Gravesend on Long Island, but then he quickly changed his strategy. General James Robertson, one of Howe's most trusted staff officers, convinced him to land the troops on Staten Island.[9] Before joining Howe's staff, Robertson had served under several British commanders in America and knew the harbor island well.[10] In 1761, while serving as the deputy quartermaster under General Jeffrey Amherst, he had established a staging area near the Watering Place on Staten Island. Now Robertson persuasively pushed Staten Island's strategic and logistical advantages. The island's proximity to New York City, Long Island, and New Jersey; its many freshwater springs; and the strong Loyalist sentiments of the majority of its residents were ideal conditions for a long-term staging area. Another British officer concurred with Robertson's assessment of the island. "Staten Island," he wrote, "is absolutely the key of this province, this great city [New York] and Amboy, in New Jersey, can in an hour be bombarded."[11]

The island also had a history of aiding the British military that dated back to the French and Indian War (1754–1763). During that conflict, the British army had allowed Staten Islanders to freely supply the troops with provisions.[12] Payment for these provisions was prompt and in the form of gold and silver specie, which was in short supply in America. This experience taught Staten Islanders that an encamped British army was always good for business.[13] Whereas civilian-military relations in many communities throughout America had been strained by the French and Indian War, this was not the case on Staten Island.[14]

Staten Islanders also helped the British in 1776. The former provincial congressman Richard Lawrence told the British that "there was nobody on the other side of the Island but a parcel of Jersey rascals . . . 500 of such."[15] The ferry operator and tavern owner Isaac Decker, who was one of four Staten Islanders arrested by Colonel Nathaniel Heard in February for Loyalist behavior but released by the Staten Island committee of safety, offered the British his services as a pilot, guiding their ships around the sandbar between Sandy Hook and Coney Island and through the Narrows.[16]

On July 2, Howe ordered three warships—*Greyhound*, *Phoenix*, and *Rose*—and several transports to sail to the Watering Place on Staten Island. As the British ships approached, the Continental troops posted there quickly abandoned their positions, surprising the British at the lack of artillery on Staten Island.[17] One British officer remarked that if the Continental army had properly fortified Staten Island's heights at the Narrows, the fleet would have been "annoyed most prodigiously, for the wind, not being favourable, we were three hours passing them."[18] But because the Whigs had decided to concentrate their available manpower and artillery on Brooklyn Heights, they did not have the means to effectively fortify Staten Island's heights. Consequently, outnumbered and lacking artillery, the Continental soldiers posted on the island retreated to New Jersey, taking some Whig refugees with them.

Among the Whigs who abandoned their homes and property and fled with the Continental army were Hendrick Garrison and his family. Garrison's slave Harry, however, stayed on the island to watch the property in his master's absence.[19] Several members of the Mersereau family also joined the Continental army in its retreat from the island. Joshua Mersereau, who operated one of Staten Island's two shipyards and was perhaps its most ardent Whig; his son John La Grange; and his brothers John and Jacob crossed over to New Jersey, where they became key operatives in a sophisticated spy ring that was headed by Colonel Elias Dayton of the First New Jersey militia and included Captain Baker Hendricks, his brother John Hendricks, and John Meeker of Elizabethtown. The Dayton-Mersereau-Hendricks spy ring secured information for Washington concerning the strength of British forces, troop deployments, and invasion plans. Operating from behind the British lines on Staten Island and in those areas of New Jersey closest to the island, the

Mersereaus and their informants, which included Abraham Bancker, the nephew of former provincial congressman Adrian Bancker, were highly effective spies for Washington until the end of the war.[20]

On July 4, the last of Howe's nine thousand troops landed on Staten Island just as the Continental Congress in Philadelphia was declaring America an independent nation. It was a brilliantly executed landing that caught Washington totally by surprise and left him guessing Howe's next move. Would the British commander in chief make a push for New York? Would he try to secure Long Island before attacking the city? Or would the rich farmlands of central New Jersey be his target? "It is difficult to determine," Washington admitted to John Hancock, "what Objects the Enemy may have in Contemplation."[21] By taking Washington to task, Howe was teaching him how to conduct a tactical war.

Strategically, the capture of Staten Island was a sound maneuver. The centrally located and weakly defended island gave the British an ideal position from which to launch a military campaign against New York City, Long Island, or New Jersey. Its location at the entrance to New York Harbor made Staten Island the geographic key to the New York region. Control of the island also gave the British open access to the farms of New Jersey, located across the narrow Kill van Kull and Arthur Kill waterways. The decision had political ramifications as well. The British military presence on Staten Island emboldened the Loyalists in the area and affected the Whigs' plans for defending New York City, Long Island, and New Jersey. Because of concerns for the security of New Jersey, the Continental troops and militia in that state were prevented from reinforcing Washington's troops on Manhattan and on Brooklyn Heights in western Long Island. The occupation of Staten Island also demonstrated that British commanders had learned a valuable lesson during the French and Indian War on the strategic use of terrain in North America. The British capture of Staten Island thus had broad ramifications for the Whigs' war effort around New York City. Now Howe had the initiative, not Washington. He would decide the next move in this chess game of military strategy.

The British troops were greeted warmly by the elated and anxious Staten Islanders. Many residents lined the island's eastern shoreline and climbed its heights to catch a glimpse of the British flotilla and the landing of the troops.[22] "The inhabitants received us with the greatest joy, seeing well the difference between anarchy and a regular mild government," wrote Major Charles Stuart of the Forty-third Regiment of Foot.[23] An-

*Delivered*

other British officer recalled that Staten Islanders demonstrated "the Greatest Satisfaction on our Arrival, which has relived them from the most horred Opresion that can be conceaved."[24] Captain John Bowater of the Royal Marines described the Staten Islanders as filled "with the Utmost Joy, having been long oppress'd for their Attachment to Government."[25] Howe was overwhelmed by the reception and wrote to the British colonial secretary Lord George Germain that the army had "landed to the great joy of a most loyal people, long suffering on that account under the oppression of the rebels stationed among them."[26] The notion that Staten Islanders were rescued from oppression was echoed by Governor William Tryon, who reported to Lord Germain that "the inhabitants of the Island came down to welcome the arrival of their deliverers."[27] King George III also commended the Staten Islanders for their warm reception.[28]

For the loyal Staten Islanders, the army of liberation had arrived, and they now were free to voice their true sentiments. A number of residents publicly cursed the Continental Congress. Others defiantly burned its paper currency.[29] Although the practice of burning effigies of royal officials and Loyalists was a common form of protest in America against British imperial policy, Staten Islanders burned several effigies of notable Whigs, symbolically demonstrating their displeasure with the rebellion. One evening in late July, Staten Islanders burned effigies of Generals Washington, Lee, and Putnam, as well as the Reverend John Witherspoon, a New Side Presbyterian of Princeton, New Jersey. As the flames from the straw figures symbolizing these four men lit up the nighttime sky, the participants cursed and damned the Whig cause.[30]

Staten Islanders then displayed their loyalty to Britain in a deeper and more odious way, by enlisting in the British army. Indeed, Isaac Decker assured Howe that four hundred to five hundred Staten Islanders were fit and ready to bear arms for the king.[31] On July 6, more than five hundred men, nearly all of them Staten Islanders and several Loyalist refugees from New Jersey, gathered in the village of Richmond and, in an elaborate ceremony attended by Howe and Tryon, happily took an oath of allegiance to King George III. These men formed the basis of a provincial corps and cavalry that were used to defend the island and to provide the army with auxiliary support. Christopher Billopp accepted the rank of lieutenant colonel with a commission to lead the provincial corps,[a] and

---

[a] This provincial unit was known as Billopp's Corps of Staten Island Militia.

Isaac Decker was given the rank of captain and command of the cavalry. The island's residents also pledged to raise £500 to equip and supply these Loyalist troops.[32]

The Whigs were not pleased with the reception that the British received on the island, and Washington declared the Staten Islanders to be "our inveterate Enemies."[33] At the Continental Congress in Philadelphia, a dismayed John Adams lambasted "the unprincipled and unfeeling and unnatural inhabitants of Staten Island . . . [for] cordially receiving the enemy." Because of their actions, he described Staten Islanders as "an ignorant, cowardly pack of scoundrels . . . [whose] numbers are small, and their spirit less."[34]

Once all the troops had landed, Howe ordered his engineers to begin setting up the army's main encampment at the Watering Place. More troops were deployed on Staten Island's heights, along its shoreline at key ferry crossings, and at the Narrows.[35] In a letter to John Hancock, Washington wrote that he had received information from General William Livingston in New Jersey indicating that Howe had no intention of constructing major fortifications.[36] But intelligence is often not perfect. In fact, Howe made extensive plans to fortify Staten Island as soon as he landed, and by the end of July, the British had completed several elaborate fortifications, earthworks, and gun placements on the island.[37] In only one month, Staten Island had been transformed into Fortress Britannia.

The nine thousand British troops and hundreds of Loyalist refugees from the surrounding area needed lodging as well, and many were billeted in private homes, barns, and commercial and public buildings. Lieutenant Loftus Cliffe of the Forty-sixth Regiment of Foot, deployed near the village of Richmond, noted that "most of us lye in Barns upon a blanket." Because of his officer's rank, however, Cliffe was fortunate "to have got into a good house and to have a Bear Skin under me."[38] But the sparsely populated island did not have enough structures to accommodate all the troops. At the main encampment, tents made of sailcloth large enough to house three hundred men were set up.[39] Some soldiers camped in open fields, orchards, and the woods, their tents a sea of white against the green and brown of the island's landscape. One Staten Islander remembered that the British pitched so many tents that "not a blade of grass could be seen."[40]

Howe made his quarters in the home of the former provincial congressman Adrian Bancker, on the main road that ran along the Kill van

Kull.[b] Before the British captured the island, Bancker had taken the opportunity to send his family to stay with relatives in New Jersey, but he remained on Staten Island with their property.[41] Bancker's nephew Abraham described how his uncle demonstrated "a degree of virtue and steadfastness in his country's cause when in the midst of his enemies."[42] On Howe's orders, Bancker was detained on a British naval vessel in New York Harbor.[43]

Although most Whig sympathizers fled Staten Island with the Continental troops, some, like Adrian Bancker, refused to abandon their homes and property to the British. Others were simply not able to leave the island before the British turned it into a garrison, shutting down its ferries and closely guarding its shoreline. As the British army settled in, their civilian supporters ferreted out and exposed adherents to the Whig cause. Loyalist mobs used physical violence and intimidation and ransacked the homes of Whig sympathizers. As one witness recounted, Cornelius Mersereau was removed from his property and "suffered everything but death." Another Staten Islander who supported the Whig cause recalled the daily insults and harassment that he and his family endured from Loyalist neighbors.[44]

In a reversal of earlier practices by Continental officers, the British authorities posted on Staten Island arrested and questioned Whig sympathizers. Among them, the brothers Hezekiah and Abraham Reckhow were apprehended in July and confined to a prison in one of the British fortifications on the island. Although Hezekiah was released because of his epilepsy, Abraham was transferred to the notorious prison ship *Jersey* in Wallabout Bay,[c] where he suffered greatly.[45] Paid

The British troops were more than adequately supplied by Staten Island's Loyalists. Even though political loyalty was mainly the reason for the Staten Islanders' willingness to provide the British troops with provisions, the lure of gold and silver specie cannot be ignored. This was hard currency that was widely accepted and easily exchanged; it was not worthless Continental paper money or undependable promissory notes. Prominent Loyalists and British commissaries went from house to house, offering residents hard currency in exchange for commodities. Staten Islanders were directed to drive their cattle to the Watering Place, where

[b] The Bancker house was located at the present-day Richmond Terrace and Bard Avenue in the New Brighton section of Staten Island.

[c] Wallabout Bay is located in the East River along the northwest shore of present-day Brooklyn, New York.

they were paid handsomely for their animals.[46] Captain John Bowater of the Royal Marines wrote that the island's residents sold "their things to the Soldiers at the most Reasonable Terms," adding that "there is fresh Provisions & Vegetables Enough for . . . six Weeks without distressing the Inhabitants who like our Gold & Silver better than the Congress paper money."[47] Shortly after his arrival on Staten Island in mid-July, Ambrose Serle, Admiral Richard Lord Howe's civilian secretary, remarked that "the Residence of the Army enriches the Island, and gives it a good Reward for its Loyalty."[48] An outraged General John Morin Scott of the New York militia reported to the New York Provincial Congress that he had been told that "the enemy . . . live in great harmony with the inhabitants" of Staten Island, "who sell them their stock for hard money, and I suppose were never so happy in their lives."[49]

In addition to fresh provisions, the British army sought horses, wagons, drivers, and flatboats to assist in hauling troops, heavy artillery, camp equipment, and baggage. General Howe turned again to prominent Loyalists to procure these items and to hire laborers. Christopher Billopp recruited "several hundred men to drive wagons and artillery for the army, as likewise many horses and wagons for their Service."[50] The former provincial congressman Richard Lawrence, who operated one of the island's two shipyards, accepted the rank of captain and the position of master carpenter of shipyards with a commission to seize vessels, naval stores, and timber belonging to Whigs and to provide the army with flatboats.[51]

The British military also was dependent on locally cut wood for fuel. Beginning in July 1776 and continuing for the duration of the war, large sections of Staten Island's forests and private woodlots were cleared for firewood. British commissaries purchased wood directly from residents such as the former assemblyman Benjamin Seaman, who willingly cleared several acres of his property.[52] But the British army's enormous need for fuel was satisfied as well through a contracting system. Private residents were issued permits to cut timber from forests that had been abandoned by or commandeered from Whig sympathizers. They also were directed to haul the wood to designated military drop-off points. Unfortunately, however, greedy individuals stripped entire sections of the island bare.[53] Staten Islander Isaac Simonson lamented that the island's forests were "all cleared during the Revolution. . . . Hundreds and Hundreds of acres were cut."[54]

Howe was very much aware of the negative effect that plundering could have on civilian support for his army, so he ordered his officers to severely punish soldiers caught looting. One British deserter remarked that Staten Islanders were "well used, no soldier dare do anything against them."[55] An officer noted that he "received very strict orders of discipline because Staten Island was still sympathetic to the Crown."[56] Although it was an unspoken rule of eighteenth-century warfare that abandoned houses were fair game and could be stripped, two British soldiers immediately learned that General Howe meant what he said. The men entered an abandoned home on the island's north shore and broke open and drank from several casks of wine and cider. Upon learning of the news, Howe ordered their arrest and court martial.[57] He also directed his officers to enforce strict curfews to prevent soldiers from attacking residents under the cover of darkness.[58] This was welcome news to Staten Islanders, who had regularly complained about Whig troops brazenly stealing their property and destroying their fields.[59]

The British presence on Staten Island attracted Loyalist refugees, both white and African American, and from New Jersey, New York City, and Long Island. The once sparsely settled island had now been transformed into a British garrison and Loyalist refugee camp. Whereas white Loyalists sought the British army's protection from Whig abuse, many African Americans on Staten Island saw it as a ticket to freedom. In November 1775, John Murray, Lord Dunmore, the royal governor of Virginia, had offered liberty to all indentured servants and slaves belonging to Whig masters who traded their servitude for military service in the king's army.[60] Hundreds of runaway slaves, women as well as men, who heard about Dunmore's offer found asylum behind British military lines on Staten Island. For example, Boston King, who had been enslaved in New Brunswick, New Jersey, set his sights on Staten Island and freedom. One evening he eluded a Whig patrol and crossed the Raritan River at low tide. "I traveled until five o'clock in the morning and then concealed myself until seven o'clock at night," he recounted, "when I proceeded forward thro' brushes and marshes for fear of being discovered." King found his way to the shore opposite Staten Island, where he found a boat that he used to take him safely across the Arthur Kill waterway to the British garrison on the island.[61] African Americans like Boston King were joined on Staten Island by others who had been born free or been manumitted who had joined the British military to fight for black freedom. One observer noted that on Staten Island he had "seen quite a number of blacks, who are just as free as the whites."[62]

The large number of African Americans—newly freed refugees and persons already free before the war—and the presence of the British mil-

*Question*

itary on Staten Island quickly brought to the surface the residents' concerns about valuable slave property. Many Staten Island Loyalists were either slave owners themselves or supported slavery as essential to their society. They worried that their slaves would be enticed to flee to the British military as a means of obtaining their freedom. But their fears were unfounded. Dunmore's proclamation, as well as future proclamations by Generals William Howe and Sir Henry Clinton, offering freedom to slaves willing to serve the Crown was born of military necessity, not humanitarianism.[63] Furthermore, the British offer of freedom applied only to the slaves of Whig masters, not to those owned by Loyalists or British officials. Indeed, this policy was formulated to disrupt an American social order based partly on racial subordination, to deprive the Whigs of a valuable source of labor, to augment British manpower, and to maintain the support of white Loyalists by guaranteeing that their slave property would be protected.[64] "The British were careful not to offend the Loyalist support they so badly needed," writes historian Gary B. Nash, noting that British officers regularly returned fugitive slaves belonging to Loyalists once their identities could be ascertained.[65] On one occasion, five male slaves ran away from Loyalist masters on Staten Island and found their way to the *Asia*, which was anchored below the Narrows in lower New York Bay. There the ship's captain, George Vandeput, returned them to their masters.[66] Even with the massive British military presence on Staten Island, slaves belonging to Loyalists there had little chance of gaining their freedom.

The British housed African American men, women, and children on Staten Island in segregated quarters and used them as guards, teamsters, woodcutters, wagon drivers, guides, messengers, pilots, spies, carpenters, blacksmiths, cooks, laundresses, housekeepers, nurses, personal servants, and in a variety of other work. According to historian Thelma Wills Foote, "For most black refugees, wartime employment presented their first opportunity to earn wages for their labors." Initially, African American adults hired by British quartermasters on Staten Island were paid less than their white counterparts, but as the war progressed and labor shortages worsened, African Americans commanded the same wages as did their white counterparts.[67]

The British quickly organized many of the white and African American refugees on Staten Island into segregated provincial units. The largest of these units, the all-white New Jersey Volunteers commanded by the former attorney general and speaker of the New Jersey assembly Cortlandt Skinner, used Staten Island as their base of operation for the duration of the war. The Black Pioneers, the African American equivalent of the New Jersey Volunteers, was organized on Staten Island in August 1776 and was commanded by white officers. Another African American unit, the Black Brigade, frequently accompanied the all-white Queen's Rangers[d] on foraging expeditions from Staten Island into New Jersey. By the winter of 1776/1777, the British were training hundreds of African Americans on Staten Island for military service.[68]

General Howe welcomed the additional manpower that the Loyalist troops provided, but the provincial troops were not professional soldiers, and he strongly believed that his planned decisive battle against Washington could not succeed before his brother's fleet arrived from Europe with reinforcements.

Making matters worse, on July 9, the Declaration of Independence was read aloud in New York City. A large, boisterous, multiethnic, and multiracial mob of men and women led by members of the Sons of Liberty marched to Bowling Green in lower Manhattan where a massive lead equestrian statue of King George III had watched over the city since 1770. Although protected by an iron fence with six-foot posts adorned by crown-shaped ornaments, the statue was no match for the mob's ropes and chains, axes, and contempt. Many of the protestors climbed the statue and beheaded it while others pulled it down. Even the crown ornaments on the fence posts were victims of this symbolic act of regicide, with much of the lead from the statue eventually melted and fashioned into musket balls for the Continental army.[69] In New York City and in communities on Long Island and in New Jersey, Whigs celebrated, cheering the Continental Congress and Washington and drinking damnation to King George III as bonfires illuminated the dark sky and the crackle of small-arms fire and the booming of cannons pierced the stillness of the summer night.

But on this momentous occasion, Staten Island stood dark and quiet. There were no celebratory bonfires here or toasts to the congress or shouts of approval for Washington and his troops. Tradition has it that General Howe and his staff read a copy of the Declaration printed in a New York newspaper while they were at the Rose and Crown Tavern,[e] a

[d] The Queen's Rangers were raised by Colonel Robert Rogers in August 1776 and, after October 1777, were commanded by Lieutenant Colonel John Graves Simcoe. They were named for Queen Charlotte, wife of King George III.

[e] The Rose and Crown Tavern was located at the intersection of present-day New Dorp Lane and Richmond Road in the New Dorp section of Staten Island.

Rose and Crown Tavern, steel engraving by J. Jordan (1839) after a painting by
James Smillie. The tavern was a popular meeting place for British officers on
Staten Island. Indeed, tradition has it that General William Howe and his staff
officers first read a copy of the Declaration of Independence at the Rose and
Crown. Courtesy of the Staten Island Historical Society.

frequent meeting place for British officers on the island. According to an eyewitness, General John Vaughan excitedly approached Howe, who was with several of his staff officers going over plans for the construction of fortifications. Vaughan handed Howe a newspaper with the headline DECLARATION OF INDEPENDENCE. After he read the opening paragraphs of the Declaration, Howe handed the newspaper to one of his subordinates and ordered him to read it aloud. After the officer finished reading, a silence fell over the room. "Those are certainly determined men," Howe said in a quiet tone. "His face was the subject of study. There was a struggle between a smile and a frown; but the latter seemed to prevail," noted the eyewitness. "There was an animated council of war ... that evening, every one present seeming to realize that the situation was becoming more and more critical."[70]

News of the Declaration of Independence prompted Howe to begin planning his next move. On July 12, the sun shone brightly in the midafternoon sky as he ordered the warships *Phoenix* and *Rose* to sail up the Hudson River from Staten Island. Their sails caught a brisk wind that propelled the ships swiftly across upper New York Bay, past lower Manhattan, and up the Hudson River. Continental signal guns thundered their warnings, frightening residents and soldiers alike in New York City. The British ships ran a gauntlet of Continental artillery from Nutten Island to Fort George in lower Manhattan to Paulus Hook at the mouth of the Hudson River and past Forts Washington and Lee. The ships answered with powerful broadsides that shook buildings and sent soldiers and civilians running for cover. By late afternoon, they were anchored near Tarrytown, in Westchester County, New York, with only minor damage. The event was Howe's way of reminding Washington and his army, as well as the Continental Congress and American civilians, that although independence had been declared, a war still had to be fought and won against the powerful British military in order to secure it. It also demonstrated that the British navy still controlled the waters around New York and that British forces still held the initiative and could attack anywhere and at any time they pleased. The inept and cowardly reaction by the American troops on this day revealed major problems in the Continental ranks and with New York City's defenses.[71]

As the British warships navigated their way up the Hudson River, a lone ship arrived off Sandy Hook. This ship, with its sails cracking in a southwest wind and the recognizable cross of St. George flying high above its masthead, was the *Eagle*, the flagship of Admiral Richard Lord

Howe. Its appearance meant that the fleet and reinforcements from Europe could not be far behind. As it sailed through the Narrows, the *Eagle* was greeted by a thunderous salute from "all the Ships of War in the Harbour [and] by the Cheers of the Sailors all along the Ships, and by those of the Soldiers on the Shore."[72] It eventually anchored in upper New York Bay opposite the Watering Place.

On July 13, General William Howe, his staff officers, and Governor William Tryon went aboard the *Eagle* and dined with the admiral, who informed them that the British government had appointed him and his brother to a peace commission. Then the discussion turned to the military situation in New York and the news of the Declaration of Independence, to which Ambrose Serle, Admiral Howe's civilian secretary, asserted was proof of "the Villainy and Madness of these deluded People."[73]

The military presence on Staten Island grew larger each day. By late July, two thousand Scots Highlanders and cavalry had arrived.[74] On July 21, General Nathanael Greene, who commanded the Continental forces on Long Island, reported that "Eight hundred Negroes Collected on Statten Island this day to be formed into a Regiment."[75] On August 1, a fleet of forty-five ships commanded by Admiral Sir Peter Parker and carrying Generals Sir Henry Clinton and Charles Lord Cornwallis and three thousand troops from the ill-fated campaign against Charleston, South Carolina, also arrived; and on August 4, twenty-one ships, the whole of Lord Howe's fleet from Europe, were spotted approaching Sandy Hook.[76] On August 12, a fleet of more than one hundred ships commanded by Commodore William Hotham and carrying ten thousand British and Hessian soldiers "made a Fine Appearance upon entering the Harbour," as Ambrose Serle described it.[77] In addition, arriving from Virginia were John Murray, Lord Dunmore, and 150 African Americans, the remnants of his all-black Ethiopian Regiment, which had been decimated by smallpox, their uniforms bearing sashes inscribed with the words LIBERTY TO SLAVES.[78]

The British assembled a force of 450 warships and transports and 32,000 soldiers, sailors, marines, and Loyalists at Staten Island. It was a sight never before seen anywhere in the eighteenth century. In fact, it was the largest British expeditionary force ever assembled until the D-Day invasion of France in June 1944.

As the British military buildup proceeded on Staten Island, Lord Howe continued peace negotiations with the Americans. He was convinced that most of them still supported reconciliation over war. But his brother disagreed. Instead, General Howe believed that the Declaration of Independence had made reconciliation almost impossible and that a swift military solution was now more than ever necessary to end the rebellion.[79]

Nonetheless, Lord Howe pushed ahead with his plans to bring the Americans to the negotiating table. He issued a proclamation announcing that he and his brother had been appointed peace commissioners with the power to grant pardons and to declare any region at peace where royal authority was restored.[80] On July 17, the Continental Congress received this proclamation and referred it to a three-man committee consisting of Charles Carroll of Maryland, Thomas Jefferson of Virginia, and Robert Treat Paine of Massachusetts. After reviewing the proclamation, the committee reported that it contained no major concessions and recommended that Congress publish it in order that

> the good People of these United States may be informed of what nature are the commissioners, and what the terms, with expectation of which, the insidious court of Britain has endeavoured to amuse and disarm them, and that the few, who still remain suspended by a hope founded either in the justice or moderation of their late king, may now, at length, be convinced, that the valour alone of their country is to save its liberties.[81]

The admiral also tried to open talks with Washington, but he rejected the overture.[82] An astonished Ambrose Serle noted that the Americans' rejection of the peace commission left "no Alternative but War and Bloodshed."[83]

Meanwhile, the British and their Hessian allies enjoyed the many comforts that Staten Island had to offer. Many of them had survived the cold and bitter winter in Boston only to spend spring in cold, damp Nova Scotia. Others had suffered through a humiliating defeat in Charleston, South Carolina, earlier that summer or had had to endure a long, tiresome, and turbulent voyage from Europe. For these men, Staten Island was paradise. "Staten Island is a hilly country, covered with beautiful forests composed mostly of a kind of fir-tree, the odor of which can be inhaled at a distance of two miles from land," noted Hessian Lieutenant Johann Heinrich. "The soil is fruitful. . . . Peaches, chestnuts, apples, pears, grapes, and various kinds of nuts grow here in wild profusion, mingled with roses and blackberry bushes."[84] Lieutenant Colonel Mungo Campbell of the Fifty-fifth Regiment of Foot described the island as "the most beautiful and fertile in the world, it supplys the Army with the very Luxuries of life."[85] Major Charles Stuart wrote to his father that he was encamped on "the most beautiful Island that nature could form or art improve, [and] we have everything we want."[86] Another British officer described the island as "the most beautiful fertile spott I was ever in, we have a good deal of fresh provisions . . . how different this is from the inhospitable coast of Nova Scotia, where nothing was to be seen but impervious Woods and barren soil and cold moist Climate even in June."[87]

But the longer the campaign against New York City was delayed, the more restless the troops on Staten Island grew.[88] Captain John Bowater of the Royal Marines spoke for many of the troops when he informed Basil Fielding, the earl of Denbigh, that "I was in hopes before this to have been able to have given your Lordship an Account of a Victory obtained by our Troops, but we have been only looking at one another for this last Month."[89]

By mid-August, the British troops finally got their wish. General William Howe and his brother Admiral Richard Lord Howe decided to commence military operations against Washington's army on Long Island. "By the best Inteligence," wrote Continental officer Colonel William Douglas of the Sixth Connecticut Regiment posted on Long Island, "the enemy are Determined to give us Battle Soon."[90] The Americans' rejection of the peace commission convinced the Howe brothers that the time had come to use their massive force to crush Washington's army and the rebellion. Not only was the military campaign against New York City about to begin, but so too was the real war for Staten Islanders.

# 5

## The Price of Loyalty

*[handwritten: Why they remained loyal]*

For many Staten Islanders, the choice to remain loyal was easy, as many in the community believed that the British army would bring the blessings of Crown rule and the British constitution, economic prosperity, and protection from "a Merciless Enemy."[1] But they soon discovered that in war, and especially one that was taking shape as a civil war, friends could quickly become enemies. The seven and a half years that the island remained under British occupation—longer than any community had endured during the American Revolution—drew Staten Islanders directly into the war, a role they originally hoped could be averted. Located on the periphery of British-occupied New York and in close proximity to Whig strongholds in New Jersey, Staten Island's resources were exploited and its residents victimized by both the warring armies and the partisan forces affiliated with them, as well as by armed gangs who wantonly terrorized, plundered, and murdered innocent civilians. The wartime experiences of Staten Islanders, like those of the residents of Westchester County in New York and Bergen County in New Jersey, were similar to those of the residents of the southern backcountry. And by the end of the war, it was these experiences that led many Staten Islanders to question their initial loyalties and to have a political change of heart.

*[handwritten: Note]*

Early on August 22, 1776, the British juggernaut began its move against George Washington's Continental army in New York. Four thousand light infantry and reserves under the command of General Sir Henry Clinton assembled at Cole's Ferry landing located near the Narrows and began to file into flat-bottomed boats. Several of these boats had been built by Richard Lawrence, the former Provincial congressman whom General William Howe had appointed to the post of master carpenter of the island's shipyards. Throughout the day, hundreds of these boats as well as naval transports carried British, Hessian, and Loyalist soldiers across the Narrows from Staten Island to Long Island. Their goal was the town of Gravesend, Brooklyn, where British commanders had decided to establish their headquarters for the next phase of the military campaign against New York City. By noon, the British military had landed fifteen thousand troops unopposed on Long Island under the cover of the guns of the British warships now anchored in Gravesend Bay.[2] The British landing concluded on August 25 when two brigades of Hessians commanded by General Leopold Philip von Heister joined the army at Gravesend.

The Battle of Long Island began on August 27, 1776. In a day of heavy fighting, British troops overwhelmed and outflanked the Continental army's forward line of defense which stretched across the Guana Heights. With the enemy in pursuit, confused and frightened Continental troops retreated to entrenchments at Brooklyn Heights where Washington, who had crossed the East River from Manhattan, watched the rout unfold. But then General Howe called off the pursuit, to the displeasure of his men and many of his officers. Instead, in an effort to force Washington to surrender, he decided to use siege warfare against the Continental troops, who now found themselves with their backs to the East River and a portion of the British navy. As Howe's men began to dig trenches toward the Continental earthworks, rain began to fall steadily and continued to fall for two days, thereby delaying the final British assault against Washington's lines at Brooklyn Heights. Finally, on August 29, the rain stopped and was followed that evening by a thick fog, which Washington used to cover the evacuation of his men across the East River, slipping past the British warships, to Manhattan. Even though the British had captured Long Island, Washington and the Continental army had escaped.[3]

On September 11, 1776, Admiral Richard Lord Howe and three delegates—John Adams, Benjamin Franklin, and Edward Rutledge—from the Continental Congress met for three hours at Christopher Billopp's Bentley Manor estate. Lord Howe expressed his friendship for America and stated that further escalation of the conflict could still be avoided if the Continental Congress would consider retracting its decision for independence. The three delegates replied that renouncing independence was not an option, and they left. The Staten Island discussions not only failed to lay the foundation for peacefully bringing the Americans back into the British imperial fold, they also delayed the British advance on New York City long enough for Washington to regroup his forces and to move the main part of his army out of the city north to Harlem Heights and King's Bridge. On September 14, the British military finally moved on New York City and secured it the next day.[4]

Even though the main British army had vacated Staten Island for Long Island and then New York City, the British still considered it an important strategic position to hold for the duration of the war. The island served the British military as a staging area and a place where sick and wounded soldiers could convalesce. To defend the island, General Howe left a force composed of a brigade of convalescents, a brigade from the Fourteenth Regiment of Foot, the Staten Island militia and its cavalry, and several Loyalist refugees. Howe ordered Lieutenant Colonel William Dalrymple, who was initially given command of the garrison, to post troops along the Staten Island shoreline opposite New Jersey, at the Narrows, and on the island's heights overlooking the area. Staten Island also served as the headquarters for the New Jersey Volunteers and the Queen's Rangers, two of the largest Loyalist regiments recruited during the war. As the American Revolution progressed, other Loyalist units and several British Regular and Hessian regiments also were stationed on the island to help guard against a Whig advance on New York from central and southern New Jersey.

The continuing British military presence on Staten Island during the American Revolution exacerbated tensions between the Loyalists and Whigs in the area, with the desire for retribution fueling violent impulses on both sides. British, Hessian, and Loyalist troops made successive raids into New Jersey, where they attacked local Whig militia, took prisoners, destroyed property, and plundered homes and businesses owned by Whigs in places such as Elizabethtown, Newark, and Rahway[a] in Essex County, Woodbridge in Middlesex County, and Shrewsbury, Colt's Neck, and Freehold in Monmouth County. New Jersey Whig partisans evened the score by frequently raiding Staten Island's farms, torturing victims, looting homes, and spreading their own form of terrorism. They also plundered valuable slave property. African American slaves who belonged to Loyalist Staten Islanders were carried off by New Jersey Whig partisans and sold for profit. In addition, Whig refugees from Staten Island who sought revenge for the abuse and intimidation that they and their families had endured at the hands of former Loyalist neighbors often accompanied the New Jersey partisans on raids of the island.

[a] Rahway was also known as Spanktown.

The Whigs, however, found it difficult to carry out raids on Staten Island in the daytime because of the British forces stationed there. They thus waited until nightfall to strike, thereby eluding the British guards and gunboats patrolling the sections of Staten Island closest to New Jersey. "The Island has been frequently visited by small parties of banditti in the night," commented one visitor.[5] Private Johann Conrad Dohla of the Fourth Company of the Hessian Bayreuth Regiment reported that on the evening of June 8, 1777, "a few rebels in boats crossed the Kills River and fired several times at our outposts, returned to their boats, and left, and this they often do, so that there is no rest in camp at night."[6] In 1777, the English traveler Nicholas Cresswell noticed that nighttime made the island's residents "very uneasy" and that they were constantly on the lookout for "a visit from the Rebels."[7] As a result, in the evenings, Staten Islanders hid their household valuables and barricaded their doors and windows in anticipation of Whig raids.

The Whigs' raiding parties caused widespread destruction on Staten Island. The farm of Roper and Rachel Dawson, which fronted the Kill van Kull, was "subject to Incursions from Jersey, and though capable of yielding great Advantages, yet little or no Benefit was derived from it during the Calamities of the War, as nothing could be preserved from plunder, which was a very great loss."[8] The store owned by John Bedell and Benjamin Micheau near the village of Richmond was a favorite target of Whig partisans because both men had been active in the Staten Island Loyalist militia and had accompanied British troops on several raids into New Jersey.[9] Another favorite target of the Whig raiders was Christopher Billopp's Bentley Manor estate. On one occasion, Whig partisans raided Billopp's manor house while he was on patrol with the Staten Island militia and "carried off a Negro, cattle, horses, carriages, bedding, and other furniture to a large amount."[10]

The family of Staten Islander Peter Houseman endured a particularly heinous robbery when Whig partisans, faces blackened with soot, broke into their house and demanded money and household valuables. When Houseman refused to turn over the items, the marauders beat him and his son-in-law John Tyson with clubs. Tyson survived the brutal assault, but Houseman died instantly. The partisans terrorized Houseman's family and slaves and ransacked the house but eventually left empty-handed.[11]

In another incident, Whig raiders entered the home of Staten Islander John Bodine Jr. and tortured him in front of his family when he refused to reveal where he had hidden his valuables. They bound his hands and feet with bed chords, suspended him from spikes in the ceiling beams, and burned him with a fireplace shovel and a set of heated fire tongs. When he still refused to disclose the location of the valuables, the raiders threatened to bayonet his wife and infant son. Fortunately, recalled one Staten Islander, they "ransacked the house instead and whatever they could not take, they destroyed." The invaders finally were scared off by a British soldier on patrol who heard the noise and fired his gun.[12]

Kidnapping also was common. Usually the abductees were turned over to the Continental army and eventually exchanged for prisoners held by the British. On June 5, 1778, a raiding party of Whig partisans led by Captain Nathaniel Fitz Randolph[b] of Woodbridge captured Christopher Billopp and several members of the Staten Island Loyalist militia who were on patrol. Billopp was held in a New Jersey prison for nine months before he was exchanged.[13] Then again, in June 1779, Billopp was abducted by Whig partisans led by Fitz Randolph's brother-in-law Captain David Coddington. Billopp was taken to a jail in Burlington, New Jersey, where he was chained to the floor and allowed only bread and water. After several months, Billopp was again exchanged.[14]

Captain Nathaniel Fitz Randolph had been a member of the New Jersey militia and commanded one of the most active Whig partisan bands during the internecine war that took place around Staten Island. His exploits became legendary, and the mention of his name brought terror to both Staten Islanders and soldiers of the British occupation forces alike. Fitz Randolph was effective because he obtained valuable assistance and information from Whig refugees and sympathizers who were still living on the island. Thus he and his men were well acquainted with Staten Island's topography and its roads and buildings, and they also knew the locations of British, Hessian, and Loyalist guard posts and encampments and the patrol's popular routes taken around the island.

Fitz Randolph's partisans often crossed the Arthur Kill at night in a whaleboat; their oars wrapped in either rags or leather to muffle the splashing. They debarked at one of the many secluded bays, inlets, and tidal marshes dotting Staten Island's shoreline, surprised and captured lone sentries, ambushed patrols, plundered residents of livestock, horses, and valuables, and kidnapped prominent Loyalists. During the course of the war, Fitz Randolph was wounded four times and captured twice by the British. He spent months in the Provost, one of the worst British pris-

[b] Staten Islanders often referred to him as Captain Randle.

ons in New York City, where he was beaten and nearly died from starvation. Tradition has it that a British officer offered Fitz Randolph "a far better position in our ranks" if he renounced his support of American independence and joined the British army. To this, Fitz Randolph replied: "The King is not rich enough to buy me." In June 1780, he was mortally wounded in a skirmish near Elizabethtown against British and Hessian troops who were returning from a humiliating defeat at the hands of New Jersey militia at the town of Connecticut Farms.[c15]

After Nathaniel's death, his cousin Asher Fitz Randolph of Woodbridge, New Jersey, who also was a captain in the New Jersey militia, led clandestine operations against Staten Island. Picking up where his cousin had left off, he attacked British guard posts along the island's shoreline, apprehended prominent Loyalists and British officers, and carried off livestock and other property belonging to Staten Islanders. Asher Fitz Randolph and his partisans proved useful in gathering forage, provisions, horses, and supplies for the Continental army and the New Jersey militia. Moreover, he utilized a network of informants on the island to collect intelligence about the strength of British troops and their plans for deployment. One of his main operatives was believed to have been Peter Latourette, who lived near the village of Richmond and the British encampment there. Latourette often passed along information by leaving a letter in a designated spot either along the shoreline or on one of the hummocks in the salt meadows opposite New Jersey. In January 1781, Asher Fitz Randolph was captured on Staten Island by a Loyalist patrol but was exchanged a few months later. After his release from British custody, he resumed leading partisan raids against the island for the duration of the war.[16]

Another active Whig partisan who caused panic among Staten Islanders was Captain Baker Hendricks of Elizabethtown. Before his partisan activities, Hendricks and his brother John had been employed by General George Washington as spies in New Jersey and on Staten Island. They were members of the spy ring coordinated by Colonel Elias B. Dayton of the New Jersey militia and included Joshua, John, John La Grange, and Jacob Mersereau from Staten Island. As a Whig raider, Hendricks was known for conducting hit-and-run raids on civilian property and British occupation forces on Staten Island and for plundering enemy shipping in the waterways around the island. In late April 1781, troops from

[c] Present-day Union, New Jersey.

the Loyalist New Jersey Volunteers and the Staten Island Loyalist militia raided Elizabethtown, looting and ransacking homes, farms, and businesses and carrying off fifty head of cattle. On May 9, 1781, Hendricks and a party of thirteen men responded in kind, plundering several homes on Staten Island before a patrol from the First Battalion of the New Jersey Volunteers was alerted to their whereabouts and set out after them. The New Jersey provincials chased Hendricks and his small party into a woods, but eventually they broke off their pursuit. After a short time, Hendricks and his men reemerged from the thicket and had begun to plunder a house nearby when they were surprised by the patrol, which had suddenly turned back. A fierce gun battle ensued that led to the death of one of Hendricks's men and the capture of two others. Although Hendricks escaped, he was wounded during the melee.[17]

The opportunity to make a quick profit and disrupt trade with the British on Staten Island led Hendricks to petition for and to obtain a commission from Governor William Livingston of New Jersey to outfit two whaleboats—the *Flying Squirrel* and the *Charming Betsey*—as privateers. The commission gave him, as a captain of whaleboat privateers, the right to seize enemy property. In March 1781, Hendricks and his men sailed to Staten Island and surprised the crew of a sloop that had run aground in the Kill van Kull. They seized two cannons and several firearms and carried the sloop and its crew and cargo back to New Jersey, an operation repeated several times by Hendricks and his whaleboat crew.[18]

Using his official capacity as a commissioned whaleboat privateer, Hendricks plundered homes along Staten Island's shoreline. Eventually, Governor Livingston revoked Hendricks's commission, charging that Hendricks abused his privilege as a whaleboat captain by attacking civilians on land and accused him of engaging in and profiting from illegal trade with the enemy. This practice, known as the "London Trade," was smuggling beef, poultry, vegetables, firewood, and forage for the British army on Staten Island where these items could be sold for hard currency or exchanged for luxury goods. For New Jersey Whig farmers, the London Trade provided a tempting choice: they could sell produce to the British army on Staten Island, for which they were paid in gold and silver, or they could continue to provide provisions to the American army in exchange for depreciated Continental paper money, military script, or promissory notes. New Jersey whaleboat captains often charged a fee or took a commission to carry farmers to Staten Island at night, where they could sell or barter their goods. This illegal trade angered Whig leaders, who argued that it helped the enemy, hurt American soldiers' morale to see civilians enjoying British luxuries while they suffered, and provided a conduit for valuable intelligence to the British.[19]

Another commissioned whaleboat captain, Adam Hyler, was one of Staten Island's most prolific and daring Whig raiders. At all times of day, Hyler's whaleboats sailed out of his hometown of New Brunswick, New Jersey, on the Raritan River and often attacked and captured small crafts anchored along the island's shoreline that were either fishing or oystering or engaged in the London Trade. Hyler's whaleboaters also surprised isolated British gunboats. Their booty was sold on the open market, and the men shared the profits. Occasionally, Hyler and his crew sailed into one of Staten Island's many inlets, brought their boats ashore, and hid them in the underbrush. They then proceeded to seize supplies from the British military and to plunder civilian property. Hyler also participated in the kidnapping of prominent civilians and British military personnel, often turning over his victims to Continental authorities in New Jersey as prisoners of war to be exchanged for persons held by the British. He died in September 1782 of complications resulting from injuries sustained in an accident.[20]

In addition to raids by Whig partisans, Staten Islanders also endured assaults on their persons and property during invasions of the island by Continental forces. For example, on October 15, 1776, Continental troops commanded by General Hugh Mercer crossed the Kill van Kull and Arthur Kill waterways from various points in New Jersey and attacked British posts in the southern and western sections of Staten Island. Mercer's men cut a swath through the island, plundering homes and fields and penetrating as far inland as the village of Richmond before being forced to retreat.[21] This October 1776 attack set a pattern. In August 1777, more than one thousand Continental soldiers under the command of General John Sullivan crossed the Kill van Kull from Elizabethtown and attacked the British garrison on Staten Island. Although Sullivan's troops plundered every home in their path, they met fierce resistance, suffering several casualties and the capture of about 140 men. The poor performance of Sullivan's troops led to many questions and much debate about the general's skills as a commander.[22] Then in late November 1777, General Philemon Dickinson led a detachment of 1,400 soldiers from Halstead's Point near Elizabethtown to Staten Island. Dickinson's foray onto the island caused the destruction of several homes and netted numerous prisoners, including Lieutenant Jacob Van Buskirk, the son of Lieutenant Colonel Abraham Van Buskirk of the Loyalist New Jersey Volunteers.[23]

The largest invasion of Staten Island by Continental forces took place in January 1780. During the severe winter of 1779/1780, a heavy snowfall blanketed the New York City region, and frigid temperatures caused the waterways around the city to freeze so completely that infantry, artillery, and cavalry all were able to easily traverse them. At his winter quarters in Morristown, New Jersey, George Washington decided to launch a surprise attack on the British garrison on Staten Island. It would be a jab in the belly of the British army, like his attacks on the Hessians at Trenton, New Jersey, and the British troops at Princeton, New Jersey, during the winter of 1776/1777. Such an attack would remind British military and political officials in America and Britain that the Continental army was willing to attack British forces anywhere and at anytime in America.[24]

Washington chose Lord Stirling to lead the attack. He was reliable and knew the topography of Staten Island better than did most Continental officers, having attempted to defend the island against a British landing in 1776. On January 14, three thousand Continental soldiers and their equipment were crammed onto three hundred sleds provided by New Jersey Whig farmers and began the trek to Staten Island. But British spies in New Jersey had warned the British forces on the island of an impending attack, and lookouts posted on Staten Island's heights noticed an unusual amount of activity on the New Jersey side of the Kill van Kull. As the Continental troops began to cross the frozen waterway, British, Hessian, and Loyalist troops on Staten Island positioned themselves behind stone walls, in earthworks dug into the snow and ice, and in homes and barns along the shoreline. Without the element of surprise, Stirling's men were heading into a hornet's nest. As soon as the Continental soldiers landed on the island, they were met by several volleys from the muskets of the well-positioned enemy. "When we arrived we found Johnny Bull prepared for our reception," remembered Continental Private Joseph Plumb Martin of the Eighth Connecticut Regiment. "We accordingly found them all waiting for us, so that we could not surprise them."[25] Stirling's advance was therefore quickly halted, and the attack ended soon after it had begun.

In an effort to prevent his men from pillaging farms and businesses on Staten Island, Stirling had announced before the attack that

any man Quitting his post or Ranks in Order to plunder is to be punished with Instant Death—no private property of the Inhabitants is to be
medled with or Brought off, on any pretense what ever, excepting fat
Cattle and Sheep, of which regular accounts are to be taken with the
names of the persons from whom taken, and to whom Delivered.[26]

Although Stirling scrutinized the actions of the Continental troops under
his command, the same could not be said of the actions of the Whig partisans who had joined the attack for the opportunity to loot the Staten Islanders' homes. During the attack, hundreds of Whig partisans crossed
the Kill van Kull and plundered farms, homes, and businesses; destroyed
property; and carried off slaves belonging to Loyalist residents. Staten Islanders "were plundered without mercy," observed the Moravian Reverend Hector Gambold.[27] One Staten Island resident stood helplessly as
partisans plundered his store.[28] Another resident watched as partisans set
fire to both his sloops.[29] After the war, Pompey Prall, a former slave, recalled that "the ice being so strong, the Americans . . . come over and
steal coloured people and sell them for slaves."[30] Whig partisans burned
the sloop belonging to Captain Isaac Decker, who commanded Staten Island's Loyalist cavalry, and they also destroyed his crops and pulled up
and burned his fences. Most disturbing, the partisans forced Decker's
wife to strip to her underpetticoat and, as she stood almost naked before
them, verbally abused her.[31] Such an action, which was commonly used
by both sides against women and men, humiliated and tore away at the
victim's dignity and self-respect.

After the January 1780 attack, Stirling ordered that all plundered
items from Staten Island be turned over to the acting assistant quartermaster general, the Presbyterian Reverend James Caldwell of Elizabethtown, New Jersey. Caldwell, who was nicknamed the "Fighting Parson,"
was charged with returning the items to their rightful owners. But this
policy proved unrealistic and difficult to enforce, and in the end, only a
few plundered items were returned to their Staten Island owners.[32]

Although the Staten Islanders expected hostile behavior from the
Whigs, they had not anticipated the abuses on their persons and property
from the British and their Hessian and Loyalist allies who were supposed
to be their liberators and protectors. Now, however, the liberators quickly
became occupiers, and Staten Islanders were forced to suffer abuse at the
hands of their protectors.

The British occupying forces plundered and physically attacked Staten Islanders, regardless of their declarations of loyalty. Britain's Hessian allies, in particular, had a reputation for indiscriminate plundering. They thought that no American could be trusted because at heart all Americans were rebels. A Hessian officer wrote that although Staten Islanders "claim to have nothing in common with the rebels . . . [they] are basically the same."[33] Staten Islanders who lived along the shoreline refused to burn lights at night, terrified that they could be accused by British authorities of sending signals to the Whigs on the opposite shore in New Jersey and suffer the destruction of their homes, imprisonment, physical violence, or, even worse, death. Other residents were afraid to talk too much in public for fear that they might say something that could be construed as pro-Whig and thus provoke retaliation.[34] The Moravian Reverend Hector Gambold noted that a complaint by civilians to British officers or soldiers "commonly makes bad worse."[35] One Staten Islander remembered that his family had to obey, without complaint, the commands of and endure the verbal abuse from two British officers quartered in their house. "There was no use in complaining or remonstrating," he noted, "if we had done so, we should have been requited with a curse and a blow of their swords."[36]

Soldiers from the occupation forces often ignored curfews and disobeyed orders against public intoxication. They roamed around the island causing mayhem, destroying property, and committing heinous acts of violence against civilians. "Several of the inhabitants have been murdered, innumerable robberies committed publicly," wrote an anguished Rev. Gambold, adding that soldiers from the occupation forces "go a number of them blackened in the night, surround a house and threaten the people with immediate death if they make any resistance."[37] One evening, four soldiers entered the home of Christian Jacobson, the former chairman of the committee of safety, as its occupants slept. They awoke Jacobson's slaves, who were sleeping in the kitchen and threatened to kill them if they did not reveal where their master had hidden his money. Bet, a female slave, managed to alert Jacobson, who was sleeping in the next room, to the invasion. Jacobson rushed into the kitchen and startled one of the soldiers, who shot him dead. As he lay on the kitchen floor, his wife and another female slave "attempted to stanch the blood which flowed from two orifices." After an investigation into the incident, the soldier who murdered Jacobson was arrested after Bet identified him, was found

guilty by a court martial, and was hanged.[38] Although British officers
made an effort to find and punish the perpetrators of such crimes, more
often than not they went free.

Confronted daily by a guerrilla-style war, many British and Hessian
troops who were trained in the conventional European linear style of
warfare began to break down mentally under the pressure. "The *petite
guerre* that made up much of the fighting in America," historian Stephen
Conway explained, "generated pressures that inclined soldiers to take revenge, or relieve frustrations, on innocent civilians."[39] One Hessian soldier stationed on Staten Island commented that a person can easily un-
derstand the difference between the guerrilla war being fought in America and war in Europe. "The rebels seldom attack a large army," he
wrote, "because, in general, they only go out widely dispersed and, more
often, only seek to cause alarm."[40] British occupation forces guarding
Staten Island's western and southern shorelines as well as British patrol
boats in the Arthur Kill and the Kill van Kull waterways were constantly
threatened by elusive Whig riflemen, who fired at them from buildings,
salt marshes, and woodlands located on the opposite shore in New Jersey. "A young officer in the Army . . . was shot at by a large party of the
Rebels concealed on the opposite shore, and mortally wounded,"
recorded Ambrose Serle, Lord Howe's civilian secretary. "They [the
rebels] are fond of carrying on this unmanly and infamous kind of War,
which no civilized Nation will allow."[41] This unseen enemy frustrated
and angered British troops, who took out their frustrations on the island's
residents. An informant notified Washington that British soldiers stationed on Staten Island were growing more impatient and disillusioned
with the nature of warfare in America and the war's progress. The British
soldiers on Staten Island "are prodigiously incensed against the Tories
and curse them as the instruments of the war now raging," the informant
reported.[42]

The damage caused by the regular British forces on Staten Island was
extensive. One resident remembered that British troops had "destroyed
all the fences, and when they went to Jersey, proclamation was made to
put them up again, but when they [British] returned from Jersey they destroyed them again."[43] After the war, Ann Perine filed a claim for damages with the British government, which explained that she and her late
husband Edward had been loyal subjects and that their woodland "was
entered into by a body of the British Troops and great Quantities cut by
Order of Sir Henry Clinton for the purpose of erecting Works." She re-

The Billiou/Stillwell/Perine House, Richmond Road, Dongan Hills, Staten Island, New York. Home of Ann and Edward Perine. Photo courtesy of the Staten Island Historical Society.

ceived neither a response from the British government nor compensation for her losses.[44] Staten Islander Peter Wandel recalled his father's anger after he had complied with British regulations by turning over two hundred cords of wood from his property to the army only to receive no payment for it.[45] On the eve of the Battle of Long Island, Washington had been informed that the British on Staten Island "have eat up all the Cattle and are now killing & barreling up all the Horses . . . They [the British] take from them [Staten Islanders] every Thing they choose, and no one has any Thing they can call their own."[46]

Even property belonging to notable Staten Island Loyalists like Alexander McDonald and Christopher Billopp was not safe from the British occupying forces. In June 1777, McDonald requested a leave of absence for two or three months from his post in Halifax, Nova Scotia, in order to return to Staten Island to inspect his property and tend to any damages. "I am told that £1000 will not indemnify me for the Damages I sustained," he wrote, "All my fences burned & my Woods cut down which render the place unfit for any use and makes me Loser of £200 Sterling pr year."[47] In a letter to General Sir Jeffrey Amherst, McDonald lamented that his farm on Staten Island "is totally ruined as well by our own troops as by the Rebells."[48] Christopher Billopp, who filed for compensation for losses after the war, asserted that "the British Army & Sailors" had caused £1441.16s in damages to his estate. General Cortlandt Skinner, the commander of the Loyalist New Jersey Volunteers, testified that Billopp "was plundered by the Hessians and the Rebels."[49]

Beginning in July 1776, the British military presence on Staten Island had attracted hundreds of white and African American Loyalist refugees from New York City, Long Island, and Whig strongholds in New Jersey. They enlisted in the British army, joined provincial regiments, and supported British forces in a noncombat role. But these Loyalists had no stake in Staten Island and thus contributed to the abuse of the island's residents. British commanders on the island frequently listened to civilians' complaints against Loyalist refugees, who, like many British and Hessian troops, ignored the strict orders against plundering and looting homes of livestock, firewood, foodstuffs, and valuables.[50] The soldiers regarded looting and plunder as a means to supplement their meager military pay, to find sustenance during food shortages, and to meet fuel needs for cooking and warmth.[51]

During the British occupation, Staten Island became home to several gangs of Loyalist freebooters and bands who were loosely affiliated with

*Note*

the British military and formed a major component of the internecine warfare in Staten Island and New Jersey during the American Revolution. Although many of their members sought revenge for the loss of property, homes, businesses, or family members at the hands of Whig committees or partisans, others joined for the "spoils of war." They moved freely about the area, committing murder, robbery, arson, kidnappings, and rape. These gangs used Staten Island's many secluded areas to launch their attacks on unsuspecting victims or to hide from Whig authorities. The British garrison on Staten Island and the island's topography provided these gangs with sanctuary, and Staten Islanders became the innocent victims caught between Loyalist freebooters and the Whig partisans who sought to avenge their actions and bring them to "justice."

One of the most notorious Loyalist freebooters was the former Elizabethtown resident Cornelius Hatfield Jr., whose property in Essex County, New Jersey, was confiscated because of his Loyalist sympathies. Shortly after the British army arrived in 1776, Hatfield fled to Staten Island and organized a gang of raiders that included several family members and close friends. Hatfield's raiders were known for their many daring raids on Elizabethtown and other sections of New Jersey closest to the island. They terrorized civilians and Whig militia, and their actions earned them a reputation as one of the war's most violent partisan bands. Hatfield's gang plundered Whig farms, physically assaulted and abducted prominent Whig civilians and military officials, and committed arson and murder. In February 1781, they captured, robbed, and hanged Whig farmer Stephen Ball from Essex County, New Jersey, who was engaged in the London Trade on Staten Island, an action that violated an order issued by the British military to allow all such persons engaged in this activity to return to their homes unmolested.[52] Hatfield's exploits, furthermore, were not restricted to New Jersey; his gang victimized Staten Island residents as well. One Staten Islander remembered that Hatfield was "a noble-looking fellow but capable of doing almost anything" and that the members of his gang were "a rough set of men, with no grace or shame, and feared neither God nor Devil."[53] Private Joseph Plumb Martin, who was posted with his Connecticut regiment in the vicinity of Elizabethtown in 1780, described Hatfield and his gang as "notorious rascals" and "miscreants."[54]

Although Hatfield provided reconnaissance for British raiding parties and was paid handsomely in gold and silver for forage, cattle, firewood, and intelligence, he often worked independently of the British. But on

January 25, 1780, the British military attached Hatfield and his raiders to a party of New Jersey Volunteers, commanded by Lieutenant Colonel Abraham Van Buskirk, who were ordered to raid the Whig garrison at Elizabethtown in retaliation for Lord Stirling's invasion of the British garrison on Staten Island eleven days earlier. During the Elizabethtown attack, Hatfield's gang went on a rampage. They assaulted civilians, kidnapped prominent Whigs, plundered homes and businesses, and burned several buildings in the town including the courthouse, schoolhouse, and the First Presbyterian Church where Hatfield's father, Cornelius Sr., had served as deacon. Hatfield's actions that day provoked several retaliatory strikes against Staten Islanders and their property by New Jersey Whig gangs, who forayed onto the island in search of Hatfield and his band of freebooters.[55]

Captain Nathaniel Robbins, a native of Britain who had settled on Staten Island shortly before the American Revolution, was the leader of another gang of Loyalist marauders who used the island as their sanctuary. In notoriety, Robbins's guerrilla band rivaled that of Hatfield. They made frequent incursions into New Jersey foraging for food and fuel, destroying fields, committing robberies, and threatening Whig families with death if they did not make a sincere effort to change their political views. Robbins and his men sold the provisions that they plundered from New Jersey Whig farms to the British military in exchange for hard currency. One evening Robbins and his gang crossed the Kill van Kull to Rahway, New Jersey, where they captured fourteen suspected Whig partisans who were betting on a cockfight in an abandoned house. Robbins believed that the partisans—most of them under the age of fifteen—were responsible for firing shots at British patrols on the Staten Island side of the Kill. He carried them back to the island where they were held for questioning at the British redoubt situated on the bluff overlooking the village of Richmond.[d] After several weeks, Robbins brought the young men to the British encampment at the Narrows[e] where they were questioned and eventually released by General Sir Henry Clinton. Robbins's gang terrorized not only New Jersey residents but also Staten Islanders. They ventured out in the evenings in disguise, indiscriminately robbed island homes, and preyed on lone travelers along its roads. One Staten Islander remembered that Robbins "had a bad name" on the island and in New

[d] Fort Richmond.

[e] At the present site of Fort Wadsworth National Historic Park.

Jersey and that although he remained on Staten Island after the war, he never dared to go into New Jersey.[56]

One of the most important Loyalist partisans to use Staten Island as a base for banditry and commissioned military operations was a fugitive slave from Monmouth County, New Jersey, named Titus who had run away from the farm of John Corlies in Colt's Neck. Titus had heard about Lord Dunmore's proclamation in November 1775 and joined the British military as a means to gain his freedom permanently. Because of his gallantry at the Battle of Monmouth in June 1778, the British army bestowed on him the ceremonial title of "Colonel Tye." Corlies's farm was situated along the Navesink River near the town of Shrewsbury in Monmouth County. Tye learned to navigate the river and gained knowledge of the property, wealth, commodities, and political leanings of the families in the area. Accordingly, Tye became an invaluable source of information for the British regarding the county's topography, residents, and forage.[57]

Colonel Tye and his small band of African American Loyalists used Staten Island and a Loyalist refugee settlement known as Refugeetown in Sandy Hook, New Jersey, as a base to launch raids against Whig farms in Monmouth County. They carried off valuables and badly needed foodstuffs, horses, and cattle for the British forces on Staten Island and in New York City; kidnapped several prominent Whigs; and liberated many slaves.[58] On March 30, 1780, Colonel Tye and his men raided the home of John Russell in the town of Shrewsbury. Russell was known for participating in Whig raids on Staten Island. During the raid, Tye's gang burned Russell's house, killed his father, and wounded him and his son.[59] Like their white counterparts, Tye and his men were paid handsomely in hard currency for their work on behalf of the British war effort.

By the summer of 1780, Colonel Tye's gang had demonstrated that they could strike into New Jersey at will, and the fear of seeing African Americans under arms was no doubt palpable to white New Jerseyans who had heard rumors of a plot among slaves in Elizabethtown to rise up, destroy the town, and murder whites.[60] In July 1780, Monmouth County Whigs, led by the former New Jersey militia officer David Forman, organized the Association for Retaliation to protect themselves against Loyalist raids, especially those conducted by Tye's gang.[61] On September 1, 1780, Colonel Tye was struck in the wrist by a musket ball during a gun battle with Retaliators at the Colt's Neck home of Whig partisan Captain Joshua Huddy, who was responsible for raids on Staten Island and

Refugeetown. Tye and other Loyalists attempted to apprehend Huddy, who was accused of executing several Loyalists captured during the raids. Although Tye's wound was initially thought to be minor, he contracted tetanus, and after several days he died.[62]

The internecine warfare and the British occupation of Staten Island made life for Staten Island women precarious. Along with the men, they endured inflation, food shortages, physical threats and humiliation, and the continual disruption of their homes by the war. Many Staten Island women were forced to stand by helplessly as their homes were requisitioned for officers' quarters or, worse, ransacked. Their personal items were often stolen; their crops were destroyed; they and their children were threatened with physical harm and humiliation; and their fathers, sons, husbands, and brothers were kidnapped, beaten, or murdered by Whig and Loyalist partisans and British occupation forces. In effect, their homes were their battlefields.

Nonetheless, Staten Island women did their best to manage their households, to protect their families, and to survive the daily pressures that came with the realities and uncertainties of the British military occupation of the island and the internecine warfare that surrounded it. Occasionally Staten Island women challenged and confounded the British occupation troops. Kitty Jackson was left alone with her young daughter for nine months while her husband, the miller Gilbert Jackson, was imprisoned for his Whig sympathies in the Provost, the British prison in New York City. During her husband's incarceration, Kitty and her young daughter were forced to share their home with several British officers and soldiers. Kitty Jackson, however, did not allow the British troops in her home intimidate her or make her change her Whig political sympathies. One Staten Islander recalled her catching a soldier taking her milk pail to his commanding officer, who wanted to use it to bathe his feet. She confronted the soldier, fearlessly chastised him in front of his comrades, and tore the pail out of his hands. Kitty also sent one of her slaves to New Jersey with provisions and information for the Whig forces posted there. To distract the British soldiers, she often started up her husband's grist mill.[f] The loud grinding of the millstones enabled her slave to avoid detection by the British as he rowed across the Arthur Kill to New Jersey.[63]

[f] Gilbert Jackson operated Disosway's Mill in the current Tottenville section of Staten Island.

Kitty and her family also endured abuse from the gangs of Loyalist marauders. One evening shortly after Gilbert's release from prison, the family was visited by several Loyalist partisans, who demanded the family's valuables. When Gilbert refused, one of the men pointed a pistol at his head and threatened to shoot him if he did not comply. Seeing her father with a pistol pointed at his head frightened the Jacksons' young daughter, who began to cry wildly. Concerned that the child's screams could draw attention to the commotion inside the home, one of the intruders struck her on the head with a blunt object before Kitty could comfort and protect her. As Kitty and Gilbert tended to their daughter, who lay unconscious on the floor, their home was ransacked and plundered.[64]

Tradition has it that one morning when a British soldier stopped at the home of the widow Ann Perine for a drink of water, he noticed the large silver buckles on her shoes. After the soldier left, she replaced the buckles with a pair made from a common metal and hid the silver ones with her other valuables in a secret compartment in her house. That evening, the soldier returned and demanded the silver buckles that he had seen on Perine's shoes earlier in the day. She denied owning such a pair of buckles and lifted her skirt slightly to reveal the replacements. When the intruder insisted that those were not the buckles that he had seen in the morning, she kept to her story. Frustrated, the soldier took out a pistol and began to load it in an attempt to frighten her. Before he could finish loading the pistol, however, a passerby who had heard the commotion entered the house, and the startled soldier fled the premises empty-handed.[65]

On another occasion, two British soldiers confronted a Staten Island woman as she was boiling soap in her kitchen. The soldiers demanded that she prepare them a meal. When the woman refused, one of the men lunged at her. Before he could reach her, she grabbed a large ladle filled with hot liquid and threw it at him, scalding his head and neck. The soldier quickly fled the house in pain. His accomplice, who did not want to suffer the same fate, followed close behind.[66]

Rape also was a very real danger for Staten Island women. Victims of rape suffered not only physically from sexually transmitted diseases, trauma, and pregnancy but also psychologically.[67] According to historian Mary Beth Norton, rape on Staten Island in particular was systematic and brutal because the continued presence of troops in the community provided "the opportunity to sexually exploit the local female population."[68] Sexual assaults of the island's female residents, especially by troops affiliated with the British occupation, grew in frequency as the war progressed, and their officers did little to stop it. Lieutenant Colonel Francis Lord Rawdon of the British army was amused by the Staten Island women's complaints of sexual assault against his men. "The fair nymphs of this isle are in wonderful tribulation, as the fresh meat our men have got here has made them as riotous as satyrs," he commented. "A girl cannot step into the bushes to pluck a rose without running the most imminent risk of being ravished, and they are so little accustomed to these vigorous methods that they don't bear them with the proper resignation, and of consequence we have most entertaining courts-martial every day." Rawdon joked about a Staten Island woman who had accused members of the British grenadier corps of raping her. According to Rawdon, General Hugh Lord Percy asked the victim how she knew that they were grenadiers, since the alleged rape had occurred in the dark, to which she replied: "Oh, good God, they could be nothing else, and if your Lordship will examine I am sure you will find it so."[69]

Because most rape victims were not inclined to testify, fewer rapes were reported than were actually committed. While murder and plunder were rightfully treated as major crimes by the British army and convicted perpetrators quickly punished, British military officials often suppressed reports of rape and took very few steps to bring the accused rapists to trial.[70] This discrepancy could be explained in several ways: from the small number of rape cases that were officially reported, to the cavalier attitudes of British officers like Rawdon who did not take reports of rape seriously, to the popular view among soldiers and their officers that rape was a natural feature and an approved tactic of warfare, to the possibility that accused rapists were tried by informal regimental courts whose proceedings often were not recorded.[71]

Staten Islanders living under British occupation also suffered from the threat of communicable diseases. Like the residents of British-held Boston in 1775, Staten Islanders were vulnerable to infectious diseases associated with military camp life.[72] The large concentration of soldiers in cramped and unsanitary barracks, redoubts, tents, huts, barns, private residences, public buildings, and churches created the perfect environment for the spread of such diseases as dysentery, typhus, and smallpox. In July 1776, dysentery and smallpox had struck almost sixty British soldiers on the island.[73] By August, two thousand British and Hessian troops were sick with the disease.[74] A Hessian officer noted that soon after arriving on Staten Island "some kind of red dysentery started to show very much among the ranks."[75] Hessian Private Johann Conrad Dohla described the conditions in the military encampments on the island as so unhealthy that "sicknesses such as putrid fever, diarrhea, and dysentery" spread quickly.[76] The island's children were particularly vulnerable to communicable diseases. A British official on Staten Island remarked that he had seen several mothers leaving a hospital with their children who had "just emerged . . . from a dreadful Fit of Sickness."[77] Many Staten Islanders died during the dysentery epidemic of 1779/1780, which ravaged the civilian and military populations in the New York City region.[78]

Staten Islanders also were subjected to restrictive British economic policies. Although the British were initially more than willing to give Staten Islanders fair market value for livestock, firewood, foodstuffs, and other provisions, by 1777 the British military had implemented price regulations, restricted the number of markets where Staten Islanders could sell their produce, and enacted policies requiring residents to provide troops with hay, grain, and cordwood.[79] In September 1777, George Brindley, the British deputy commissary general of forage, announced that Staten Islanders immediately had to deliver to the army "all the straw they have already thresh'd, and that they without delay get the remainder ready." He warned that any person who ignored this order would be swiftly punished by the most "disagreeable methods."[80] Even ferry rates were regulated. In January 1779, the *Royal Gazette* published a proclamation issued by General Alexander Leslie, the British commander on Staten Island, that addressed "the exorbitant price . . . extracted by the different proprietors of the Ferry Boats, for the fare of passengers between Staten Island and New York." Leslie fixed ferry rates at two shillings for each passenger and six shillings for each horse and stipulated that ferry boats had to be large enough to accommodate at least six passengers. Ferry operators who did not comply with the new regulations could lose their license to conduct business.[81]

Historian Judith L. Van Buskirk described the substantial number of civilians that crisscrossed the military lines that surrounded New York City during the American Revolution: "Civilians crossed the terrain of the two armies ringing New York City on a continuous basis, electing to pursue their private concerns with or without the permission of authorities."[82] Because of Staten Island's location, in some places a mere five hundred feet from Whig-controlled areas of New Jersey, it had a significant amount of traffic. Staten Islanders joined the movement of people who crossed the military lines to visit relatives and friends or to conduct business in New York City and the market towns of New Jersey. This pattern of migration, however, was problematic for authorities on both sides, as not only people and goods but also political and military intelligence crossed the lines.

British officers on Staten Island complained about the numbers of people who passed through the lines, conveying a stream of intelligence to the Whigs in New Jersey. In an effort to stop this flow of information, the British regulated movement on and off the island. They implemented civilian curfews and new regulations for procuring passes and safe-conduct permits, designated a special ferry to provide service between Staten Island and Elizabethtown under a flag of truce for persons holding authorized passes, and restricted access to the island through three landings: Cole's Ferry near the Narrows, Decker's Ferry on the Kill van Kull opposite Bergen Point, New Jersey, and the New Blazing Star Ferry on the island's west shore opposite Elizabethtown and Rahway. British authorities at these landings monitored all activities and closely inspected the mails.[83]

As in other British-occupied communities in America, Staten Island's dissenter churches were labeled as "rebel churches" and singled out for destruction by the British forces. The wood-frame United Reformed Church in the village of Richmond was plundered and demolished by British soldiers, who used the wood to reinforce their earthworks and for firewood. The British converted the small meetinghouse on the island's south shore[g] into a hospital before it, too, was torn down and used for firewood. The Dutch Reformed Church located in Decker's Ferry, where the New Jersey evangelical Reverend Theodore J. Frelinghuysen had once held several revivals, was plundered and requisitioned for barracks and stables.[84]

The war also affected regular services at the island's Moravian church.[h] Built in 1763, the church, which also served as the parsonage for the Reverend Hector Gambold and his family, was damaged by fire and plundered by British troops. A group of British soldiers broke into the parsonage one evening, frightened its occupants, destroyed their furniture, and took several items, including the church's early records.[85]

Staten Island's dominant congregation, the Anglican St. Andrew's, was affected by the war as well. Although at first the services at the church in the village of Richmond were held unimpeded, the pressures of having to

[g] The area of Staten Island where the meetinghouse was located is now called Rossville.

[h] The Moravian church was located on the grounds of the present-day Moravian Cemetery in the New Dorp section of Staten Island.

deal with Whig raiding parties and British occupation forces eventually caused much hardship for the congregation. Its minister, the Reverend Richard Charlton, filed a complaint with the SPG[i] against British and Hessian troops that laid waste to the church's glebe,[j] which was located on the island's eastern shore near the Watering Place.[86] In January 1778, the Reverend Dr. Samuel Seabury of Westchester County traveled to Staten Island to minister to the congregation and reported that St. Andrew's glebe "had suffered very much from the troops . . . the fences being demolished, the timber, which was of considerable value, cut off so that scarce a single tree is left, and a fine young orchard of 500 or 600 apple trees nearly destroyed."[87] By 1781, the entire glebe had been cleared. This was the second time that encamped British troops had caused much destruction to the church's glebe; the first was during the French and Indian War.[88] St. Andrew's was also requisitioned by the British for use as a military hospital, and its edifice sustained severe damage during General Hugh Mercer's attack against the British garrison on the island in October 1776 as well as during General John Sullivan's raid in August 1777.[89]

Under British occupation, Staten Islanders not only were the victims of violence and abuse; they also were subjected to martial law. The island's civil government ceased to exist. Civil courts, which were held in the county courthouse in the village of Richmond, were closed, leaving residents without legal recourse in civil matters or cases involving the British occupation forces. The courthouse was burned by British troops during the war. In February 1778, Frederick Howard, the earl of Carlisle, who headed a failed attempt to open peace talks with the Americans, recommended to British Colonial Secretary Lord George Germain that civil government be restored in all British-occupied areas. Germain supported the proposal and incorporated it into a new strategy designed to reduce the British military presence in America.[90]

By March 1780, Germain had begun to implement the new strategy in New York. He appointed General James Robertson as governor and ordered him to restore civil government there. In February 1781, Robertson began to take the necessary steps to restore civil government on Staten Island. He created a police court and appointed Christopher Billopp as the

---

[i] Society for the Propagation of the Gospel in Foreign Parts.

[j] A *glebe* is a piece of church-owned land that provided an income in rent for the resident minister or the entire parish.

superintendent of police at a salary of £350.[91] Billopp had the authority "to hear and determine Controversies, maintain Peace and good Order, and regulate the Police . . . until Civil Government in all Forms can take Place."[92] He enforced regulations, served as a community liaison, heard complaints against military personnel, and tried cases involving civilians. The police court was located in the village of Richmond and heard cases every Monday. Billopp served as the island's police superintendent until 1782. He was immediately succeeded by Richard Conner and eventually by Paul Micheau Jr., who held the post until the British evacuated Staten Island in early December 1783.[93] Although British officials portrayed the creation of a police court and the appointment of a police superintendent as steps toward the revival of civil government on the island, the functions of the court and the superintendent were still largely military in nature.

Staten Island was situated in the middle of a civil war battlefield where no rules existed and where everyone and everything were fair game. It was a community laid to waste by internecine warfare and the wanton cruelty and destruction committed by British occupation forces. One observer noted that Staten Island was in "an uncivilized and poverty-stricken state, for the foraging parties of the rebels and the different encampments of his Majesty's troops have stripped the country of all the necessary articles of life."[94] In 1780, Rev. Gambold wrote to a friend that

> the middle part of the Island has yet some timber for fire and fencing, but by the waterside and where the forts are, all is gone. The inhabitants are harassed and oppressed daily with taking away their hay and corn, drawing their forage and provisions in the worst of weather, and quartering of their men upon them. These are some of the difficulties, but you can hardly conceive of the distressed condition the Island is in.[95]

The vicious acts of plunder, property destruction, rape, and murder committed by members of the British occupation forces, the restrictive economic regulations implemented by the military and its failure to provide security against partisan Whig raids, and the suspension of civil government complicated the relationship between the British authorities and the Staten Islanders and severely damaged their trust in each other. The situation heightened the tensions between civilians and the military on Staten Island and weakened the British hold on the residents' "hearts and minds."

The mounting public disgust with the British occupation triggered a wave of anti-British sentiment among Staten Islanders. Once hailed as liberators, the British and their Hessian and Loyalist allies were now scorned on the island. As the situation deteriorated, many residents questioned their initial political loyalties, defied British orders, and committed acts of violence and sabotage against the occupation forces. A New Jersey militia officer reported that "the Tories on the Island are very ill treated . . . so that the Inhabitants who at first were pleased, would now be willing to poison them all."[96] During the frigid winter of 1779/1780, General James Pattison, the British commandant for New York, wrote to General Cortlandt Skinner of the New Jersey Volunteers, charging Staten Islanders with hoarding firewood in order to drive up its price in the city. In addition, Pattison accused the Staten Islanders of blackmail and directed Skinner "to oblige them to dispose of it immediately at the Established Rate," adding that if they refused, he was to order his men to seize the firewood.[97] One resident recalled that a member of the Dupuy family was shot by a British officer for refusing to obey an order to carry a load of wood to the British encampment at the Watering Place.[98] In a show of defiance against British military policy, several Staten Islanders refused to continue their service in the Loyalist Staten Island militia, and other residents passed vital information to the Whigs about the strength and condition of the British troops on the island.[99] Hessian Private Johann Conrad Dohla criticized British military authorities for failing to properly control the number of passes and safe-conduct permits issued to Staten Islanders, whom he accused of spying for the enemy. Moreover, he reported that residents ambushed patrols and took every opportunity to shoot at soldiers affiliated with the occupation.[100]

The surrender of British General Charles Lord Cornwallis at Yorktown, Virginia, in October 1781 forced all Loyalists in America to make the difficult choice between accepting the reality of Whig victory and the new state governments that were created during the war or entering a life of exile. By 1783, only the staunchest Staten Island Loyalists had chosen to sell their homes and lands and to leave the island rather than to live under a government controlled by their wartime enemies. Joining thousands of other white Loyalists, their families and slaves, and African American refugees who had been promised freedom by the British, they waited in New York City to board evacuation ships to take them to various destinations within the British Empire. For these Loyalists, these were chaotic and confusing times. "The last Division of Refugees are . . .

preparing for Embarkation," wrote the Staten Island Whig Abraham Bancker. "Many families on Long Island, Staten Island, and New York are struck with a Panick & making preparations to go off, Some of them I think might stay in Safety but are frightened away by others."[101] One Loyalist described his plight and the plight of others as filled with "Anarchy and Confusion."[102]

In July 1783, Staten Islander John M. Mersereau, who had served as a captain in Oliver De Lancey's Loyalist regiment, the New York Volunteers, departed from New York City on board the *Lord Townsend* bound for Nova Scotia, Canada. He was joined by his two sons Andrew and Lawrence. All three men eventually settled in Maugerville on the St. John River in Sunbury County, New Brunswick.[103] Another Staten Island Loyalist, Peter Guyon, sold his property on the island and migrated with his wife Jane and their children to Shelburne, Nova Scotia.[104] Alexander McDonald also sold his property on Staten Island and chose to remain in Halifax where he had been posted for most of the war. In late 1776, his wife Susannah and their children had joined him there; she died three years later.[105] In November 1784, McDonald and his children sailed for Britain. He never returned to Staten Island.[106]

We do not know precisely how many Loyalists fled Staten Island at the end of the American Revolution. Political divisions within families and the decision to leave the island for a new life in Canada or Britain or some other region of the British Empire brought both hardship and heartache to the refugees as well as their relatives and friends. In January 1785, Staten Islander Lettie Heslop, who had married a British officer during the war and eventually settled with him in Britain, wrote to her aunt Ann Perine that it gave her "great pleasure to hear from you as it is the only letter I have received from any of my Friends since I left New York." She lamented that many of her letters had gone unanswered and pleaded with Ann "to give me the particulars about my Mother and sister and friends."[107] Staten Islander Richard Decker exchanged letters with his former neighbors Abraham and Jane Jones, who had settled near Shelburne, Nova Scotia. Abraham Jones had served as a captain in the Staten Island Loyalist militia during the war. "I imbrace this opportunity to inform you that we are all in good health, am sorry any Evil should subsist between you and any of your former Friends. Hope the true Friendship subsisting between your family & mine may never be dissolved." Decker closed by asking Jane "to give our best Respects to Captain Jones, to Mr.

and Mrs. [Peter] Guyon, Captain Isaac Decker, his Family and all Friends."[108]

Some Loyalists voluntarily departed from Staten Island, whereas others were forced to leave. New York State confiscated the landholdings of and banished Loyalists who were considered to be too dangerous to the stability and security of the government. Under the state law known as the Confiscation Act, passed in October 1779, fifty-nine prominent New York Loyalists, including Christopher Billopp and Benjamin Seaman of Staten Island, were branded as Loyalist felons; their estates were confiscated; and they were banished from the state.[109] The law was designed to undermine Loyalist political power and to raise revenue for New York State from the sale of confiscated property. Staten Island, however, was under British occupation at the time of its enactment, and so the state could not immediately enforce the law against Staten Islanders. In May 1780, Billopp began to sell his lands on Staten Island for about two-thirds their value rather than to risk losing the property to New York State without compensation if the British occupation ended.[110] Seaman also sold his land at a reduced price because it still was subject to confiscation by the state.[111]

Following the British evacuation of Staten Island in early December 1783, New York State confiscated and sold at public auction the estates belonging to Christopher Billopp and Benjamin Seaman. Most of the land on these estates was bought by well-to-do speculators who became embroiled in legal disputes with the persons who had privately purchased the same land from the two men during the war. The disputed claims took years to settle, with varying results.[112]

A second state law, the Trespass Act of 1783, was designed to punish the Loyalists. Under this law, Whigs who had fled British-occupied areas of New York State could sue Loyalists for their unauthorized occupation of and damage to their property during the war. In two separate lawsuits, Whigs John and Samuel Broome of New York City accused Staten Islander Richard Conner of cutting down thousands of trees on their property on the island, valued at £7,000, for use by the Staten Island militia and the British occupation forces. John and Samuel Broome were represented by Aaron Burr, and Conner retained the legal services of Henry Brockholst Livingston, the son of New Jersey Governor William Livingston and the husband of Benjamin Seaman's granddaughter Catherine. A jury found Conner guilty of violating the Trespass Act, and he was assessed damages.[113] In a second trespass case, several Staten Island Whigs accused Richard Lawrence, who had served as the master carpenter of the island's shipyards under the British occupation, of cutting wood from their property for use in the construction of flat-bottomed boats for the British military and for the repair of British vessels. Lawrence, who received legal advice from Alexander Hamilton, pleaded not guilty on the grounds that the Trespass Act had violated the peace treaty that ended the war.[114] In 1786, a jury found Lawrence guilty and sentenced him to prison. In prison, he futilely wrote to members of the Articles of Confederation government and to several British officials, including King George III, seeking relief.[115] After his release in 1788 Lawrence, his wife, and their nine children immigrated to Britain, where he died the following year, "advanced in life and impaired by hard toil."[116]

In July 1783, Christopher Billopp and Benjamin Seaman joined fifty-three other Loyalists in a petition to General Sir Guy Carleton, now commander in chief of the British forces in America. The men sought special consideration in the allocation of 250,000 acres of land in Nova Scotia, Canada. Carleton referred the petition to Governor John Parr of Nova Scotia, who refused their request on the grounds that it would disrupt the orderly and expeditious settlement of his province.[117] Billopp, Seaman, and several members of their families eventually moved to Nova Scotia, settling in the refugee community of Parrtown. In 1784, Parrtown was combined with another refugee community, Carleton, to form the city of Saint John, in what became the province of New Brunswick. Both Billopp and Seaman immediately assumed prominent public roles in their new home. Seaman died in 1785. Billopp served in the First New Brunswick Assembly and was appointed in 1796 to its council by King George III. He died in 1827 at the age of ninety.[118]

By 1784, Whigs who had fled the island when the British landed in 1776 returned to the community to reclaim their houses, farms, and businesses. One of those Whigs who returned was Hendrick Garrison, who discovered that his slave Harry had chosen not to leave the island on a British evacuation ship nor had he been forcibly taken by a British officer or Loyalist civilian. Instead, Harry had remained with his master's property throughout the war, selling "the produce of the farm to the British." Upon reuniting with Garrison, Harry turned over "a hoard of many hundred pounds which he had thus accumulated." Unfortunately, Harry's devotion to his master and business acumen did not immediately earn him his freedom; he was eventually manumitted in 1807.[119]

Civil government was restored on Staten Island. Civil courts were re-opened, but because the county courthouse had been destroyed during the war, they were held in private homes that also served as inns. Elections were held for local and state offices, and the town supervisors began to meet regularly as they had done before the war. Although Staten Island's political culture continued to reflect deference to prominent families and the educated and wealthier members of the community, the American Revolution had nonetheless brought important changes. Men from families who actively supported the Whig cause replaced the prewar political leadership provided by the families of Loyalists Christopher Billopp and Benjamin Seaman. Whigs such as Adrian and Abraham Bancker and Joshua and John Mersereau were the new political power brokers in postwar Staten Island. Moreover, Britain's defeat had weakened the influence of the Anglican Church on the island, and political leadership now devolved to men affiliated with the dissenter faiths.[120]

Except for the confiscation and dissolution of the Billopp and Seaman estates by New York State, the American Revolution did not noticeably change Staten Island's socioeconomic structure. Instead, the island remained a predominantly agrarian, slaveholding, middle-class community. Its population had grown slightly from 2,847 residents before the war to 3,835 in 1790, the year of the first federal census. This slight growth could be attributed to the losses during the war. Of the island's 3,835 residents in 1790, 886 were African American, of whom 759 were slaves.[121]

On December 3, 1783, the British army evacuated Staten Island. Several residents stood on the shoreline and the island's heights to watch the British vessels sail through the Narrows into the Atlantic Ocean. "We were very boisterous in our demonstrations of joy," remembered one Staten Islander. "We clapped our hands, we waved our hats, we sprang into the air, and some few, who had brought muskets with them, fired a *feu-de-joie*; a few others, in the exuberance of their gladness, indulged in gestures, which though very expressive, were neither polite nor judicious."[122] Seven and a half years of military occupation had taken an emotional and physical toll on Staten Island's residents. Their fields had been left in ruins and their homes ransacked and plundered by marauding bands of Whigs and Loyalists, by Hessians, and by the regular armies of Britain and America. In addition to suffering the destruction of their property, Staten Islanders endured physical and verbal abuse, rape and murder. Although callous acts of violence by Whig partisans and Continental forces angered Staten Islanders, it was not unexpected. But when similar acts were committed by British soldiers, who had been warmly welcomed by the community and hailed as liberators, residents felt betrayed and abandoned. The daily demands made by the British occupation forces, the rough treatment of male and female residents, and the British military's inability to subdue the rebellion, bring security to their lives, and reassert imperial power in America cooled the Loyalist ardor of most Staten Islanders. By 1783, many of the island's residents had embraced the Whig cause. Only the most vocal and active Loyalists had departed from Staten Island, leaving behind a community physically and emotionally scarred by the war. For the Staten Islanders who remained, it was time to heal old wounds, to rebuild their community, and to give their loyalty to their new country: the United States.

# APPENDIX 1

*Population of Staten Island, New York, 1698–1800*

| Year | Total Population |
|------|------------------|
| 1698 | 727 |
| 1703 | 504 |
| 1712 | 1,279 |
| 1723 | 1,506 |
| 1731 | 1,817 |
| 1737 | 1,889 |
| 1746 | 2,073 |
| 1749 | 2,154 |
| 1756 | 2,132 |
| 1771 | 2,847 |
| 1786 | 3,152 |
| 1790 | 3,835 |
| 1800 | 4,564 |

*Sources:* Evarts B. Greene and Virginia D. Harrington, eds., *American Population before the Federal Census of 1790* (Gloucester, Mass.: Peter Smith, 1966), 92–105; and Kenneth T. Jackson, ed., *The Encyclopedia of New York* (New Haven, Conn.: Yale University Press, 1995), 923.

# APPENDIX 2

*Population of Staten Island, New York, by Race, 1698–1800*

| Year | Number of Whites | Number of African Americans |
|------|------------------|------------------------------|
| 1698 | 654 | 73 |
| 1703 | 407 | 97 |
| 1712 | n/a | n/a |
| 1723 | 1,251 | 255 |
| 1731 | 1,513 | 304 |
| 1737 | 1,540 | 349 |
| 1746 | 1,691 | 382 |
| 1749 | 1,745 | 409 |
| 1756 | 1,667 | 465 |
| 1771 | 2,253 | 594 |
| 1786 | 2,459 | 693 |
| 1790 | 2,949 | 886[a] |
| 1800 | 3,806 | 758[b] |

*Sources:* Evarts B. Greene and Virginia D. Harrington, eds., *American Population before the Federal Census of 1790* (Gloucester, Mass.: Peter Smith, 1966), 92–105; Vivienne L. Kruger, "Born to Run: The Slave Family in Early New York, 1626 to 1827" (PhD diss., Columbia University, 1985), 924; and Ira Rosenwaike, *Population History of New York City* (Syracuse, N.Y.: Syracuse University Press, 1972), 32.

[a] Includes 127 free African Americans.

[b] Includes 83 free African Americans.

# APPENDIX 3

## African Americans as a Percentage of the Total Population of Staten Island, New York, 1698–1800

| Year | Total Population | African Americans (%) |
|------|------------------|----------------------|
| 1698 | 727 | 10.0 |
| 1703 | 504 | 19.2 |
| 1712 | 1,279 | n/a |
| 1723 | 1,506 | 16.9 |
| 1731 | 1,817 | 16.7 |
| 1737 | 1,889 | 18.5 |
| 1746 | 2,073 | 18.4 |
| 1749 | 2,154 | 19.0 |
| 1756 | 2,132 | 21.8 |
| 1771 | 2,847 | 20.9 |
| 1786 | 3,152 | 22.0 |
| 1790 | 3,835 | 23.1[a] |
| 1800 | 4,564 | 16.6[b] |

*Sources:* Evarts B. Greene and Virginia D. Harrington, eds., *American Population before the Federal Census of 1790* (Gloucester, Mass.: Peter Smith, 1966), 92–105; and Kenneth T. Jackson, ed., *The Encyclopedia of New York City* (New Haven, Conn.: Yale University Press, 1995), 921–923.

[a] 3.3% = free African Americans.

[b] 1.8% = free African Americans.

# Notes

INTRODUCTION

1. Captain Alexander McDonald to Walter and Thomas Buchannon, 4 November 1775, in *The Letter-Book of Captain Alexander McDonald of the Royal Highland Emigrants, 1775–1779* (New York: New York Historical Society, 1882), 215 (hereafter cited as *Letter-Book*).

2. Christopher Moore, *The Loyalists: Revolution, Exile, Settlement* (Toronto: McClelland and Stewart, 1984), 22.

3. Captain Alexander McDonald to General William Howe, n.d., *Letter-Book*, 275.

4. Ibid.

5. This interpretation is popularly known as the Whig school of American historiography and is represented by Mercy Otis Warren's *The History of the Rise, Progress, and Termination of the American Revolution*, 2 vols. (Boston: Manning and Loring, 1805); and George Bancroft's *History of the United States from the Discovery of the American Continent*, 10 vols. (Boston: C. C. Little and J. Brown, 1842–1874).

6. Lorenzo Sabine, *Biographical Sketches of Loyalists of the American Revolution with an Historical Essay*, 2 vols. (Boston: Little, Brown, 1864).

7. See Moses C. Tyler, "The Party of the Loyalists in the American Revolution," *American Historical Review* 1 (1895): 24–45; Claude H. Van Tyne, *The Loyalists in the American Revolution* (New York: Macmillan, 1902); and Alexander C. Flick, *Loyalism in New York during the American Revolution* (1901; repr., New York: AMS Press, 1970).

8. See James H. Stark, *The Loyalists of Massachusetts and the Other Side of the American Revolution* (Boston: W. B. Clarke, 1907); Otis G. Hammond, *The Tories of New Hampshire* (Concord: New Hampshire Historical Society, 1917); Isaac S. Harrell, *Loyalism in Virginia* (Durham, N.C.: Duke University Press, 1926); E. Alfred Jones, *The Loyalists of New Jersey: The Memorials, Petitions, Claims* (Newark: New Jersey Historical Society, 1927); Robert O. De Mond, *The Loyalists of North Carolina during the Revolution* (Durham, N.C.: Duke University Press, 1940); Harold B. Hancock, *The Delaware Loyalists* (1940; repr., Boston: Gregg Press, 1972), and *The Loyalists of Revolutionary Delaware*

(Newark: University of Delaware Press, 1977); and Robert W. Barnwell, "Loyalism in South Carolina, 1765–1785" (PhD diss., Duke University, 1941).

9. Leonard W. Labaree, *Conservatism in Early American History* (New York: New York University Press, 1948), 150–151, 161, 165.

10. William H. Nelson, *The American Tory* (Boston: Beacon Press, 1968), 12.

11. Robert M. Calhoon, *The Loyalists in Revolutionary America, 1760–1781* (New York: Harcourt Brace Jovanovich, 1973), 505–506.

12. See Ann G. Condon, "Marching to a Different Drummer: The Political Philosophy of the American Loyalists," in *Red, White, and True Blue: The Loyalists in the Revolution*, edited by Esmond Wright (New York: AMS Press, 1976), 1, 18; and Janice Potter, *The Liberty We Seek: Loyalist Ideology in Colonial New York and Massachusetts* (Cambridge, Mass.: Harvard University Press, 1983).

13. Potter, *The Liberty We Seek*, 11.

14. Bernard Bailyn, *The Ordeal of Thomas Hutchinson* (Cambridge, Mass.: Harvard University Press, 1974), xi.

15. See William A. Benton, *Whig-Loyalism: An Aspect of Political Ideology in the American Revolutionary Era* (Teaneck, N.J.: Fairleigh Dickinson University Press, 1969); Leslie F. S. Upton, *The Loyal-Whig: William Smith of New York and Quebec* (Toronto: University of Toronto Press, 1969); Mary Beth Norton, *The British-Americans: The Loyalist Exiles in England, 1774–1789* (Boston: Little, Brown, 1972); and Carol Berkin, *Jonathan Sewall: Odyssey of an American Loyalist* (New York: Columbia University Press, 1974). See also James Thomas Flexner, *States Dyckman: American Loyalist* (Boston: Little, Brown, 1980); and Elizabeth P. McCaughey, *From Loyalist to Founding Father: The Political Odyssey of William Samuel Johnson* (New York: Columbia University Press, 1980).

16. See Rick J. Ashton, "The Loyalist Experience: New York, 1763–1789" (PhD diss., Northwestern University, 1973); Robert S. Lambert, *South Carolina Loyalists in the American Revolution* (Columbia: University of South Carolina Press, 1987); Anne M. Ousterhut, *A State Divided: Opposition in Pennsylvania to the American Revolution* (Westport, Conn.: Greenwood Press, 1987); Philip Ranlet, *The New York Loyalists* (Knoxville: University of Tennessee Press, 1986); and Dennis P. Ryan, *New Jersey Loyalists* (Trenton: New Jersey Historical Commission, 1975). Ranlet also assessed the numerical strength of Loyalism in New York and found that historians had overestimated the number of Loyalists in that state.

17. See Ruth M. Keesey, "Loyalism in Bergen County, New Jersey," *William and Mary Quarterly*, 3rd ser., 18 (1961): 558 (hereafter cited as *WMQ*); Adrian C. Leiby, *The Revolutionary War in the Hackensack Valley: The Jersey Dutch and the Neutral Ground* (New Brunswick, N.J.: Rutgers University Press, 1992); Bruce G. Merritt, "Loyalism and Social Conflict in Revolutionary Deerfield,

Massachusetts," *Journal of American History* 57 (1970): 277–289 (hereafter cited as *JAH*); Joseph S. Tiedemann, "Communities in the Midst of the American Revolution: Queens County, New York, 1774–1775," *Journal of Social History* 18 (1984): 57–78, "Patriots by Default: Queens County, New York, and the British Army, 1776–1783," *WMQ*, 3rd ser., 43 (1986): 35–63, and "A Revolution Foiled: Queens County, New York, 1775–1776," *JAH* 75 (1988): 417–444; and Judith L. Van Buskirk, *Generous Enemies: Patriots and Loyalists in Revolutionary New York* (Philadelphia: University of Pennsylvania Press, 2002).

18. See Albert H. Tillson Jr., "The Localist Roots of Backcountry Loyalism: An Examination of Popular Political Culture in Virginia's New River Valley," *Journal of Southern History* 54 (1988): 387–404 (hereafter cited as *JSH*); Adele Hast, *Loyalism in Revolutionary Virginia: The Norfolk Area and the Eastern Shore* (Ann Arbor, Mich.: UMI Research Press, 1982); Ronald Hoffman, Thad W. Tate, and Peter J. Albert, eds., *An Uncivil War: The Southern Backcountry during the American Revolution* (Charlottesville: University Press of Virginia, 1985); Keith Mason, "Localism, Evangelicalism, and Loyalism: The Sources of Discontent in the Revolutionary Chesapeake," *JSH* 56 (1990): 23–54; Rebecca Starr, "Little Bermuda: Loyalism on Daufuskie Island, South Carolina, 1775–1783," in *Loyalists and Community in North America*, edited by Robert M. Calhoon, Timothy M. Barnes, and George A. Rawlyk (Westport, Conn.: Greenwood Press, 1994), 55–63; Edward J. Cashin, *The King's Ranger: Thomas Brown and the American Revolution on the Southern Frontier* (New York: Fordham University Press, 1999); and Walter Edgar, *Partisans and Redcoats: The Southern Conflict That Turned the Tide of the American Revolution* (New York: Morrow, 2001).

19. For a study that focuses mainly on partisan warfare in the north, see Harry M. Ward, *Between the Lines: Banditti of the American Revolution* (Westport, Conn.: Greenwood Press, 2002). For a treatment of partisan operations in the context of conventional warfare, see Mark V. Kwasny, *Washington's Partisan War, 1775–1783* (Kent, Ohio: Kent State University Press, 1996).

CHAPTER 1

1. Adolph B. Benson, ed., *The America of 1750: Peter Kalm's Travels in North America, the English Version of 1770*, 2 vols. (New York: Wilson-Erickson, 1937), vol. 1, 124.

2. Bartlett B. James and J. Franklin Jameson, eds., *Journal of Jasper Danckaerts, 1679–1680* (New York: Scribner, 1913), 70.

3. Captain Philipp Waldeck is quoted in Gertrude L. Calhoun, ed., "Excerpts from Philipp Waldeck's Diary of the American Revolution," *Proceedings of the*

*Union County Historical Society of Union County, New Jersey* 2 (1923–1924): 142.

4. For discussions of fishing, oystering, crabbing, and clamming as leisure and economic activities for eighteenth-century Staten Islanders, see Burton A. Kollmer, "The Yesterday of the Oysterman," *Staten Island Historian*, 1st ser., 3 (1940): 17, 19–24 (hereafter cited as *SIH*); Clyde L. Mackenzie, *The Fisheries of the Raritan Bay* (New Brunswick, N.J.: Rutgers University Press, 1992), 17–19; and Charles L. Sachs, *Made on Staten Island: Agriculture, Industry, and Suburban Living in the City* (Staten Island, N.Y.: Staten Island Historical Society, 1988), 17, 20, 27.

5. See John Waldman, *Heartbeats in the Muck: A Dramatic Look at the History, Sea Life, and Environment of New York Harbor* (New York: Lyons Press, 1999), 99–103; and Elizabeth Barlow, *The Forests and Wetlands of New York City* (Boston: Little, Brown, 1969), 95–96.

6. Benson, *The America of 1750*, vol. 1, 124.

7. James and Jameson, *Journal of Jasper Danckaerts*, 69.

8. See Charles E. Anthon, ed., "Anthon's Notes," *Proceedings of the Staten Island Institute of Arts and Sciences* 3–6 (1924–1932): 158 (hereafter cited as *PSIIAS*).

9. Daniel Denton, *A Brief Description of New York: Formerly Called New Netherland* (London: Printed for John Hancock, 1670), 13.

10. James and Jameson, *Journal of Jasper Danckaerts*, 71.

11. A parcel of land on Staten Island was advertised in the *New-York Journal*, 31 December 1791, as having "60 acres of the first quality of wood land, which may be easily transported to the City of New York, or to Amboy [Perth Amboy], at very little expense."

12. See Sachs, *Made on Staten Island*, 33; and Loring McMillen, "An Island Saga: The Mersereau Family: Part 2," *Chronicles of Staten Island* 1 (1989–1990): 156 (hereafter cited as *COSI*).

13. Lieutenant Johann Heinrich to August Ludwig Schlozer, 18 September 1776, in *Letters of Brunswick and Hessian Officers during the American Revolution*, edited by William L. Stone (New York: Da Capo Press, 1970), 194 (hereafter cited as *Letters*).

14. *New-York Daily Advertiser*, 15 January 1791.

15. Two manorial estates were established on Staten Island before the American Revolution: the 5,100-acre Cassiltowne Manor, which belonged to Thomas Dongan, the proprietary governor of New York, and the 1,600-acre Bentley Manor. By the American Revolution, Cassiltowne Manor had been divided and subdivided several times. The reduction of the Dongan landholdings left the Billopps as the largest landowners on Staten Island. For a discussion of Cassiltowne Manor, see William E. McGinn, "John Palmer, Thomas Dongan, and the Manor of Cassiltowne," *SIH*, 1st ser., 29 (1968): 9–13. For a discussion of Bentley

Manor, see William T. Davis, *The Conference/Billopp House* (Staten Island, N.Y.: Staten Island Historical Society, 1926), 50–51, 79–83; and Field Horne, *The Conference House Revisited: A History of the Billopp Manor House* (Staten Island, N.Y.: Conference House Association, 1990), 1–11.

16. Benson, *The America of 1750*, vol. 1, 124.

17. Lincoln MacVeagh, ed., *Journal of Nicholas Cresswell, 1774–1777* (New York: Dial Press, 1924), 243.

18. For a discussion of milling on Staten Island, see Loring McMillen, "Old Mills of Staten Island," *SIH*, 1st ser., 10 (1949): 1–4, 9, 15–16, and "Dongan's Mills," *SIH*, 1st ser., 1 (1938): 25–27, 31. See also Harlow McMillen, "Richmondtown: The First 160 Years, Part VII: The Residents of Richmondtown— The Millers," *SIH*, 1st ser., 23 (1962): 14–16; Charles W. Leng and William T. Davis, *Staten Island and Its People: A History, 1609–1929*, 3 vols. (New York: Lewis Historical Publishing, 1930), vol. 2, 610; and Sachs, *Made on Staten Island*, 18. For a discussion and complete listing of Staten Island's colonial ferries, see Kenneth Scott, "The Colonial Ferries of Staten Island," *PSIIAS* 14 (1951): 45–68, and "The Colonial Ferries of Staten Island: Part II," *PSIIAS* 15 (1952), 9–31. For the island's early road system, see Leng and Davis, *Staten Island and Its People*, vol. 1, 141; and Herbert B. Reed, "The Early Staten Island Roads," *SIH*, 1st ser., 26 (1965): 17–21.

19. See Sherene Baugher, "Trade Networks: Colonial and Federal Period (1680–1815)," *PSIIAS* 34 (1989): 33–37; Robert W. Venables, "A Historical Overview of Staten Island's Trade Networks," *PSIIAS* 34 (1989): 1–24; and Sherene Baugher and Robert W. Venables, "Ceramics as Indicators of Status and Class in Eighteenth Century New York," in *Consumer Choice in Historical Archaeology*, edited by Suzanne M. Spencer-Wood (New York: Plenum Press, 1987), 31–53. On the consumer revolution of the eighteenth century, see T. H. Breen, "'Baubles of Britain': The American and British Consumer Revolution of the Eighteenth Century," *Past and Present* 119 (1988): 73–104; and Carole Shammas, *The Pre-Industrial Consumer in England and America* (New York: Oxford University Press, 1990).

20. Anthon, "Anthon's Notes," 155.

21. See Charles F. Billopp, *A History of Thomas and Anne Billopp Farmar and Some of Their Descendants in America* (New York: Grafton Press, Genealogical Publishers, 1908); Marjorie Johnson, *Christopher Billopp Family Genealogy: Captain Christopher Billopp (1631–1725) and His Descendants and the Allied Farmar Family* (Staten Island, N.Y.: Conference House Association, 1991); and William A. Whitehead, *Contributions to the Early History of Perth Amboy and Adjoining Country* (New York: D. Appleton, 1856), 53, 92–120.

22. Anthon, "Anthon's Notes," 133.

23. Horne, *The Conference House Revisited*, 14.

24. "Petition of Peter Billou, Claude Le Maitre, and Others, All Recently Ar-

rived Emigrants, for Land on Staten-Island," 22 August 1661, in *Documents Relative to the Colonial History of the State of New York*, edited by E. B. O'-Callaghan, 15 vols. (Albany, N.Y.: Weed, Parsons Printers, 1853–1887), vol. 13, 206 (hereafter cited as *NYCD*).

25. See Field Horne, *A Social-Historical Context of the Voorlezer's House at Richmond Town, Staten Island, New York: A Guide for Interpretation* (Saratoga Springs, N.Y.: Public History and Museum Services, 1986), 16–18.

26. See Edward Countryman, *A People in Revolution: The American Revolution and Political Society in New York, 1760–1790* (Baltimore: Johns Hopkins University Press, 1981), 24.

27. See Evarts B. Greene and Virginia D. Harrington, eds., *American Population before the Federal Census of 1790* (Gloucester, Mass.: Peter Smith, 1966), 92–105; and Kenneth T. Jackson, ed., *The Encyclopedia of New York City* (New Haven, Conn.: Yale University Press, 1995), 923.

28. Anglicanism had been established in the counties of New York, Queens, Westchester, and Richmond (on Staten Island) by the Ministry Act of 1693, which is reprinted in Edward T. Corwin, ed., *Ecclesiastical Records of the State of New York*, 7 vols. (Albany, N.Y.: J. B. Lyon, State Printer, 1901–1916), vol. 2, 1042–1043.

29. For a discussion of the 1713 charter, see Rev. Charles S. Burch, "History of Saint Andrew's Church, Richmond, Staten Island," *Grafton Magazine of History and Genealogy* 1 (1908): 5. St. Andrew's Church was built on land deeded to the parish by William and Mary Tillyer. A transcript of the Tillyer deed can be found in the Saint Andrew's Church Collection, box 1, folder 1, Staten Island Historical Society (hereafter cited as SI-HS). The quotation is from Lewis Morris to John Chamberlayne, 1707 September, in *The Papers of Lewis Morris*, edited by Eugene R. Sheridan, 3 vols. (Newark: New Jersey Historical Society, 1991), vol. 1, 58.

30. Rev. Aeneas Mackenzie to the SPG, 8 November 1705, in Burch, "History of Saint Andrew's," 3.

31. See Rev. Aeneas Mackenzie to the SPG, 13 June 1709, in *Church of St. Andrew, Richmond, Staten Island: Its History, Vital Records, and Gravestone Inscriptions*, edited by William T. Davis, Charles W. Leng, and Royden W. Vosburgh (Staten Island, N.Y.: Staten Island Historical Society, 1925), 50 (hereafter cited as *Church of St. Andrew*). See also Burch, "History of Saint Andrew's," 4; *Church of St. Andrew*, 22; and Jean Paul Jordan, "The Anglican Establishment in Colonial New York, 1693–1783" (PhD diss., Columbia University, 1971), 168.

32. John Calam, *Parsons and Pedagogues: The SPG Adventure in American Education* (New York: Columbia University Press, 1971), writes that "the predominant task was to teach children the three R's together with religious and social conformity" (104).

33. Rev. Aeneas Mackenzie to the SPG, 4 May 1711, in *Church of St. Andrew*, 52.

34. For general discussions of slavery on Staten Island during the eighteenth century, see John J. Clute, *Annals of Staten Island: From Its Discovery to the Present Time* (New York: Press of Charles Vogt, 1877), 70–71, 76, 513; Ira K. Morris, *Morris's Memorial History of Staten Island, New York*, 2 vols. (New York: Memorial Publishing Company, 1898–1900), vol. 1, 6; Ronald David Jackson and Evelyn E. Jackson, eds., *African American History in Staten Island: Slave Holding Families and Their Slaves, Raw Notes* (Staten Island, N.Y.: Staten Island Historical Society, 1995); Ronald David Jackson, "The Freedom Seekers: Staten Island's Runaway Slaves," *SIH*, 2nd ser., 14 (1996): 1–12, 16; Edgar J. McManus, *A History of Negro Slavery in New York* (Syracuse, N.Y.: Syracuse University Press, 1966), 42, 45; and Graham Russell Hodges, *Root and Branch: African Americans in New York and East New Jersey, 1613–1863* (Chapel Hill: University of North Carolina Press, 1999), 104, 164.

35. There were 73 slaves on Staten Island in 1698, 709 in 1749, and 594 by 1771. See Horne, *A Social-Historical Context*, 18; Hodges, *Root and Branch*, 104; Vivienne L. Kruger, "Born to Run: The Slave Family in Early New York, 1626–1827" (PhD diss., Columbia University, 1985), 91, 131; McManus, *History of Negro Slavery*, 42; and Greene and Harrington, *American Population*, 93, 100, 102.

36. See Jackson, "The Freedom Seekers," 1–2; Kruger, "Born to Run," 93, 150; and Hodges, *Root and Branch*, 75.

37. Calhoun, "Excerpts from Philipp Waldeck's Diary," 142.

38. For general discussions of the revocation of the Edict of Nantes and its effect on the Huguenots, see Jon Butler, *The Huguenots in America: A Refugee People in New World Society* (Cambridge, Mass.: Harvard University Press, 1983), chap. 1; and Louis Mettam, "Louis XIV and the Huguenots," *History Today* 35 (1985): 15–21.

39. Rev. David de Bonrepos's support of SPG-sponsored education and his close working relationship with Anglicans are discussed in Butler, *Huguenots in America*, 169; and Jordan, "Anglican Establishment," 201–208. See also Rev. Aeneas Mackenzie to the SPG, 8 November 1705, in Burch, "History of Saint Andrew's," 3.

40. Elders and Members of the French Congregation to the SPG, 1735, transcript, Charles W. Leng Collection, box 1, folder 60B, Staten Island Institute of Arts and Sciences (hereafter cited as SIIAS).

41. See *Church of St. Andrew*, 131–132; and Clute, *Annals*, 257, 396, 424–425. French surnames outnumbered those of English origin in a list of subscribers for the salary of Rev. John H. Rowland, dated 10 April 1787.

42. For a brief history of the Dutch Reformed congregation on Staten Island, see Cornelius Vander Naald, "History of the Reformed Church on Staten Is-

land," *SIH*, 1st ser., 16 (1955): 1–5. See also Henry Delavan Frost, "The Church on Staten Island," in *Tercentenary Studies, 1928: Reformed Church in America, a Record of Beginnings*, compiled by the Tercentenary Committee on Research and Publication (New York: Published by the church, 1928), 89–90; and Leng and Davis, *Staten Island and Its People*, vol. 1, 435. For a discussion of the life and career of Rev. Cornelius Van Santvoord, see Edward T. Corwin, *A Manual of the Reformed Church in America: 1628–1902* (New York: Board of Publication of the Reformed Church of America, 1902), 851–852; William Sprague, *Annals of the American Reformed Dutch Pulpit; Or Commemorative Notices of Distinguished Clergymen of That Denomination in the United States from Its Commencement to the Close of the Year Eighteen Hundred and Fifty-five* (New York: Carter, 1869), 6–7; and Frederick L. Weis, *The Colonial Clergy of the Middle Colonies: New York, New Jersey, and Pennsylvania, 1628–1776* (Worcester, Mass.: American Antiquarian Society, 1957), 334. On the relationship between the Huguenots and the Dutch Reformed congregation, see Butler, *Huguenots in America*, 192.

43. See Corwin, *A Manual*, 472–477; Weis, *Colonial Clergy*, 221; Douglas G. Jacobsen, *Unprov'd Experiment: Religious Pluralism in Colonial New Jersey* (Brooklyn, N.Y.: Carlson Publishers, 1991), 75–83; and James Tanis, *Dutch Calvinistic Pietism in the Middle Colonies: A Study of the Life and Theology of Theodorus Jacobus Frelinghuysen* (The Hague: Nijhoff, 1967).

44. This interpretation is similar to that of F. J. Schrag, "Theodorus Jacobus Frelinghuysen, the Father of American Pietism," *Church History* 14 (1945): 201–216; and Patricia U. Bonomi, *Under the Cope of Heaven: Religion, Society, and Politics in Colonial America* (New York: Oxford University Press, 1986), 131–132. For an opposing view, see Herman Harmelink III, "Another Look at Frelinghuysen and His 'Awakening,'" *Church History* 37 (1968): 423–438; and M. Eugene Osterhaven, "The Experimental Theology of Early Dutch Calvinism," *Reformed Review* 27 (1974): 186–192.

45. See Luke Tyerman, *The Life of the Reverend George Whitefield, B.A., of Pembroke College, Oxford*, 2 vols. (New York: Anson D. F. Randolph, 1877), vol. 1, 433. Rev. George Whitefield is quoted in Leng and Davis, *Staten Island and Its People*, vol. 1, 444–445.

46. See Martin E. Lodge, "The Great Awakening in the Middle Colonies" (PhD diss., University of California at Berkeley, 1964), 140, 190; and Rev. Gilbert Tennent to Rev. George Whitefield, 25 April 1741, in Tyerman, *The Life of the Reverend George Whitefield*, vol. 1, 477.

47. Rev. Jonathan Arnold to the SPG, 10 November 1742, transcript, Charles W. Leng Collection, box 2, folder 60B, SIIAS.

48. *New-York Gazette*, 15–22 January 1740.

49. See Bonomi, *Under the Cope of Heaven*, chap. 7; and Frank Lambert, *The Founding Fathers and the Place of Religion in America* (Princeton, N.J.:

Princeton University Press, 2003), 127–129, 145. See also Jonathan Clark, "The American Revolution: A War of Religion?" *History Today* 39 (1989): 10–16; and Timothy D. Hall, *Contested Boundaries: Itinerancy and the Reshaping of the Colonial American Religious World* (Durham, N.C.: Duke University Press, 1994).

50. For a general discussion of the Great Awakening and the divisions that it caused in many congregations throughout America, see Bonomi, *Under the Cope of Heaven*, chap. 5; and Charles H. Maxson, *The Great Awakening in the Middle Colonies* (Chicago: University of Chicago Press, 1920). For the schism in the Dutch Reformed Church, see Adrian C. Leiby, "The Coetus-Conferentie Controversy: Part I—Events up to the Time the Conferentie Was Formed, 1755," *De Halve Maen* 38 (1963): 11–13, and "The Coetus-Conferentie Controversy: Part II—The Conferentie Faction Is Overthrown, 1771," *De Halve Maen* 39 (1964): 13–14. See also Gerald F. De Jong, *The Dutch Reformed Church in the American Colonies* (Grand Rapids, Mich.: Eerdmans, 1978), chap. 11.

51. Rev. Jonathan Arnold to the SPG, 10 November 1742, transcript, Charles W. Leng Collection, box 2, folder 60B, SIIAS.

52. Rev. Jonathan Arnold is quoted in Jordan, "The Anglican Establishment," 209.

53. Henry Holland was a native of Albany, New York. In the late 1740s, he relocated to New York City and purchased a large tract of land on the northwest shore of Staten Island. His estate was known as Morning Star.

54. Rev. Richard Charlton to James Duane, 12 February 1768, James Duane Papers, 1680–1853, reel 1, New York Historical Society (hereafter cited as NY-HS).

55. Henry Holland is quoted in Clute, *Annals*, 264.

56. *New-York Gazette and Weekly Mercury*, 13 October 1777. In 1747, Charlton recommended Chandler to the vestry of St. John's Church in Elizabethtown, New Jersey, to replace the deceased Reverend Edward Vaughn. See Samuel A. Clark, *The History of St. John's Church, Elizabeth Town, New Jersey, from the Year 1703 to the Present Time* (Philadelphia: Lippincott, 1857), 57–60. For a discussion of the Anglican movement to create an American episcopate, see Arthur L. Cross, *The Anglican Episcopate and the American Colonies* (Cambridge, Mass.: Harvard University Press, 1902); and Nancy L. Rhoden, *Revolutionary Anglicanism: The Colonial Church of England during the American Revolution* (New York: New York University Press, 1999), chap. 3. See also Jordan, "The Anglican Establishment," 437, 441.

57. See Loring McMillen, "The First Presbyterian Church of Staten Island, 1717–1776–1808: Part I," *COSI* 1(1985): 4.

58. For a discussion of the life and career of the Reverend William Jackson, see Richard M. Bayles, *History of Richmond County, Staten Island, New York: From Its Discovery to the Present Time* (New York: L. E. Preston, 1887), 356;

Frost, "The Church on Staten Island," 92–93; and Daniel Van Winkle, *Old Bergen: History and Reminiscences* (Jersey City, N.J.: J. W. Harrison, 1902), 171–174. The quotation is from Corwin, *A Manual*, 540.

59. See McMillen, "Presbyterian Church," 7.

60. Bonomi, *Under the Cope of Heaven*, 201.

61. See Clute, *Annals*, 256–259, 275–277; and Harry E. Stocker, *A History of the Moravian Church in New York City* (New York: Published by the author, 1922), 108–109. I am indebted to Elisabeth Sommer, the former director of research and historical interpretation at the Staten Island Historical Society for information about the Moravian Church.

62. See Leonard Lundin, *Cockpit of the Revolution: The War for Independence in New Jersey* (Princeton, N.J.: Princeton University Press, 1940), 100–101; and Van Winkle, *Old Bergen*, 173–174.

63. Ranlet, *New York Loyalists*, 71.

64. Lieutenant Loftus Cliffe to unknown, 8 July 1776, transcript, Military Collection, American Revolution, box 2, folder 2, SI-HS.

65. Rodney Atwood, *The Hessians: Mercenaries from Hessen-Kassel in the American Revolution* (Cambridge: Cambridge University Press, 1980), 160.

66. Rev. Richard Charlton to the SPG, 6 April 1770, transcript, Charles W. Leng Collection, box 2, folder 60B, SIIAS.

67. Captain Alexander McDonald to Lord Jeffrey Amherst, August 1777, *Letter-Book*, 354.

68. Atwood, *Hessians*, 160.

69. Captain Alexander McDonald to Lord Jeffrey Amherst, August 1777, *Letter-Book*, 356.

CHAPTER 2

1. See the Election Returns of the New York City Delegates, July 1774, in *American Archives: A Documentary History of the United States*, 4th ser., edited by Peter Force, 6 vols. (Washington, D.C.: Published under the authority of an Act of Congress, 1837–1846), vol. 1, 319 (hereafter cited as *Am. Arch.*).

2. Committee of Fifty-one to the Committees, or the Treasurer of the Different Counties, 29, July 1774, *Am. Arch.*, 4th ser., vol. 1, 319–322.

3. James Duane to Peter Van Schaack, 2 September [i.e., October] 1774, in *Letters of the Delegates to the Congress, 1774–1789*, edited by Paul H. Smith, 26 vols. (Washington, D.C.: Library of Congress, 1976–2000), vol. 1, 136 (hereafter cited as *LDC*).

4. Isaac Low to the Committee of Fifty-one, 17 September 1774, *Am. Arch.*, 4th ser., vol. 1, 326.

5. Ray Raphael, *A People's History of the American Revolution: How Com-*

*mon People Shaped the Fight for Independence* (New York: HarperCollins, 2002), 41.

6. See Arthur M. Schlesinger, *The Colonial Merchants and the American Revolution* (New York: Frederick Unger, 1918), 490; and Joseph S. Tiedemann, *Reluctant Revolutionaries: New York City and the Road to Independence, 1763–1776* (Ithaca, N.Y.: Cornell University Press, 1997), 205.

7. Woodbridge Committee of Observation, *Am. Arch.*, 4th ser., vol. 1, 1249.

8. See Charles Monaghan, *The Murrays of Murray Hill* (Brooklyn, N.Y.: Urban History Press, 1998), 51–52; and Tiedemann, *Reluctant Revolutionaries*, 205–206.

9. Jonathan Hampton to the Committee of Observation of New York, 10 March 1775, *Am. Arch.*, 4th ser., vol. 2, 144.

10. Ibid., 144–145. Ichabod Barnet was John Murray's son-in-law and managed Murray's store in Elizabethtown. John Graham was a partner in John Murray's New York store. Samuel Reed was the Murrays' nephew. See Monaghan, *The Murrays of Murray Hill*, 52.

11. John Murray is quoted in Monaghan, *The Murrays of Murray Hill*, 52. The Murrays apologized for their wrongdoing and agreed to donate a sum of money to repair a hospital in Elizabethtown.

12. *Rivington's Royal Gazette*, 2 March 1775, in *New Jersey Archives*, 1st ser., 42 vols. (Trenton: New Jersey State Library, Archives and History Bureau, 1880–1949), vol. 31, 75–76 (hereafter cited as *N.J. Arch.*). See also Theodore Thayer, *As We Were: The Story of Old Elizabethtown* (Elizabeth, N.J.: Grassman, 1964), 102–103.

13. Thayer, *As We Were*, 103.

14. See Dirk Hoerder, "Boston Leaders and Boston Crowds, 1765–1776," in *The American Revolution: Explorations in the History of American Radicalism*, edited by Alfred F. Young (De Kalb: Northern Illinois University Press, 1976), 240; Pauline Maier, *From Resistance to Revolution: Colonial Radicals and the Development of American Opposition to Britain, 1765–1776* (New York: Norton, 1972), 86–89; and Raphael, *People's History of the American Revolution*, 17–18.

15. Thayer, *As We Were*, 103.

16. For the public condemnation and interdiction of Staten Island by the committee of observation in Elizabethtown, New Jersey, on 13 February 1775, see *Am. Arch.*, 4th ser., vol. 1, 1234–1235.

17. For the interdiction of Staten Island by the committee of observation in Woodbridge, New Jersey, on 20 February 1775, see *Am. Arch.*, 4th ser., vol. 1, 1249.

18. *New-York Journal*, 6 April 1775, in *N.J. Arch.*, vol. 31, 105.

19. For a discussion of the De Lancey and Livingston factions, see Carl L. Becker, *The History of Political Parties in the Province of New York, 1760–*

*1776* (Madison: University of Wisconsin Press, 1909), 175–176; Patricia U. Bonomi, *A Factious People: Politics and Society in Colonial New York* (New York: Columbia University Press, 1971), 277; and Roger J. Champagne, "Family Politics versus Constitutional Principles: The New York Assembly Elections of 1768 and 1769," *William and Mary Quarterly,* 3rd ser. 20 (1963): 58 (hereafter cited as *WMQ*).

20. Quoted in the Loyalist Claim of Christopher Billopp, transcript, Staten Island Loyalist Collection, box 1, folder 1, Staten Island Historical Society (hereafter cited as SI-HS).

21. Edward H. Tatum Jr., ed., *American Journal of Ambrose Serle, Secretary to Lord Howe, 1776–1778* (San Marino, Calif.: Huntington Library, 1940), 153.

22. See Proceedings of the General Assembly of the Colony of New York, January–April 1775, *Am. Arch.,* 4th ser., vol. 1, 1286–1287, 1289–1290.

23. Nominations for the New York Provincial Convention, 6 March 1775, *Am. Arch.,* 4th ser., vol. 2, 138–139.

24. See *New-York Gazette and Weekly Mercury,* 17 April 1775; and the Loyalist Claim of Christopher Billopp, transcript, Staten Island Loyalist Collection, box 1, folder 1, SI-HS.

25. The Reverend Richard Charlton was quoted in Philip Ranlet, *The New York Loyalists* (Knoxville: University of Tennessee Press, 1986), 71.

26. Bernard Mason, *The Road to Independence: The Revolutionary Movement in New York, 1773–1777* (Lexington: University of Kentucky Press, 1966), 44, 178–179; Alexander C. Flick, ed., *The American Revolution in New York: Its Political, Social, and Economic Significance* (Albany: New York State Department of Education, Division of Archives and History, 1926), 49.

27. Thomas Jones, *History of New York during the Revolutionary War and of the Leading Events in the Other Colonies at That Period,* edited by Edward F. De Lancey, 2 vols. (New York: New York Historical Society, 1879), vol. 1, 39.

28. Ibid., 40.

29. See Lieutenant Governor Cadwallader Colden to William Legge (Lord Dartmouth), 3 May 1775, in *Documents Relative to the Colonial History of the State of New York,* edited by E. B. O'Callaghan, 15 vols. (Albany, N.Y.: Weed, Parsons Printers, 1853–1887), vol. 8, 571 (hereafter cited as *NYCD*). See also Becker, *History of Political Parties,* 193; and Mason, *Road to Independence,* 75–77. The one hundred troops stationed in New York City were from the Royal Irish Regiment.

30. Members of the New York Assembly to General Thomas Gage, 5 May 1775, *Am. Arch.,* 4th ser., vol. 2, 513.

31. Alexander McDonald to General William Howe, n.d., *The Letter-Book of Captain Alexander McDonald of the Royal Highland Emigrants, 1775–1779*

(New York: New York Historical Society, 1882), 275 (hereafter cited as *Letter-Book*).

32. Alexander McDonald to Walter and Thomas Buchannon, 4 November 1775, *Letter-Book*, 217. In January 1776, McDonald wrote to John Ogilvie, a London merchant, that "the Authors of this unhappy disaster you have among you in England. The pretty speeches that has [*sic*] been made in the house of Lords [at] the time of the Stamp Act and [by] other Gentlemen well known, out of and in the house Commons, are alone the Authors of this unnatural Rebellion, which I am very much afraid will terminate in the destruction of Great Brittain and the Colonies god forbid it should be the Case." See Alexander McDonald to John Ogilvie, 2 January 1776, *Letter-Book*, 233.

33. Rev. Richard Charlton is quoted in Ranlet, *New York Loyalists*, 71.

34. See the General Association of New York, 29 April 1775, in *Am. Arch.*, 4th ser., vol. 2, 471; and *Calendar of Historical Manuscripts Relating to the War of the Revolution in the Office of the Secretary of State*, 2 vols. (Albany, N.Y.: Weed & Parsons, 1868), vol. 1, 3–4.

35. See *Calendar of Historical Manuscripts*, vol. 1, 42; Harlow McMillen, "Green, and Red, and a Little Blue: The Story of Staten Island in the American Revolution, Part 2," *Staten Island Historian*, 1st ser., 32 (1975): 17–18. For the personal backgrounds of the five men selected to represent Staten Island at the Provincial Congress, see John J. Clute, *Annals of Staten Island: From Its Discovery to the Present Time* (New York: Press of Charles Vogt, 1877), 140–141, 148, 170, 303–304, 357–358, 396. On Richard Conner, see Oscar T. Conner, *The Genealogy of the Descendants of Richard Conner, Born in Ireland in 1723* (Ridgewood, N.J.: Published by the author, 1987), 11. On Aaron Cortelyou, see John Van Zandt Cortelyou, *The Cortelyou Genealogy: A Record of Jaques Corteljou and Many of His Descendants* (Lincoln, Neb.: Press of Brown Printing Service, 1942), 113–120; Lorenzo Sabine, *Biographical Sketches of Loyalists of the American Revolution with an Historical Essay*, 2 vols. (Boston: Little, Brown, 1864), vol. 2, 500. On Richard Lawrence, see Gregory Palmer, *Biographical Sketches of Loyalists of the American Revolution* (Westport, Conn.: Meckler Publishing, 1984), 479. On Paul Micheau Jr., see Charles W. Leng and William T. Davis, *Staten Island and Its People: A History, 1609–1929*, 3 vols. (New York: Lewis Historical Publishing, 1930), vol. 2, 165, 201; and Mary T. Seaman, *The Seaman Family in America as Descended from Captain John Seaman of Hempstead, Long Island* (New York: T. A. Wright, 1928), 79.

36. Reverend Hector Gambold to Nathaniel Seidel, 10 May 1775. I wish to thank Elisabeth Sommer, the former director of research and historical interpretation at the Staten Island Historical Society, for bringing this letter to my attention.

37. In *History of Political Parties*, Becker wrote: "Many conservatives and

loyalists . . . [hoped] that the Provincial Congress would lead New York out of revolution rather than into it" (207).

38. See Proceedings of the New York Provincial Congress, 22 May 1775, *Am. Arch.*, 4th ser., vol. 2, 1244, 1271.

39. Ibid., 1286, 1288–1290, 1308; 3: 541–542, 547–548, 568, 570.

40. See Becker, *History of Political Parties*, 212–213, 215; Flick, *American Revolution in New York*, 317–318; and Mason, *Road to Independence*, 63. See also Proceedings of the New York Provincial Congress, 22 May 1775, *Am. Arch.*, 4th ser., vol. 2, 471; and Lieutenant Governor Cadwallader Colden to William Legge (Lord Dartmouth), 7 June 1775, *NYCD*, vol. 8, 580.

41. Alexander McDonald to John Ogilvie, 3 November 1775, *Letter-Book*, 213.

42. *New-York Gazette and Weekly Mercury*, 20 July 1775.

43. Bruce Bliven Jr., *Under the Guns, New York: 1775–1776* (New York: Harper & Row, 1972), wrote that "the city was highly vulnerable to fire, as all its residents were constantly aware, a firebomb or two could start a conflagration that might burn New York to the ground" (6).

44. For the logistical problems faced by the besieged British army in Boston, see R. Arthur Bowler, "Logistics and Operations in the American Revolution," in *Reconsiderations on the Revolutionary War: Selected Essays*, edited by Don Higginbotham (Westport, Conn.: Greenwood Press, 1978), 62–64, and *Logistics and the Failure of the British Army in America, 1775–1783* (Princeton, N.J.: Princeton University Press, 1975), 41–46, 53–55, 60–65, 95–96. See also David Syrett, *The Royal Navy in American Waters, 1775–1783* (Brookfield, Vt.: Gower Publishing, 1989), 2–3. For the efforts to prevent the transfer of provisions from New York City to the British army in Boston, see Tiedemann, *Reluctant Revolutionaries*, 200–201; and Judith L. Van Buskirk, *Generous Enemies: Patriots and Loyalists in Revolutionary New York* (Philadelphia: University of Pennsylvania Press, 2002), 108–112.

45. General George Washington to the New York Provincial Congress, 8 August 1775, in *The Papers of George Washington*, Revolutionary War Series, edited by W. W. Abbot, Philander D. Chase, and Dorothy Twohig, 12 vols. (Charlottesville: University Press of Virginia, 1985–2002), vol. 1, 274 (hereafter cited as *GWPRWS*).

46. See Proceedings of the New York Provincial Congress, 22 May 1775, *Am. Arch.*, 4th ser., vol. 3, 537, 573–574.

47. See Proceedings of the New York Committee of One Hundred, 14 May 1775, *Am. Arch.*, 4th ser., vol. 2, 533.

48. David Burger to the New York Provincial Congress, 1 September 1775, *Am. Arch.*, 4th ser., vol. 3, 624–625.

49. John Wetherhead to the New York Committee of Safety, 17 September 1775, *Am. Arch.*, 4th ser., vol. 3, 724–725. For the personal threats against

Wetherhead, his family, and his property, see Catherine S. Crary, ed., *The Price of Loyalty: Tory Writings from the Revolutionary Era* (New York: McGraw-Hill, 1973), 44–47.

50. See Bliven, *Under the Guns*, 61–62; Mason, *Road to Independence*, 115; and Tiedemann, *Reluctant Revolutionaries*, 235.

51. See Proceedings of the New York Provincial Congress, 24 November 1775, *Am. Arch.*, 4th ser., vol. 3, 1754.

52. Paul Micheau Jr. to Robert Benson (secretary for the New York Provincial Congress), 1 December 1775, *Am. Arch.*, 4th ser., vol. 4, 149.

53. New York Provincial Congress to the Richmond County Committee of Safety, 2 December 1775, *Am. Arch.*, 4th ser., vol. 3, 1762–1764.

54. Richmond County Committee of Safety to Nathaniel Woodhull (president of the New York Provincial Congress), 15 December 1775, *Am. Arch.*, 4th ser., vol. 4, 428.

55. See Proceedings of the New York Provincial Congress, *Am. Arch.*, 4th ser., vol. 4, 372, 434–435; and the *New-York Journal*, 28 December 1775.

56. For Christian Jacobson's testimony before the New York committee of safety see Proceedings of the New York Committee of Safety, 12 January 1776, *Am. Arch.*, 4th ser., vol. 4, 1040. For a discussion of Christian Jacobson, see Richard M. Bayles, *History of Richmond County, Staten Island, New York: From Its Discovery to the Present Time* (New York: L. E. Preston, 1887), 426.

57. Proceedings of the New York Committee of Safety, 12 January 1776, *Am. Arch.*, 4th ser., vol. 4, 1040. Richard Lawrence had confided in Abraham Brasher of New York City.

58. Proceedings of the New York Committee of Safety, 12 January 1776, *Am. Arch.*, 4th ser., vol. 4, 1040.

59. See the Richmond County Committee of Safety to the New York Committee of Safety, 19 January, 1776, *Am. Arch.*, 4th ser., vol. 4, 1069–1070.

60. McMillen, "Green, and Red, and a Little Blue," 24.

61. See Proclamation by Governor William Tryon, 2 January 1776, *Am. Arch.*, 4th ser., vol. 4, 542; and Meeting of the New York Committee of Safety, 4 January 1776, *Am. Arch.*, 4th ser., vol. 4, 1020.

62. Alexander Hamilton to John Jay, 31 December 1775, in *The Papers of Alexander Hamilton*, edited by Harold C. Syrett, 27 vols. (New York: Columbia University Press, 1961–1987), vol. 1, 179.

63. Paul David Nelson, *William Tryon and the Course of Empire: A Life in British Imperial Service* (Chapel Hill: University of North Carolina Press, 1990), 139.

64. Mason, *Road to Independence*, 130, 131, n. 78. John Alsop from New York City and Oliver De Lancey from Westchester County were the other Loyalists elected to seats in the new assembly.

65. McMillen, "Green, and Red, and a Little Blue," 23.

66. See Nelson, *William Tryon*, 139; Becker, History of Political Parties, 242–243; and Mason, *Road to Independence*, 131–133.

67. See Tiedemann, *Reluctant Revolutionaries*, 210.

CHAPTER 3

1. General George Washington to John Hancock, 4 January 1776, in *The Papers of George Washington*, Revolutionary War Series, edited by W. W. Abbot, Philander D. Chase, and Dorothy Twohig, 12 vols. (Charlottesville: University Press of Virginia, 1985–2002), vol. 3, 19–20 (hereafter cited as *GWPRWS*).

2. General Charles Lee to General George Washington, 19 February 1776, in *The Lee Papers*, 4 vols. (New York: New York Historical Society Collections, 1871), vol. 1, 309.

3. See Don Higginbotham, *The War of American Independence: Military Attitudes, Policies, and Practice, 1763–1789* (1971; repr. Boston: Northeastern University Press, 1981), 152.

4. General Charles Lee to General George Washington, 19 February 1776, *Lee Papers*, vol. 1, 309.

5. General Charles Lee to the New York Provincial Congress, 6 March 1776, *Lee Papers*, vol. 1, 352.

6. Colonel William Douglas to Hannah Douglas, n.d., in "Letters Written during the Revolutionary War by Colonel William Douglas to His Wife Covering the Period July 19, 1775 to December 5, 1776," *New York Historical Society Quarterly* 13 (1929): 37.

7. See Worthington C. Ford et al., eds., *Journals of the Continental Congress, 1774–1789*, 34 vols. (Washington D.C.: U.S. Government Printing Office, 1907–1937), vol. 4, 45.

8. See Barnet Schecter, *The Battle for New York: The City at the Heart of the American Revolution* (New York: Walker, 2002), 76.

9. See the Proceedings of the New York Committee of Safety, 10 February 1776, in *American Archives: A Documentary History of the United States*, 4th ser., edited by Peter Force, 6 vols. (Washington, D.C.: Published under the authority of an Act of Congress, 1837–1846), vol. 4, 1120 (hereafter cited as *Am. Arch.*).

10. New York Committee of Safety to the Provincial Congress of New Jersey, 10 February 1776, *Am. Arch.*, 4th ser., vol. 4, 1120–1121.

11. For the arrival of General Sir Henry Clinton in New York and the panic it caused in the city, see Bruce Bliven Jr., *Under the Guns, New York: 1775–1776* (New York: Harper & Row, 1972), 122; Governor William Tryon to William Legge (Lord Dartmouth), 8 February 1776, in *Documents Relative*

*to the Colonial History of the State of New York*, edited by E. B. O'Callaghan, 15 vols. (Albany, N.Y.: Weed, Parsons Printers, 1853–1887), vol. 8, 667 (hereafter cited as *NYCD*); and John R. Alden, *General Charles Lee: Traitor or Patriot?* (Baton Rouge: Louisiana State University Press, 1951), 98. For the British plans to invade Charleston, South Carolina, see General William Howe to William Legge (Lord Dartmouth), 16 January 1776, *Am. Arch.*, 4th ser., vol. 4, 700; and Sir Henry Clinton, *The American Rebellion: Sir Henry Clinton's Narrative of His Campaigns, 1775–1782*, edited by William B. Willcox (New Haven, Conn.: Yale University Press, 1954), 24. See also General Charles Lee to General George Washington, 5 February 1776, *Lee Papers*, vol. 1, 271.

12. See the Testimony of Colonel Abraham Lott before the New York Committee of Safety, 11 February 1776, in *Naval Documents of the American Revolution*, edited by William B. Clark and William J. Morgan, 10 vols. (Washington, D.C.: U.S. Government Printing Office, 1964–1996), vol. 3, 1215 (hereafter cited as *NDAR*).

13. Provincial Congress of New Jersey to Pierre Van Cortlandt, 12 February 1776, *Am. Arch.*, 4th ser., vol. 5, 263.

14. New York Committee of Safety to the Elizabethtown Committee of Observation, 11 February 1776, *Am. Arch.*, 4th ser., vol. 4, 1123. See also *New-York Gazette and Weekly Mercury*, 19 February 1776; *New-York Gazette*, 19 February 1776; and Rev. Edwin F. Hatfield, *History of Elizabeth, New Jersey: Including the Early History of Union County* (New York: Charlton and Lanahan, 1868), 427.

15. Joseph S. Tiedemann, "Response to Revolution: Queens County, New York during the Era of the American Revolution" (PhD diss., City University of New York, 1977), 121–124.

16. Bliven, *Under the Guns*, 148; and *New-York Gazette and Weekly Mercury*, 19 February 1776.

17. Adrian Bancker and Richard Lawrence to Robert Benson, 17 February 1776, *Am. Arch.*, 4th ser., vol. 5, 283.

18. New York Provincial Congress to Adrian Bancker and Richard Lawrence, 19 February 1776, *Am. Arch.*, 4th ser., vol. 5, 283–284.

19. Colonel Nathaniel Heard to the New York Provincial Congress, 16 February 1776, *Am. Arch.*, 4th ser., vol. 4, 1163.

20. Richmond County Committee of Safety to the New York Provincial Congress, 7 March 1776, *Am. Arch.*, 4th ser., vol. 5, 102–103.

21. Robert Ogden to the New York Provincial Congress, 22 February 1776, *Am. Arch.*, 4th ser., vol. 5, 309. Ogden had replaced Jonathan Hampton as chairman of the Elizabethtown committee of observation.

22. New York Provincial Congress to the Elizabethtown Committee of Observation, 21 February 1776, *Am. Arch.*, vol. 5, 293.

23. Hendrick Garrison to the New York Provincial Congress, 8 March 1776, *Am. Arch.*, vol. 5, 136–137.

24. Alexander C. Flick, *Loyalism in New York during the American Revolution* (1901; repr., New York: AMS Press, 1970), 93.

25. Alexander McDonald to Susannah McDonald, 22 February 1776, in *The Letter-Book of Captain Alexander McDonald of the Royal Highland Emigrants, 1775–1779* (New York: New York Historical Society, 1882), vol. 1, 250 (hereafter cited as *Letter-Book*).

26. See John Hancock to General Charles Lee, 1 March 1776, *Lee Papers*, vol. 1, 342–343. For further discussion of Lee's new command, see John Shy, *A People Numerous and Armed: Reflections on the Military Struggle for American Independence* (Ann Arbor: University of Michigan Press, 1990), 141; and Alden, *General Charles Lee*, 105–110. The Continental Congress had originally assigned Lee to command the Continental troops in the Canadian theater, but his orders were changed when reports reached the congress of a British expedition sailing for the Carolinas.

27. See Alan Valentine, *Lord Stirling* (New York: Oxford University Press, 1969), 169–170; Mark V. Kwasny, *Washington's Partisan War, 1775–1783* (Kent, Ohio: Kent State University Press, 1996), 39; and John Hancock to Colonel William Alexander (Lord Stirling), 1 March 1776, in *Letters of the Delegates to the Congress, 1774–1789*, edited by Paul H. Smith, 26 vols.(Washington, D.C.: Library of Congress, 1976–2000), vol. 3, 317 (hereafter cited as *LDC*). Stirling had recently been promoted to brigadier general by the Continental Congress.

28. See Alden, *General Charles Lee*, 110; and Harlow McMillen, "Green, and Red, and a Little Blue: The Story of Staten Island in the American Revolution, Part 4," *Staten Island Historian*, 1st ser., 32 (1975): 24 (hereafter cited as *SIH*).

29. See *Report on the Defence of New York*, March 1776, Lee Papers, vol. 1, 354–357.

30. Valentine, *Lord Stirling*, 168.

31. General William Alexander (Lord Stirling) to General Philip Schuyler, 10 March 1776, *Am. Arch.*, 4th ser., vol. 5, 174.

32. John Hancock to General William Alexander (Lord Stirling), 15 March 1776, *LDC*, vol. 3, 378–379.

33. General William Alexander (Lord Stirling) to John Hancock, 14 March 1776, *Am. Arch.*, 4th ser., vol. 5, 217.

34. Valentine, *Lord Stirling*, 173.

35. Alden, *General Charles Lee*, 99.

36. Bliven, *Under the Guns*, 186.

37. Colonel William Alexander (Lord Stirling) to the New York Committee of Safety, 12 January 1776, *Am. Arch.*, 4th ser., vol. 4, 655.

38. General William Alexander (Lord Stirling) to Samuel Tucker, 2 March 1776, *Am. Arch.*, 4th ser., vol. 5, 132–133. See also Paul David Nelson, *William Alexander, Lord Stirling* (Tuscaloosa: University of Alabama Press, 1987), 73.

39. *Extracts from the Journal of Proceedings of the Provincial Congress of New Jersey, 1775–1776* (Woodbury, N.J.: Joseph Sailor, Printer, 1835), 181–182; and Nelson, *William Alexander*, 73.

40. General William Howe to William Legge (Lord Dartmouth), 21 March 1776, in *Documents of the American Revolution, 1770–1783*, Colonial Office Series, edited by K. G. Davies, 21 vols. (Dublin: Irish University Press, 1972–1981), vol. 12, 81–82 (hereafter cited as *Documents*).

41. See Piers Mackesy, *The War for America, 1775–1783* (1964; repr., Lincoln: University of Nebraska Press, Bison Books, 1993), 80; Christopher Hibbert, *Redcoats and Rebels: The American Revolution through British Eyes* (New York: Norton, 1990), 74; Christopher Ward, *The War of the Revolution*, edited by John R. Alden, 2 vols. (New York: Macmillan, 1952), vol. 1, 114–116.

42. General George Washington to John Hancock, 13 March 1776, *GWPRWS*, vol. 3, 461.

43. General George Washington to General William Alexander (Lord Stirling), 19 March 1776, *GWPRWS*, vol. 3, 497–498.

44. Lieutenant Stephen Moylan to General William Alexander (Lord Stirling), 9 March 1776, *Am. Arch.*, 4th ser., vol. 5, 374. Lieutenant Stephen Moylan served as one of Washington's military secretaries.

45. General William Alexander (Lord Stirling) to Captain John Warner, 14 March 1776, *Am. Arch.*, 4th ser., vol. 5, 222.

46. Proceedings of the New York Provincial Congress, 14 March 1776, *Am. Arch.*, 4th ser., vol. 5, 383.

47. New York Committee of Safety to the Richmond County Committee of Safety, 30 March 1776, *Am. Arch.*, 4th ser., vol. 5, 1417.

48. See Kwasny, *Partisan War*, 43; Nelson, *William Alexander*, 77; and Valentine, *Lord Stirling*, 173.

49. General William Alexander (Lord Stirling) to General William Livingston, 24 March 1776, in *The Papers of William Livingston*, edited by Carl E. Prince and Dennis P. Ryan, 4 vols. (Trenton: New Jersey Historical Commission, 1979–1987), vol. 1, 44–45 (hereafter cited as *PWL*).

50. General William Heath to General William Livingston, 1 April 1776, *PWL*, vol. 1, 46.

51. General William Alexander to General George Washington, 1 April 1776, *GWPRWS*, vol. 4, 13–14.

52. See Bliven, *Under the Guns*, 211–212; Malcolm Decker, *Brink of Revolution: New York in Crisis, 1765–1776* (New York: Argosy Antiquarian LTD, 1964), 230; and General Israel Putnam to John Hancock, 7 April 1776, *Am. Arch.*, 4th ser., vol. 5, 811.

53. Andrew Eliot to William Tryon, 8 April 1776, *NDAR*, vol. 4, 724.

54. Charles E. Anthon, ed., "Anthon's Notes," *Proceedings of the Staten Island Institute of Arts and Sciences* 3–6 (1924–1932): 158 (hereafter cited as *PSIIAS*).

55. General Israel Putnam to John Hancock, 7 April 1776, *Am. Arch.*, 4th ser., vol. 5, 811.

56. Captain Hugh Stephenson to General Israel Putnam, 8 April 1776, *Am. Arch.*, 4th ser., vol. 5, 820–821. For a discussion of the skirmish see Bliven, Jr., *Under the Guns*, 210–211; and McMillen, "Green, and Red, and a Little Blue . . . Part 4," 25.

57. General Israel Putnam to John Hancock, 7 April 1776, *Am. Arch.*, 4th ser., vol. 5, 811.

58. See General Orders for New York, 8 April 1776, *Am. Arch.*, 4th ser., vol. 5, 1455.

59. Danske Dandridge, ed., *Historic Shepherdstown* (Charlottesville: University Press of Virginia, 1910), 139.

60. Proceedings of the New York Committee of Safety, 19 April 1776, *Am. Arch.*, 4th ser., vol. 5, 1455.

61. Christian Jacobson to the New York Committee of Safety, 16 April 1776, *Am. Arch.*, 4th ser., vol. 5, 955–956.

62. Captain Alexander McDonald to Thomas and Walter Buchannon, 4 November 1775, *Letter-Book*, vol. 1, 216.

63. Captain Alexander McDonald to Major John Small, 15 September 1775, *Letter-Book*, vol. 1, 212.

64. Captain Alexander McDonald to Pedro de Mendonzo, 11 January 1777, *Letter-Book*, vol. 1, 313.

65. General William Alexander (Lord Stirling) to the New York Committee of Safety, 12 April 1776, *Am. Arch.*, 4th ser., vol. 5, 1439.

66. New York Committee of Safety to the Richmond County Committee of Safety, 12 April 1776, *Am. Arch.*, 4th ser., vol. 5, 1439.

67. Christian Jacobson to the New York Committee of Safety, 16 April 1776, *Am. Arch.*, 4th ser., vol. 5, 955–956.

68. Lieutenant Loftus Cliffe to unknown, 8 July 1776, transcript, Military Collection, American Revolution, box 2, folder 2, Staten Island Historical Society (hereafter cited as SI-HS).

69. See Carl L. Becker, *The History of Political Parties in the Province of New York, 1760–1776* (Madison: University of Wisconsin Press, 1909), 261; Alexander C. Flick, ed., *The American Revolution in New York: Its Political, Social, and Economic Significance* (Albany: New York State Department of Education, Division of Archives and History, 1926), 213; Flick, *Loyalism in New York*, 66–69; and *Calendar of Historical Manuscripts Relating to the War of the Revolution in the Office of the Secretary of State*, 2 vols. (Albany, N.Y.: Weed & Parsons, 1868), vol. 1, 338–339, 341. The New York Provincial Congress ordered

the immediate arrest of Christopher Billopp, Minah Burger, Isaac Decker, Abraham Harris, Benjamin Seaman, and Ephraim Taylor. These six Staten Islanders had held military or civil commissions under the royal government or had been vocal opponents of the Whig cause.

70. General George Washington to John Hancock, 15 April 1776, *GWPRWS*, vol. 4, 69–70.

71. John Ferling, *Setting the World Ablaze: Washington, Adams, Jefferson, and the American Revolution* (New York: Oxford University Press, 2000), writes: "Washington had little choice but to fight for New York. Congress demanded that the city be defended. It had lavished funds on the army for the past year and expected it to be used. Many believed Europe's statesmen would be more impressed by an American army that stood and fought, and those from the Middle Atlantic states, apprehensive at the prospect of British regulars on their doorstep in New York, insisted that the invasion be resisted" (138–139). See also Schecter, *Battle for New York*, 92.

72. David Hackett Fischer, *Washington's Crossing* (New York: Oxford University Press, 2004), 86.

73. Joseph Plumb Martin, *Private Yankee Doodle: Being a Narrative of Some of the Adventures, Dangers, and Sufferings of a Revolutionary War Soldier*, edited by George F. Scheer (Boston: Little, Brown, 1962), 20.

74. See General Orders, 2 July 1776, *GWPRWS*, vol. 5, 180.

75. For Washington's continuation and expansion of General Lee's original plan of defense for New York, see John Ferling, *The First of Men: A Life of George Washington* (Knoxville: University of Tennessee Press, 1988), 153; Willard S. Randall, *George Washington: A Life* (New York: Henry Holt, 1997), 309–310; Fischer, *Washington's Crossing*, 82–83; John J. Gallagher, *The Battle of Brooklyn, 1776* (New York: Da Capo Press, 1995), 73–75; and Schecter, *Battle for New York*, 91, 117–119. The *chevaux de fries* that were placed into the Hudson River were composed of wire nets and spikes.

76. General George Washington, quoted in Schecter, *Battle for New York*, 95. See also Generals John Sullivan, Nathanael Greene, and William Alexander (Lord Stirling) to General George Washington, 27 April 1776, *GWPRWS*, vol. 4, 145–146.

77. General George Washington to John Hancock, 3 July 1776, *GWPRWS*, vol. 4, 193.

78. See Proceedings of the New York Committee of Safety, 18 April 1776, *Am. Arch.*, 4th ser., vol. 5, 1453. See also General George Washington to the New York Committee of Safety, 17 April 1776, and New York Committee of Safety to General George Washington, 18 April 1776, *GWPRWS*, vol. 4, 77–79, 81–82.

79. General George Washington to the New York Committee of Safety, 6 May 1776, *GWPRWS*, vol. 4, 221.

80. Proceedings of the New York Committee of Safety, 8 May 1776, *Am. Arch.*, 4th ser., vol. 5, 1491.

81. Richmond County Committee of Safety to the New York Provincial Congress, 13 May 1776, *Am. Arch.*, 4th ser., vol. 6, 436–437.

82. General George Washington to Nathaniel Woodhull, 27 June 1776, *GWPRWS*, vol. 5, 128. See also Council of War, 28 June 1776, *GWPRWS*, vol. 5, 130–131.

83. See Proceedings of the New York Provincial Congress, 29 June 1776, *Am. Arch.*, 4th ser., vol. 6, 1439; and New York Provincial Congress to the Elizabethtown Committee of Observation, 29 June 1776, *Am. Arch.*, 4th ser., vol. 6, 1440.

84. General George Washington to John Hancock, 3 July 1776, *GWPRWS*, vol. 5, 193. Washington also ordered Nathaniel Heard, who had recently been promoted to brigadier general, to assist with the removal of the livestock. See Robert Hanson Harrison to General Nathaniel Heard, 29 June 1776, *Am. Arch.*, 4th ser., vol. 6, 1134–1135.

85. General John Morin Scott to the New York Provincial Congress, 5 July 1776, in *American Archives: A Documentary History of the United States*, edited by Peter Force, 5th ser. (Washington, D.C.: Published under authority of an Act of Congress, 1837–1953), vol. 1, 22 (hereafter cited as *Am. Arch.*).

86. Governor Jonathan Trumbull to Jeremiah Wadsworth, 4 July 1776, *NDAR*, vol. 5, 918.

87. Captain Alexander McDonald to Major John Small, 19 February 1776, *Letter-Book*, vol. 1, 246.

CHAPTER 4

1. General William Howe is quoted in Troyer S. Anderson, *The Command of the Howe Brothers during the American Revolution* (New York: Oxford University Press, 1936), 121.

2. General William Howe to Lord George Germain, 7 June 1776, in *Documents of the American Revolution, 1770–1783*, Colonial Office Series, edited by K. G. Davies, 21 vols. (Dublin: Irish University Press, 1972–1981), vol. 12, 83 (hereafter cited as *Documents*).

3. General William Howe to Lord George Germain, 7 July 1776, *Documents*, vol. 12, 157.

4. For suggestions that Howe land troops on Long Island and immediately strike at the Continental lines there, see Paul David Nelson, *William Tryon and the Course of Empire: A Life in British Imperial Service* (Chapel Hill: University of North Carolina Press, 1990), 142; and Joseph S. Tiedemann, "A Revolution

Foiled: Queens County, New York, 1775–1776," *Journal of American History* 75 (1988): 441 (hereafter cited as *JAH*).

5. Daniel McCurtain is quoted in *Rebels and Redcoats: The American Revolution through the Eyes of Those Who Fought and Lived It*, edited by George F. Scheer and Hugh F. Rankin (1957; repr., New York: Da Capo Press, 1988), 148.

6. Charles E. Anthon, ed., "Anthon's Notes," *Proceedings of the Staten Island Institute of Arts and Sciences* 3–6 (1924–1932): 86 (hereafter cited as *PSI-IAS*).

7. *New-York Journal*, 4 July 1776.

8. Adrian Bancker to Evert Bancker, 29 June 1776, Bancker Family Papers, Correspondence 1775–1787, folder 2, New York Historical Society (hereafter cited as NY-HS).

9. Major Charles Stuart to John Stuart (earl of Bute), 9 July 1776, in *Naval Documents of the American Revolution*, edited by William B. Clark and William J. Morgan, 10 vols. (Washington, D.C.: U. S. Government Printing Office, 1964–1996), vol. 5, 989 (hereafter cited as *NDAR*).

10. For a discussion of General James Robertson's military career, see *The Twilight of British Rule in Revolutionary America: The New York Letter Book of General James Robertson, 1780–1783*, edited by Milton M. Klein and Ronald W. Howard (Cooperstown, N.Y.: New York State Historical Association, 1983), 1–33.

11. Margaret W. Willard, ed., *Letters on the American Revolution, 1774–1776* (Boston: Houghton Mifflin, 1925), 329.

12. *New-York Mercury*, 27 July 1761.

13. See Charles W. Leng and William T. Davis, *Staten Island and Its People: A History, 1609–1929*, 3 vols. (New York: Lewis Historical Publishing, 1930), vol. 1, 272; Dorothy Valentine Smith, *Staten Island: Gateway to New York* (Philadelphia: Chilton Book Company, 1970), 51–56.

14. For civilian-military relations in America after the French and Indian War, see John Shy, *Toward Lexington: The Role of the British Army in the Coming of the American Revolution* (Princeton, N.J.: Princeton University Press, 1965).

15. See Examination of James McFarlan, a Soldier Belonging to the Fifty-fifth Regiment, Colonel Medie, 5 July 1776, *NDAR*, vol. 5, 936.

16. Anthon, "Anthon's Notes," 130.

17. Major Francis Hutcheson to General Sir Frederick Haldimand, 10 July 1776, *NDAR*, vol. 5, 1011.

18. Major Charles Stuart to John Stuart (earl of Bute), 9 July 1776, *NDAR*, vol. 5, 989.

19. Anthon, "Anthon's Notes," 20.

20. John Bakeless, *Turncoats, Traitors, and Heroes: Espionage in the American Revolution* (1959; repr., New York: Da Capo Press, 1998), 123, 166, 177–

181, 194–195, 277, 345, 364. See also Pension Claim of John L. Mersereau, in *The Revolution Remembered: Eyewitness Accounts of the War for Independence*, edited by John C. Dann (Chicago: University of Chicago Press, 1980), 347–350; Loring McMillen, "An Island Saga: The Mersereau Family: Part 2," *Chronicles of Staten Island* 1 (1989–1990): 156–159 (hereafter cited as *COSI*). See also Loring McMillen, "An Island Saga: The Mersereau Family: Part 3," *COSI* 1 (1990): 168–172, and "An Island Saga: The Mersereau Family: Part 4," *COSI* 1 (1990): 184–185; and General Hugh Mercer to General George Washington, 16 July 1776, in *The Papers of George Washington*, Revolutionary War Series, edited by W. W. Abbot, Philander D. Chase, and Dorothy Twohig, 12 vols. (Charlottesville: University Press of Virginia, 1985–2002), vol. 5, 344–346 (hereafter cited as *GWPRWS*).

21. General George Washington to John Hancock, 3 July 1776, *GWPRWS*, vol. 5, 193.

22. Henry G. Steinmeyer, *Staten Island under British Rule, 1776–1783* (Staten Island, N.Y.: Staten Island Historical Society, 1949), 3.

23. Major Charles Stuart to John Stuart (earl of Bute), 9 July 1776, *NDAR*, vol. 5, 989.

24. Major Francis Hutcheson to General Sir Frederick Haldimand, 10 July 1776, *NDAR*, vol. 5, 1011.

25. Captain John Bowater to Basil Fielding (earl of Denbigh), 7 July 1776, in *The Lost War: Letters from British Officers during the American Revolution*, edited by Marian Balderston and David Syrett (New York: Horizon Press, 1975), 88.

26. General William Howe to Lord George Germain, 7 July 1776, *Documents*, vol. 12, 157–158.

27. Governor William Tryon to Lord George Germain, 8 July 1776, in *Documents Relative to the Colonial History of the State of New York*, edited by E. B. O'Callaghan, 15 vols. (Albany, N.Y.: Weed, Parsons Printers, 1853–1887), vol. 8, 681 (hereafter cited as *NYCD*).

28. Lord George Germain to Governor William Tryon, 22 August 1776, *NYCD*, vol. 8, 685.

29. See Examination of William Ash, from Staten Island, 8 July 1776, in *American Archives: A Documentary History of the United States*, edited by Peter Force, 5th ser. (Washington, D.C.: Published under authority of an Act of Congress, 1837–1953), vol. 1, 120 (hereafter cited as *Am. Arch.*).

30. Frank Moore, ed., *Diary of the American Revolution: From Newspapers and Original Documents*, 2 vols. (New York: Scribner, 1858), vol. 1, 277.

31. See Examination of Abram Van Duzar, of New York, from Staten Island, 9 July 1776, *Am. Arch.*, 5th ser., vol. 1, 200.

32. See Governor William Tryon to Lord George Germain, 8 July 1776, *NYCD*, vol. 8, 681; and Harlow McMillen, "The Oath of Allegiance Signed by the Inhabitants of Staten Island on July 9, 1775," *Staten Island Historian*, 1st

ser., 32 (1976): 52 (hereafter cited as *SIH*). For the pledge of £500, see Harlow McMillen, "Red, Green, and a Little Blue: The Story of Staten Island in the American Revolution, Part 8," *SIH*, 1st ser., 32 (1977): 91.

33. General George Washington to General William Livingston, 6 July 1776, *GWPRWS*, vol. 5, 223.

34. John Adams to Abigail Adams, 11 July 1776, *Am. Arch.*, 5th ser., vol. 1, 183.

35. See General William Livingston to General George Washington, 4 July 1776, *GWPRWS*, vol. 5, 202.

36. General George Washington to John Hancock, 4–5 July 1776, *GWPRWS*, vol. 5, 216. See also General William Livingston to General George Washington, 4 July 1776, in *The Papers of William Livingston*, edited by Carl E. Prince and Dennis P. Ryan, 4 vols. (Trenton: New Jersey Historical Commission, 1979–1987), vol. 1, 64–65 (hereafter cited as *PWL*).

37. *Kemble Papers, 1773–1789*, 2 vols. (New York: New York Historical Society Collections, 1883), vol. 1, 82.

38. Lieutenant Loftus Cliffe to unknown, 8 July 1776, transcript, Military Collection, American Revolution, box 2, folder 2, Staten Island Historical Society (hereafter cited as SI-HS).

39. Anthon, "Anthon's Notes," 155.

40. Ibid.

41. Adrian Bancker to Evert Bancker, 29 June 1776, Bancker Family Papers, Correspondence 1775–1787, folder 2, NY-HS.

42. Abraham Bancker to Evert Bancker, 25 January 1777, Miscellaneous Genealogical Files Collection, box 1, Bancker folder, SI-HS.

43. Major Francis Hutcheson to General Sir Frederick Haldimand, 10 July 1776, *NDAR*, vol. 5, 1011. See also the Examination of William Ash, from Staten Island, 8 July 1776, *Am. Arch.*, 5th ser., vol. 1, 120; and Harlow McMillan, *History of Staten Island, New York, during the American Revolution* (Staten Island, N.Y.: Staten Island Historical Society, 1976), 9.

44. See General William Livingston to General George Washington, 5 July 1776, *GWPRWS*, vol. 5, 215–216.

45. Anthon, "Anthon's Notes," 133–134.

46. Ibid., 130.

47. Captain John Bowater to Basil Fielding (earl of Denbigh), 7 July 1776, in Balderston and Syrett, *Lost War*, 88–89.

48. Edward H. Tatum Jr., ed., *American Journal of Ambrose Serle, Secretary to Lord Howe, 1776–1778* (San Marino, Calif.: Huntington Library, 1940), 37.

49. General John Morin Scott to the New York Provincial Congress, 5 July 1776, *Am. Arch.*, 5th ser., vol. 1, 22.

50. Loyalist Claim of Christopher Billopp, transcript, Staten Island Loyalist Collection, box 1, folder 1, SI-HS.

51. See Leng and Davis, *Staten Island and Its People*, vol. 1, 201; Lorenzo Sabine, *Biographical Sketches of Loyalists of the American Revolution with an Historical Essay*, 2 vols. (Boston: Little, Brown, 1864), vol. 2, 6; Harlow McMillen, "Green and Red, and a Little Blue: The Story of Staten Island in the American Revolution, Part 5," *SIH*, 1st ser., 32 (1976): 48; Examination of Emanuel Josephson, of New York, deserter, 10 July 1776, transcript, Military Collection, American Revolution, box 2, folder 1, SI-HS; and Examination of William Ash, from Staten Island, 8 July 1776, *Am. Arch.*, 5th ser., vol. 1, 120. Ash told Continental interrogators in Elizabethtown, New Jersey, that the British had appointed Lawrence as a collector.

52. "1783—To the King—One Bill for 1017 Cords of Wood," *SIH*, 1st ser., 31 (1972): 79.

53. See Kenneth Scott, "Cutting of Staten Island Forests during the Revolution," *Proceedings of the Staten Island Institute of Arts and Sciences* 17 (1955): 8–13 (hereafter cited as *PSIIAS*). The British also used local timber to construct pickets, fascines, palisades, and pontoon bridges and to repair the keels and masts on their ships.

54. Anthon, "Anthon's Notes," 160.

55. See Examination of James McFarlan, a soldier belonging to the Fifty-fifth Regiment, *Am. Arch.*, 5th ser., vol. 1, 199.

56. Walter G. Buchholz et al., eds., *Journal of the Grenadier Battalion von Minnigerode, 1776–1784* (Staten Island, N.Y.: Staten Island Historical Society, 1976), 7.

57. For the unspoken rules concerning plunder by eighteenth-century armies, see David Hackett Fischer, *Washington's Crossing* (New York: Oxford University Press, 2004), 176–177. For the court martial of the two British soldiers, see Bruce Bliven Jr., *Under the Guns, New York: 1775–1776* (New York: Harper & Row, 1972), 332–333; McMillen, "Red, Green, and a Little Blue . . . Part 5," 48; and McMillen, *History of Staten Island*, 13.

58. See British Order Book no. 13, transcript, Military Collection, American Revolution, box 2, folder 4, SI-HS. See also Ira D. Gruber, *The Howe Brothers and the American Revolution* (New York: Atheneum, 1972), 92; and Sylvia R. Frey, *The British Soldier in America: A Social History of Military Life in the Revolutionary Period* (Austin: University of Texas Press, 1981), 40.

59. Lieutenant Loftus Cliffe to unknown, 8 July 1776, transcript, Military Collection, American Revolution, box 2, folder 2, SI-HS.

60. Thelma Wills Foote, *Black and White Manhattan: The History of Racial Formation in Colonial New York City* (New York: Oxford University Press, 2004), 212; and Graham Russell Hodges, *Root and Branch: African Americans in New York and East New Jersey, 1613–1863* (Chapel Hill: University of North Carolina Press, 1999), 139–140. Before his appointment as royal governor of

Virginia, Lord Dunmore served as royal governor of New York from 1770 to 1771.

61. Boston King, quoted in Hodges, *Root and Branch*, 139. See also Judith L. Van Buskirk, *Generous Enemies: Patriots and Loyalists in Revolutionary New York* (Philadelphia: University of Pennsylvania Press, 2002), 136.

62. Lieutenant Johann Heinrich to August Ludwig Schlozer, 18 September 1776, in *Letters of Brunswick and Hessian Officers during the American Revolution*, edited by William L. Stone (New York: Da Capo Press, 1970), 195 (hereafter cited as *Letters*).

63. Ray Raphael, *A People's History of the American Revolution: How Common People Shaped the Fight for Independence* (New York: HarperCollins, 2002), 331.

64. Ibid., 321, 332.

65. Gary B. Nash, *The Unknown American Revolution: The Unruly Birth of Democracy and the Struggle to Create America* (New York: Viking, 2005), 331.

66. See Danske Dandridge, ed., *Historic Shepherdstown* (Charlottesville: University Press of Virginia, 1910), 140–141.

67. See Foote, *Black and White Manhattan*, 216; and Hodges, *Root and Branch*, 149. For a discussion of the experiences of African Americans behind British lines in New York City and its surrounding communities, see also Van Buskirk, *Generous Enemies*, chap. 5.

68. For a discussion of the organization and recruitment of white Loyalist units in 1776, see Paul H. Smith, *Loyalists and Redcoats: A Study in British Revolutionary Policy* (New York: Norton, 1964), 48–49. For African American Loyalist units, see Todd W. Braisted, "The Black Pioneers and Others: The Military Role of Black Loyalists in the American War for Independence," in *Moving On: Black Loyalists in the Afro-Atlantic World*, edited by John W. Pulis (New York: Garland, 1999), 3–37; Benjamin Quarles, *The Negro in the American Revolution* (Chapel Hill: University of North Carolina Press, 1961), chap. 8; Foote, *Black and White Manhattan*, 212–214; and Hodges, *Root and Branch*, 144, 147–153.

69. See David McCullough, *1776* (New York: Simon & Schuster, 2005), 137–138; and Stanley Weintraub, *Iron Tears: America's Battle for Freedom, Britain's Quagmire: 1775–1783* (New York: Free Press, 2005), 70.

70. For a retelling of the story associated with General William Howe's reading of the Declaration of Independence at the Rose and Crown Tavern, see Ira K. Morris, *Morris's Memorial History of Staten Island, New York*, 2 vols. (New York: Memorial Publishing Company, 1898–1900), vol. 1, 207–208. For clarification on the use of the Rose and Crown and other Staten Island taverns for meetings by Howe and his staff, see McMillen, "Green, and Red, and a Little Blue . . . Part 5," 50.

71. Barnet Schecter, *The Battle for New York: The City at the Heart of the American Revolution* (New York: Walker, 2002), 104–106; McCullough, *1776*, 139–140; and Fischer, *Washington's Crossing*, 83–84.

72. Tatum, *American Journal*, 28.

73. Ibid., 30.

74. Harlow McMillen, "Green, and Red, and a Little Blue: The Story of Staten Island in the American Revolution, Part 6," *SIH*, 1st ser., 32 (1976): 72.

75. General Nathanael Greene to General George Washington, 21 July 1776, *GWPRWS*, vol. 5, 414.

76. General George Washington to John Hancock, 7 August 1776, *GWPRWS*, vol. 5, 606; and General George Washington to General William Livingston, 8 August 1776, *PWL*, vol. 1, 112.

77. Tatum, *American Journal*, 62.

78. See Hodges, *Root and Branch*, 144; Edwin G. Burrows and Michael Wallace, *Gotham: A History of New York City to 1898* (New York: Oxford University Press, 1998), 248; Schecter, *Battle for New York*, 113–114; and General George Washington to John Hancock, 14 August 1776, *GWPRWS*, vol. 6, 49.

79. See Gruber, *Howe Brothers*, 92–93; Thomas Fleming, *1776: Year of Illusions* (New York: Norton, 1975), 281; and Schecter, *Battle for New York*, 106.

80. Ira D. Gruber, "Lord Howe and Lord George Germain: British Politics and the Winning of American Independence," *William and Mary Quarterly*, 3rd ser., 22 (1965): 233.

81. The committee's recommendation is quoted in Gruber, *Howe Brothers*, 98–99. See also Weldon A. Brown, *Empire or Independence: A Study in the Failure of Reconciliation, 1774–1783* (Baton Rouge: Louisiana State University Press, 1941), 113.

82. Memorandum of an interview with Lieutenant Colonel James Paterson, 20 July 1776, *GWPRWS*, vol. 5, 398–403.

83. Tatum, *American Journal*, 33.

84. Lieutenant Johann Heinrich to August Ludwig Schlozer, 18 September 1776, *Letters*, 194.

85. Lieutenant Colonel Mungo Campbell is quoted in "A 1776 Item," *SIH*, 1st ser., 23 (1962): 22.

86. Major Charles Stuart to John Stuart (earl of Bute), 9 July 1776, *NDAR*, vol. 5, 989.

87. Lieutenant Loftus Cliffe to unknown, 8 July 1776, Military Collection, American Revolution, box 2, folder 2, SI-HS.

88. Tatum, *American Journal*, 37.

89. Captain John Bowater to Basil Fielding (earl of Denbigh), 15 August 1776, in Balderston and Syrett, *Lost War*, 95.

90. Colonel William Douglas is quoted in "Letters Written during the Revolutionary War by Colonel William Douglas to His Wife Covering the Period July

19, 1775 to December 5, 1776," *New York Historical Society Quarterly* 13 (1929): 80.

CHAPTER 5

1. Captain Alexander McDonald to John Ogilvie, 24 April 1776, in *The Letter-Book of Captain Alexander McDonald of the Royal Highland Emigrants, 1775–1779* (New York: New York Historical Society, 1882), 267 (hereafter cited as *Letter-Book*).

2. *Kemble Papers, 1773–1789*, 2 vols. (New York: New York Historical Society Collections, 1883), vol. 1, 84.

3. For a detailed discussion of the events surrounding the Battle of Long Island see Barnet Schecter, *The Battle for New York: The City at the Heart of the American Revolution* (New York: Walker, 2002), 126–167; and John J. Gallagher, *The Battle of Brooklyn, 1776* (New York: Da Capo Press, 1995), 87–154.

4. For the Staten Island peace talks, see Ernest Schimizzi and Gregory Schimizzi, *The Staten Island Peace Conference: September 11, 1776* (Albany: New York State American Revolution Bicentennial Commission, 1976); Lyman H. Butterfield, ed., *The Diary and Autobiography of John Adams*, 4 vols. (Cambridge, Mass.: Harvard University Press, 1961), 419–420; *The Papers of Benjamin Franklin*, 37 vols. (New Haven, Conn.: Yale University Press, 1959–2004), vol. 22, 598–609, and Henry Steele Commager and Richard B. Morris, eds., *The Spirit of Seventy-Six: The Story of the American Revolution as Told by Participants* (1967; repr., New York: Da Capo Press, 1995), 448–456. See also David McCullough, *John Adams* (New York: Simon & Schuster, 2001), 154–158, and *1776* (New York: Simon & Schuster, 2005), 208.

5. Rev. Dr. Samuel Seabury is quoted in Rev. Charles S. Burch, "History of Saint Andrew's Church, Richmond, Staten Island," *Grafton Magazine of History and Genealogy* 1 (1908): 17.

6. Bruce Burgoyne, ed., *A Hessian Diary of the American Revolution* (Norman: University of Oklahoma Press, 1990), 37.

7. Lincoln MacVeagh, ed., *Journal of Nicholas Cresswell, 1774–1777* (New York: Dial Press, 1924), 217.

8. Memorial of Thomas McDonogh on behalf of Rachel Dawson, transcript, Staten Island Loyalist Collection, box 1, folder 4, Staten Island Historical Society (hereafter cited as SI-HS).

9. Loyalist Claim of John Bedell and Benjamin Micheau, transcript, Staten Island Loyalist Collection, box 1, folder 2, SI-HS.

10. Loyalist Claim of Christopher Billopp, transcript, Staten Island Loyalist Collection, box 1, folder 1, SI-HS.

11. Charles E. Anthon, ed., "Anthon's Notes," *Proceedings of the Staten Island Institute of Arts and Sciences* 3–6 (1924–1932): 82–83.

12. Ibid., 82, 108–109.

13. Field Horne, *The Conference House Revisited: A History of the Billopp Manor House* (Staten Island, N.Y.: Conference House Association, 1990), 24; and William T. Davis, *The Conference/Billopp House* (Staten Island, N.Y.: Staten Island Historical Society, 1926), 133–144.

14. See Lieutenant Colonel John Graves Simcoe, *Simcoe's Military Journal: A History of the Operations of a Partisan Corps, Called the Queen's Rangers, Commanded by Lieut. Col. J. G. Simcoe, during the War of the American Revolution* (New York: Bartlett and Welford, 1844), 268–286. Billopp shared a prison cell with the commander of the Loyalist Queen's Rangers Lieutenant Colonel John Graves Simcoe.

15. See Anthon, "Anthon's Notes," 143, 149–150, 152–154; and Thomas Fleming, *The Battle of Springfield* (Trenton: New Jersey Historical Commission, 1975), 13.

16. See Harlow McMillen, *A History of Staten Island, New York, during the American Revolution* (Staten Island, N.Y.: Staten Island Historical Society, 1976), 44; and Anthon, "Anthon's Notes," 143–146, 149–154.

17. *New-York Gazette and Weekly Mercury*, 14 May 1781.

18. Rev. Edwin F. Hatfield, *History of Elizabeth, New Jersey: Including the Early History of Union County* (New York: Charlton and Lanahan, 1868), 503, 509–510.

19. Harry M. Ward, *Between the Lines: Banditti of the American Revolution* (Westport, Conn.: Greenwood Press, 2002), 41; Hatfield, *History of Elizabeth*, 510; Alexander Rose, *Washington's Spies: The Story of America's First Spy Ring* (New York: Bantam, 2006), 72–74.

20. Anthon, "Anthon's Notes," 84–85, 126–127; Ward, *Between the Lines*, 40–41; and McMillen, *History of Staten Island*, 45.

21. See McMillen, *History of Staten Island*, 31; Mark V. Kwasny, *Washington's Partisan War, 1775–1783* (Kent, Ohio: Kent State University Press, 1996), 63, 73, 81–82; and Frank Moore, ed., *Diary of the American Revolution: From Newspapers and Original Documents*, 2 vols. (New York: Scribner, 1858), vol. 1, 325. See also General Hugh Mercer to General George Washington, 16 October 1776, in *The Papers of George Washington*, Revolutionary War Series, edited by W. W. Abbot, Philander D. Chase, and Dorothy Twohig, 12 vols. (Charlottesville: University Press of Virginia, 1985–2002), vol. 6, 577 (hereafter cited as *GWPRWS*).

22. Walter T. Dornfest, "Sullivan's Raid on Staten Island: August 22, 1777," *Staten Island Historian*, 1st ser., 31 (1972): 97–102 (hereafter cited as *SIH*); Charles P. Whittemore, *A General of the Revolution: John Sullivan of New Hampshire* (New York: Columbia University Press, 1961), 54–55, 64, 67, 75–

76; McMillen, *History of Staten Island*, 33–35; Kwasny, *Partisan War*, 160–161; Burgoyne, *A Hessian Diary*, 45–46. For a civilian's account of Sullivan's raid, see the Loyalist Claim of Frances Dongan, widow of Lieutenant Edward Vaughan Dongan of the Third Battalion of the New Jersey Volunteers, transcript, Staten Island Loyalist Collection, box 1, folder 2, SI-HS.

23. See McMillen, *History of Staten Island*, 35; Kwasny, *Partisan War*, 178–180. See also General Philemon Dickinson to General George Washington, 28 November 1777, *GWPRWS*, vol. 8, 434–435; and General William Livingston to General George Washington, 1 December 1777, *GWPRWS*, vol. 12, 470–472.

24. Bruce Chadwick, *George Washington's War: The Forging of a Revolutionary Leader and the American Presidency* (Naperville, Ill.: Sourcebooks, 2004), 336.

25. Joseph Plumb Martin, *Private Yankee Doodle: Being a Narrative of Some of the Adventures, Dangers, and Sufferings of a Revolutionary War Soldier*, edited by George F. Scheer (Boston: Little, Brown, 1962), 171.

26. Lord Stirling's orders are reprinted in "A Hitherto Unpublished Item Relating to the American Revolution," edited by Elmer G. Van Name, *SIH*, 1st ser., 22 (1961): 19.

27. See Excerpt from the Moravian Congregation Diary, 15 January 1780, Military Collection, American Revolution, box 2, folder 19, SI-HS.

28. Peter W. Coldham, ed., *American Migrations, 1765–1799: The Lives, Times, and Families of Colonial Americans Who Remained Loyal to the British Crown before, during, and after the Revolutionary War, as Related in Their Own Words and through Their Correspondence* (Baltimore: Genealogical Publishing, 2000), 385.

29. Ibid., 342.

30. Anthon, "Anthon's Notes," 141–142.

31. See the Memorial of Isaac Decker, transcript, Staten Island Loyalist Collection, box 1, folder 1, SI-HS.

32. Ward, *Between the Lines*, 55.

33. Burgoyne, *A Hessian Diary*, 36.

34. Anthon, "Anthon's Notes," 109.

35. Rev. Hector Gambold to Nathaniel Seidel, 13 March 1780, excerpt, Military Collection, American Revolution, box 2, folder 19, SI-HS.

36. John J. Clute, *Annals of Staten Island: From Its Discovery to the Present Time* (New York: Press of Charles Vogt, 1877), 118.

37. Rev. Hector Gambold to Nathaniel Seidel, 13 March 1780, excerpt, Military Collection, American Revolution, box 2, folder 19, SI-HS.

38. A description of the events surrounding the murder of Christian Jacobson can be found in Anthon, "Anthon's Notes," 87. Jacobson's home was located in what is today the New Dorp section of Staten Island.

39. Stephen Conway, "'The Great Mischief Complain'd Of': Reflections on the Misconduct of British Soldiers in the Revolutionary War," *William and Mary Quarterly*, 3rd ser., 47 (1961): 377 (hereafter cited as *WMQ*).

40. Burgoyne, *A Hessian Diary*, 43.

41. Edward H. Tatum Jr., ed., *American Journal of Ambrose Serle, Secretary to Lord Howe, 1776–1778* (San Marino, Calif.: Huntington Library, 1940), 35.

42. See General William Livingston to General George Washington, 21 August 1776, *GWPRWS*, vol. 6, 99, n. 2.

43. Anthon, "Anthon's Notes," 139–140.

44. Memorial of Ann Perine, Perine Collection, box 1, folder 1, SI-HS.

45. Ibid., 158.

46. General William Livingston to General George Washington, 21 August 1776, *GWPRWS*, vol. 6, 99.

47. Captain Alexander McDonald to Captain Robert McKenzie, 11 June 1777, *Letter-Book*, 340.

48. Captain Alexander McDonald to Lord Jeffrey Amherst, August 1777, *Letter-Book*, 361.

49. Loyalist Claim of Christopher Billopp, transcript, Staten Island Loyalist Collection, box 1, folder 1, SI-HS.

50. Anthon, "Anthon's Notes," 139–140. The most frequently cited units were those commanded by Abraham Van Buskirk and Joseph Barton.

51. Conway, "'The Great Mischief Complain'd Of,'" 381–384.

52. For a detailed description of the capture and hanging of Stephen Ball, see "Stephen Ball Hung by Tories," Military Collection, American Revolution, box 2, folder 17. See also Anthon, "Anthon's Notes," 135; Hatfield, *History of Elizabeth*, 650–651; and Ward, *Between the Lines*, 58–59.

53. Anthon, "Anthon's Notes," 111, 135–136, 158.

54. Martin, *Private Yankee Doodle*, 180.

55. For the Hatfield gang's rampage against Elizabethtown, see Theodore Thayer, *As We Were: The Story of Old Elizabethtown* (Elizabeth, N.J.: Grassman, 1964), 133; Hatfield, *History of Elizabeth*, 479–483; and Ellis L. Derry, *Old and Historic Churches of New Jersey*, 2 vols. (Medford, N.J.: Plexus Publishing, 1994), vol. 2, 75. See also Coldham, *Migrations*, 403. After the war, Cornelius Hatfield Jr. settled in Nova Scotia, Canada.

56. See Clute, *Annals*, 114; and Anthon, "Anthon's Notes," 85–86, 137.

57. See Graham Russell Hodges, *Slavery and Freedom in the Rural North: African Americans in Monmouth County, New Jersey, 1665–1865* (Madison, Wis.: Madison House Publishers, 1997), 97; and Ward, *Between the Lines*, 61–62.

58. Hodges, *Slavery and Freedom*, 97–98.

59. Ward, *Between the Lines*, 62–63; and Hodges, *Slavery and Freedom*, 100.

60. For the rumored slave insurrection in Elizabethtown, see Hodges, *Slavery and Freedom*, 98; Thayer, *As We Were*, 131; and Hatfield, *History of Elizabeth*, 476.

61. For the Monmouth County Whigs' response to the raids conducted by Colonel Tye and other Loyalist partisans, see Michael S. Adelberg, "'A Combination to Trample All Law Underfoot': The Association for Retaliation and the American Revolution in Monmouth County," *New Jersey History* 115 (1997): 3–35.

62. Hodges, *Slavery and Freedom*, 103–104; Ward, *Between the Lines*, 63–64.

63. Richard M. Bayles, *History of Richmond County, Staten Island, New York: From Its Discovery to the Present Time* (New York: L. E. Preston, 1887), 233.

64. Ibid.

65. Charles G. Hine, ed., *The Story and Documentary History of the Perine House* (Staten Island, N.Y.: Staten Island Antiquarian Society, 1915), 30–31.

66. Clute, *Annals*, 118–119.

67. Ray Raphael, *A People's History of the American Revolution: How Common People Shaped the Fight for Independence* (New York: HarperCollins, 2002), 170.

68. Mary Beth Norton, *Liberty's Daughters: The Revolutionary Experience of American Women, 1750–1800* (New York: HarperCollins, 1980), 203–204.

69. Lieutenant Colonel Francis Lord Rawdon to the earl of Huntington, 5 August 1776, in Commager and Morris, *The Spirit of Seventy-Six*, 424.

70. See Sylvia R. Frey, *The British Soldier in America: A Social History of Military Life in the Revolutionary Period* (Austin: University of Texas Press, 1981), 78; Carol Berkin, *Revolutionary Mothers: Women in the Struggle for America's Independence* (New York: Knopf, 2005), 40–41; Jerome J. Nadelhaft, *The Disorders of War: The Revolution in South Carolina* (Orono: University of Maine at Orono Press, 1981), 68; and Conway, "'The Great Mischief Complain'd Of,'" 385–389.

71. Frey, *The British Soldier in America*, 79.

72. For the spread of smallpox in British-occupied Boston, see Elizabeth A. Fenn, *Pox Americana: The Great Smallpox Epidemic of 1775–82* (New York: Hill & Wang, 2001), 45–55, 264–265.

73. See Examination of James MacFarlan, A Soldier Belonging to the 55th Regiment, Colonel Medie, 5 July 1776, in *Naval Documents of the American Revolution*, edited by William B. Clark and William J. Morgan, 10 vols. (Washington, D.C.: U.S. Government Printing Office, 1964–1996), vol. 5, 936 (hereafter cited as *NDAR*); and the Examinations of Elijah Stephens and Chauncey Smith, Deserters from the Enemy's Fleet, New York, 11 July 1776, in *American Archives: A Documentary History of the United States*, edited by Peter Force,

5th ser. (Washington, D.C.: Published under authority of an Act of Congress, 1837–1953), vol. 1, 198 (hereafter cited as *Am. Arch.*).

74. See General Hugh Mercer to General George Washington, 7 August 1776, *Am. Arch.*, 5th ser., vol. 1, 813.

75. Mary Ann Furetti, ed., *Lossberg Journal, 1776–1783* (Staten Island, N.Y.: Staten Island Historical Society, 1976), 23.

76. Burgoyne, *A Hessian Diary*, 44.

77. Tatum, *American Journal*, 65.

78. Frey, *The British Soldier in America*, 42.

79. See British Order Book no. 13, transcript, Military Collection, American Revolution, box 2, folder 4, SI-HS.

80. *New-York Gazette and Weekly Mercury*, 22 September 1777.

81. *Royal Gazette*, 13 January 1779.

82. Judith L. Van Buskirk, *Generous Enemies: Patriots and Loyalists in Revolutionary New York* (Philadelphia: University of Pennsylvania Press, 2002), 47.

83. Van Buskirk, *Generous Enemies*, 67; Harlow McMillen, "Green, and Red, and a Little Blue: The Story of Staten Island in the American Revolution," *SIH*, 1st ser., 32 (1977): 105; and McMillen, *History of Staten Island*, 13. For the British inspection of the Staten Island mails, see Abraham Bancker to Abraham Bancker, 10 November 1779, Bancker Family Papers, correspondence, 1775–1787, folder 14, New York Historical Society (hereafter cited as NY-HS).

84. See Thomas Jones, *History of New York during the Revolutionary War and of the Leading Events in the Other Colonies at That Period*, edited by Edward F. De Lancey, 2 vols. (New York: New York Historical Society, 1879), vol. 1, 337; Loring McMillen, "The First Presbyterian Church of Staten Island, 1717–1776–1808: Part I," *Chronicles of Staten Island* 1(1985): 7 (hereafter cited as *COSI*); Cornelius Vander Naald, "History of the Reformed Church on Staten Island," *SIH*, 1st ser., 16 (1955): 4; and Harlow McMillen, "Richmondtown: The First 160 Years, Part IV: The Dutch Congregation," *SIH*, 1st ser., 22 (1961): 22.

85. Charles W. Leng and William T. Davis, *Staten Island and Its People: A History, 1609–1929*, 3 vols. (New York: Lewis Historical Publishing, 1930), vol. 2, 463; and Clute, *Annals*, 278.

86. See Jean Paul Jordan, "The Anglican Establishment in Colonial New York, 1693–1783" (PhD diss., Columbia University, 1971), 560.

87. Rev. Dr. Samuel Seabury is quoted in Burch, "History of Saint Andrew's," 17.

88. See Burch, "History of Saint Andrew's," 17–18; Archbishop Thomas Secker to Rev. Dr. Samuel Johnson, 6 October 1762, in *Documents Relative to the Colonial History of the State of New York*, edited by E. B. O'Callaghan, 15 vols. (Albany, N.Y.: Weed, Parsons Printers, 1853–1887), vol. 7, 508 (hereafter cited as *NYCD*); Archbishop Thomas Secker to Rev. Dr. Samuel Johnson, 30 March

1763, *NYCD*, vol. 7, 517–519; and William T. Davis, Charles W. Leng, and Royden W. Vosburgh, eds., *Church of St. Andrew, Richmond, Staten Island: Its History, Vital Records, and Gravestone Inscriptions* (Staten Island, N.Y.: Staten Island Historical Society, 1925), 37 (hereafter cited as *Church of St. Andrew*).

89. See Harlow McMillen, "Richmondtown: The First 160 Years, Part V: The Church of St. Andrew," *SIH*, 1st ser., 22 (1961): 28; and *Church of St. Andrew*, 38–39.

90. Milton M. Klein and Ronald W. Howard, eds., *The Twilight of British Rule in Revolutionary America: The New York Letter Book of General James Robertson, 1780–1783* (Cooperstown, N.Y.: New York State Historical Association, 1983), 7–9.

91. Klein and Howard, *The Twilight of British Rule*, 58, 188, 189, n. 3. See also General James Robertson to General Sir Guy Carleton, 16 March 1782, Sir Guy Carleton Papers, 1724–1808, reel 14, Harriet Irving Library, University of New Brunswick, Fredericton, New Brunswick, Canada.

92. Klein and Howard, *The Twilight of British Rule*, 188.

93. See McMillen, *History of Staten Island*, 29.

94. Lieutenant Johann Heinrich to August Ludwig Schlozer, 18 September 1776, in *Letters of Brunswick and Hessian Officers during the American Revolution*, edited by William L. Stone (New York: Da Capo Press, 1970), 194–195.

95. Rev. Hector Gambold to Nathaniel Seidel, 13 March 1780, excerpt, Military Collection, American Revolution, box 2, folder 19, SI-HS.

96. General William Livingston to General George Washington, 21 August 1776, *GWPRWS*, vol. 6, 99.

97. General James Pattison to General Cortlandt Skinner, 22 December 1779, in *The Official Letters of Major General James Pattison* (New York: New York Historical Society Collections, 1875), 319 (hereafter cited as *Official Letters*).

98. Anthon, "Anthon's Notes," 121.

99. General James Pattison to Major Frederick Bowes, 25 July 1779, *Official Letters*, 230.

100. Burgoyne, *A Hessian Diary*, 37.

101. Abraham Bancker to Abraham Bancker, 28 August 1783, Bancker Family Papers, correspondence, 1775–1787, folder 14, NY-HS.

102. Stephen Skinner to Effingham Lawrence, 11 June 1783, Stephen Skinner Letter-Book, 1780–1793, NY-HS.

103. See Loring McMillen, "An Island Saga: The Mersereau Family, Part 5," *COSI* 1 (1990–1991): 202; and Esther Clark Wright, *The Loyalists of New Brunswick*, 5th ed. (Yarmouth, Nova Scotia: Sentinel Printing, Ltd., 1985), 80, 245.

104. Charlotte M. Hix, *The Crocheron Family of Staten Island, New York* (Garden City, N.Y.: Published by the author, 1979), 35.

105. Captain Alexander McDonald to William McAdam, 19 January 1779, *Letter-Book*, 496.

106. Loyalist Claim of Captain Alexander McDonald, transcript, Staten Island Loyalist Collection, box 1, folder 2, SI-HS. See also Loring McMillen, "Captain Alexander McDonald: Part II," *COSI* 1 (1986–1987): 51; and Christopher Moore, *The Loyalists: Revolution, Exile, Settlement* (Toronto: McClelland and Stewart, 1984), 216.

107. Lettie Heslop to Ann Perine, 23 January 1785, Perine Collection, box 1, folder 1, SI-HS.

108. Richard Decker to Jane Jones, 1 August 1788, Decker/Prall/Hillyer Collection, box 19, folder 12, SI-HS.

109. See Loyalist claim of Christopher Billopp, transcript, box 1, folder 1, Staten Island Loyalist Collection, SI-HS; Harry B. Yoshpe, *The Disposition of Loyalist Estates in the Southern District of the State of New York* (1939; repr., New York: AMS Press, 1967), 48; Horne, *Conference House Revisited,* 26; Alexander C. Flick, ed., *The American Revolution in New York: Its Political, Social, and Economic Significance* (Albany: New York State Department of Education, Division of Archives and History, 1926), 221–222. Flick contends that revenge was also a major factor in the passage of the Confiscation Act of 1779. See Alexander C. Flick, *Loyalism in New York during the American Revolution* (1901; repr., New York: AMS Press, 1970), 146–150.

110. See Loyalist claim of Christopher Billopp, transcript, Staten Island Loyalist Collection, box 1, folder 1, SI-HS. See also Horne, *Conference House Revisited,* 26.

111. See Loyalist claim of Benjamin Seaman, transcript, Staten Island Loyalist Collection, box 1, folder 1, SI-HS.

112. Horne, *Conference House Revisited,* 26–27.

113. Kenneth Scott, "Cutting of Staten Island Forests during the Revolution," *Proceedings of the Staten Island Institute of Arts and Sciences* 17 (1955): 11–12.

114. Forrest McDonald, *Alexander Hamilton: A Biography* (New York: Norton, 1979), 73–74.

115. See Philip Ranlet, *The New York Loyalists* (Knoxville: University of Tennessee Press, 1986), 173; John Jay to Alexander Hamilton, 15 May 1783, in *The Papers of Alexander Hamilton,* edited by Harold C. Syrett, 27 vols. (New York: Columbia University Press, 1961–1987), vol. 4, 648–649.

116. Coldham, *Migrations,* 273.

117. Ranlet, *The New York Loyalists,* 175; Wright, *The Loyalists of New Brunswick,* 60, 175–177.

118. For Christopher Billopp's life and career after the American Revolution, see Lorenzo Sabine, *Biographical Sketches of Loyalists of the American Revolution with an Historical Essay,* 2 vols. (Boston: Little, Brown, 1864), vol. 1, 229–230; and Sharon Dubeau, *New Brunswick Loyalists: A Bicentennial Tribute* (Agincourt, Ontario: Generation Press, 1983), 11. See also Joseph W. Lawrence, *The Judges of New Brunswick and Their Times,* edited by Alfred A. Stockton

(Saint John, New Brunswick: Acadiensis, 1907), 212–215, 230. For Billopp's death, see *City Gazette* (Saint John, New Brunswick), 29 March 1827. For Benjamin Seaman's life after the American Revolution, see Sabine, *Biographical Sketches*, 271–272. For a general description of the lives of both men after the American Revolution, see Gregory Palmer, ed., *Biographical Sketches of Loyalists of the American Revolution* (Westport, Conn.: Meckler, 1984), 67, 769. The struggles experienced by the Loyalists who settled the many refugee communities in Nova Scotia, Canada, are discussed in Neil MacKinnon, *This Unfriendly Soil: The Loyalist Experience in Nova Scotia, 1783–1791* (Kingston, Ontario: McGill–Queen's University Press, 1986).

119. Anthon, "Anthon's Notes," 20. See also *African American History on Staten Island*, 38 and *Wills of Richmond County, 1787–1763* (Staten Island, N.Y.: Staten Island Historical Society, 1941), 86.

120. Of the ten men who represented Staten Island in the New York State Assembly from 1777 to 1800, six were affiliated with the Reformed Church.

121. See Charles L. Sachs, *Made on Staten Island: Agriculture, Industry, and Suburban Living in the City* (Staten Island, N.Y.: Staten Island Historical Society, 1988), 15. For the slight growth in population, see Evarts B. Greene and Virginia D. Harrington, eds., *American Population before the Federal Census of 1790* (Gloucester, Mass.: Peter Smith, 1966), 105. See also Hodges, *Root and Branch*, who writes: "In Richmond and in the rural parts of Kings County, almost 60 percent of the white households in 1790 used black laborers, most of them enslaved. . . . Nearly 40 percent of the households in Kings, Queens, and Richmond Counties owned slaves, a higher ratio than in South Carolina, North Carolina, or Maryland" (164). The federal census of 1790 counted 127 free African Americans living on Staten Island (Richmond County).

122. Clute, *Annals*, 126.

# Bibliography

MANUSCRIPTS

Harriet Irving Library, University of New Brunswick, Fredericton, New
  Brunswick, Canada
Sir Guy Carleton Papers
Edward Winslow Papers
New Brunswick Museum and Archives, Saint John, New Brunswick,
  Canada
H. T. Hazen Papers
New York Historical Society, New York, New York
Bancker Family Papers
James Duane Papers
John Rutherford Papers
Stephen Skinner Letter-Book
Saint John Public Library, Saint John, New Brunswick, Canada
Graves Papers
Staten Island Historical Society, Staten Island, New York
Decker/Prall/Hillyer Collection
Dubois Collection
Dupuy Collection
Genealogical Vertical Files
Mersereau Collection
Military Collection, American Revolution
Miscellaneous Genealogical Files Collection
Poillon Collection
Richmond County Public Records Collection
Saint Andrew's Church Collection
Staten Island Loyalist Collection
Staten Island Institute of Arts and Sciences, Staten Island, New York
Charles W. Leng Collection
Trade Networks Files

PRINTED PRIMARY SOURCES

Abbot, W. W., Philander D. Chase, and Dorothy Twohig, eds. *The Papers of George Washington*. Revolutionary War Series. 12 vols. Charlottesville: University Press of Virginia, 1985–2002.

Anthon, Charles E., ed. "Anthon's Notes." *Proceedings of the Staten Island Institute of Arts and Sciences* 3–6 (1924–1932).

"A 1776 Item." *Staten Island Historian*, 1st series, 23 (1962): 22–23.

Balderston, Marion and David Syrett, eds. *The Lost War: Letters from British Officers during the American Revolution*. New York: Horizon Press, 1975.

Bangs, Edward, ed. *Journal of Lieutenant Isaac Bangs: April 1 to July 29, 1776*. 1890. Reprint, New York: Arno Press, 1968.

Benson, Adolph B., ed. *The America of 1750: Peter Kalm's Travels in North America, the English Version of 1770*. New York: Wilson-Erickson, 1937.

Buchholz, Walter G., et al., eds. *Journal of the Grenadier Battalion von Minnigerode, 1776–1784*. Staten Island, N.Y.: Staten Island Historical Society, 1976.

Burgoyne, Bruce, ed. *A Hessian Diary of the American Revolution*. Norman: University of Oklahoma Press, 1990.

Butterfield, L. H., ed. *The Diary and Autobiography of John Adams*. 4 vols. Cambridge, Mass.: Harvard University Press, 1961.

*Calendar of Historical Manuscripts Relating to the War of the Revolution*. Albany, N.Y.: Weed & Parsons, 1868.

Calhoun, Gertrude L., ed. "Excerpts from Philipp Waldeck's Diary of the American Revolution." *Proceedings of the Union County Historical Society of Union County, New Jersey* 2 (1923–1924): 137–143.

Clark, William B., and William J. Morgan, eds. *Naval Documents of the American Revolution*. 10 vols. Washington, D.C.: U.S. Government Printing Office, 1964–1996.

Clinton, Sir Henry. *The American Rebellion: Sir Henry Clinton's Narrative of His Campaigns, 1775–1782*. Edited by William B. Willcox. New Haven, Conn.: Yale University Press, 1954.

Coldham, Peter W., ed. *American Migrations, 1765–1799: The Lives, Times, and Families of Colonial Americans Who Remained Loyal to the British Crown before, during, and after the Revolutionary War, as Related in Their Own Words and through Their Correspondence*. Baltimore: Genealogical Publishing, 2000.

*Collections of the Protestant Episcopal Historical Society for the Year 1851*. 2 vols. New York: Protestant Episcopal Historical Society, 1851.

Commager, Henry Steele, and Richard B. Morris, eds. *The Spirit of Seventy-Six: The Story of the American Revolution as Told by Participants*. 1967. Reprint, New York: Da Capo Press, 1995.

Corwin, Edward T., ed. *Ecclesiastical Records of the State of New York.* 7 vols. Albany, N.Y.: J. B. Lyon, State Printer, 1901–1916.

Crary, Catherine S., ed. *The Price of Loyalty: Tory Writings from the Revolutionary Era.* New York: McGraw-Hill, 1973.

Dann, John C., ed. *The Revolution Remembered: Eyewitness Accounts of the War for Independence.* Chicago: University of Chicago Press, 1980.

Davies, K.G., ed. *Documents of the American Revolution, 1770–1783.* Colonial Office Series. 21 vols. Dublin: Irish University Press, 1972–1981.

Davis, William T., Charles W. Leng, and Royden Woodward Vosburgh, eds. *The Church of St. Andrew, Richmond, Staten Island: Its History, Vital Records, and Gravestone Inscriptions.* Staten Island, N.Y.: Staten Island Historical Society, 1925.

Denton, Daniel. *A Brief Description of New York: Formerly Called New Netherland.* London: Printed for John Hancock, 1670.

*Extracts from the Journal of Proceedings of the Provincial Congress of New Jersey, 1775–1776.* Woodbury, N.J.: Joseph Sailor, Printer, 1835.

Force, Peter, ed. *American Archives: A Documentary History of the United States.* 4th and 5th series. Washington, D.C.: Published under authority of an Act of Congress, 1837–1953.

Ford, Worthington C., ed. *Correspondence and Journals of Samuel Blachley Webb.* 3 vols. Lancaster, Pa.: Wickersham Press, 1893–1894.

Ford, Worthington C., et al., eds. *Journals of the Continental Congress, 1774–1789.* 34 vols. Washington, D.C.: U.S. Government Printing Office, 1907–1937.

Furetti, Mary Ann, ed. *Lossberg Journal, 1776–1783.* Staten Island, N.Y.: Staten Island Historical Society, 1976.

Gerlach, Larry R., ed. *New Jersey in the American Revolution, 1763–1783: A Documentary History.* Trenton: New Jersey Historical Commission, 1975.

Greene, Evarts B., and Virginia D. Harrington, eds. *American Population before the Federal Census of 1790.* Gloucester, Mass.: Peter Smith, 1966.

Hine, Charles G., ed. *The Story and Documentary History of the Perine House.* Staten Island, N.Y.: Staten Island Antiquarian Society, 1915.

Hix, Charlotte M. *Staten Island Wills and Letters of Administration: Richmond County, 1670–1800.* Bowie, Md.: Heritage Books, 1993.

Humphreys, David. *Historical Account of the Incorporated Society for the Propagation of the Gospel in Foreign Parts.* London: Joseph Downing, Printer, 1730.

Jackson, Ronald D., and Evelyn E. Jackson, eds. *African American History in Staten Island: Slave Holding Families and Their Slaves, Raw Notes.* Staten Island, N.Y.: Staten Island Historical Society, 1995.

James, Bartlett B., and J. Franklin Jameson, eds. *Journal of Jasper Danckaerts, 1679–1680.* New York: Scribner, 1913.

Jameson, J. Franklin, ed. *Narratives of New Netherland, 1609–1664.* New York: Scribner, 1909.

Jones, E. Alfred, ed. *The Loyalists of New Jersey: Their Memorials, Petitions, Claims.* Newark: New Jersey Historical Society, 1927.

Jones, Thomas. *History of New York during the Revolutionary War and of the Leading Events in the Other Colonies at That Period.* Edited by Edward F. De Lancey. 2 vols. New York: New York Historical Society, 1879.

*Kemble Papers, 1773–1789.* In New York Historical Society Collections. 2 vols. New York: Printed for the Society, 1883.

Klein, Milton M., and Ronald W. Howard, eds. *The Twilight of British Rule in Revolutionary America: The New York Letter Book of General James Robertson, 1780–1783.* Cooperstown: New York State Historical Association, 1983.

*Lee Papers.* In New York Historical Society Collections. 4 vols. New York: Printed for the Society, 1871.

*The Letter-Book of Captain Alexander McDonald of the Royal Highland Emigrants, 1775–1779.* In New York Historical Society Collections. New York: Printed for the Society, 1882.

"Letters of William Alexander, Lord Stirling." *Proceedings of the New Jersey Historical Society* 60 (1942): 171–179.

"Letters Written during the Revolutionary War by Colonel William Douglas to His Wife Covering the Period July 19, 1775 to December 5, 1776." *New York Historical Society Quarterly* 12–14 (1928–1929).

MacVeagh, Lincoln, ed. *The Journal of Nicholas Cresswell, 1774–1777.* New York: Dial Press, 1924.

Martin, Joseph Plumb. *Private Yankee Doodle: Being a Narrative of Some of the Adventures, Dangers and Sufferings of a Revolutionary War Soldier.* Edited by George F. Scheer. Boston: Little, Brown, 1962.

McMillen, Harlow. "The Oath of Allegiance Signed by the Inhabitants of Staten Island on July 9th 1776." *Staten Island Historian,* 1st series, 32 (1976): 50–57.

Moore, Frank, ed. *Diary of the American Revolution: From Newspapers and Original Documents.* 2 vols. New York: Scribner, 1858.

*New Jersey Archives,* 1st series. 42 vols. Trenton: New Jersey State Library, Archives and History Bureau, 1880–1949.

O'Callaghan, E. B., ed. *Documentary History of the State of New York.* 4 vols. Albany, N.Y.: Weed, Parsons Printers, 1849–1850.

———, ed. *Documents Relative to the Colonial History of the State of New York.* 15 vols. Albany, N.Y.: Weed, Parsons Printers, 1853–1887.

*The Official Letters of Major General James Pattison.* In New York Historical Society Collections. New York: Printed for the Society, 1875.

*The Papers of Benjamin Franklin.* 37 vols. New Haven, Conn.: Yale University Press, 1959–2004.

Prince, Carl E., and Dennis P. Ryan, eds. *The Papers of William Livingston, 1774–1783.* 4 vols. Trenton: New Jersey Historical Commission, 1979–1987.

Scheer, George F., and Hugh F. Rankin, eds. *Rebels and Redcoats: The American Revolution through the Eyes of Those Who Fought and Lived It.* 1957. Reprint, New York: Da Capo Press, 1988.

*Selections from the Correspondence of the Executive of New Jersey: From 1776 to 1786.* Newark, N.J.: Newark Daily Advertiser, 1848.

"1783—To the King—One Bill for 1017 Cords of Wood." *Staten Island Historian,* 1st series (1972): 79–80.

Sheridan, Eugene R., ed. *The Papers of Lewis Morris.* 3 vols. Newark: New Jersey Historical Society, 1991.

Simcoe, Lieutenant Colonel John Graves. *Simcoe's Military Journal: A History of the Operations of a Partisan Corps, Called the Queen's Rangers, Commanded by Lieut. Col. J. G. Simcoe, during the War of the American Revolution.* New York: Bartlett and Welford, 1844.

Smith, Paul H., ed. *Letters of the Delegates to the Congress, 1774–1789.* 25 vols. Washington, D.C.: Library of Congress, 1976–1998.

Smith, William Jr. *The History of the Province of New York.* Edited by Michael Kammen. 2 vols. Cambridge, Mass.: Harvard University Press, 1972.

Stone, William L., ed. *Letters of Brunswick and Hessian Officers during the American Revolution.* New York: Da Capo Press, 1970.

Stowe, Walter H., ed. "The Seabury Minutes of the New York Clergy Conventions of 1766 and 1767." *Historical Magazine of the Protestant Episcopal Church* 10 (1941): 124–162.

Syrett, Harold C., ed. *The Papers of Alexander Hamilton.* 27 vols. New York: Columbia University Press, 1961–1987.

Tatum, Edward H. Jr., ed. *The American Journal of Ambrose Serle, Secretary to Lord Howe, 1776–1778.* San Marino, Calif.: Huntington Library, 1940.

Van Name, Elmer G., ed. "A Hitherto Unpublished Item Relating to the American Revolution." *Staten Island Historian,* 1st series, 22 (1961): 19–20.

Willard, Margaret W., ed. *Letters on the American Revolution, 1774–1776.* Boston: Houghton Mifflin, 1925.

*Wills of Richmond County, 1787–1863.* Staten Island, N.Y.: Staten Island Historical Society, 1941.

Wood-Holt, B., ed. *The King's Loyal Americans: The Canadian Fact, Marriage Licenses for Sunbury County, 1788–1829, Passenger Lists, and Other Lists, etc.* Saint John, New Brunswick: Holland House, 1990.

Wright, Tobias A., ed. *Staten Island Church Records.* Bowie, Md.: Heritage Books, 1997.

NEWSPAPERS

*American Minerva*
*City Gazette* (Saint John, New Brunswick, Canada)
*New York Daily Advertiser*
*New York Gazette*
*New York Gazette and Weekly Mercury*
*New York Gazette and Weekly Post-Boy*
*New York Journal*
*New York Journal or General Advertiser*
*New York Mercury and General Advertiser*

SECONDARY SOURCES

Adelberg, Michael S. "'A Combination to Trample All Law Underfoot': The Association for Retaliation and the American Revolution in Monmouth County." *New Jersey History* 115 (1997): 3–35.

Alden, John R. *General Charles Lee: Traitor or Patriot?* Baton Rouge: Louisiana State University Press, 1951.

Anderson, Fred. *Crucible of War: The Seven Years' War and the Fate of Empire in British North America, 1754–1766.* New York: Vintage Books, 2000.

Anderson, Troyer S. *The Command of the Howe Brothers during the American Revolution.* New York: Oxford University Press, 1936.

Atwood, Rodney. *The Hessians: Mercenaries from Hessen-Kessel in the American Revolution.* Cambridge: Cambridge University Press, 1980.

Bailyn, Bernard. *The Ordeal of Thomas Hutchinson.* Cambridge, Mass.: Harvard University Press, 1974.

Bakeless, John. *Turncoats, Traitors, and Heroes: Espionage in the American Revolution.* 1959. Reprint, New York: Da Capo Press, 1998.

Balmer, Randall H. *A Perfect Babel of Confusion: Dutch Religion and English Culture in the Middle Colonies.* New York: Oxford University Press, 1989.

Bancroft, George. *History of the United States from the Discovery of the American Continent.* 10 vols. Boston: C. C. Little and J. Brown, 1842–1874.

Barck, Oscar T. *New York City during the War for Independence: With Special Reference to the Period of British Occupation.* New York: Columbia University Press, 1931.

Barlow, Elizabeth. *The Forests and Wetlands of New York City.* Boston: Little, Brown, 1969.

Baugher, Sherene. "Trade Networks: Colonial and Federal Period (1680–1815)." *Proceedings of the Staten Island Institute of Arts and Sciences* 34 (1989): 33–37.

Bayles, Richard M. *History of Richmond County, Staten Island, New York: From Its Discovery to the Present Time.* New York: L. E. Preston and Company, 1887.

Becker, Carl L. *The History of Political Parties in the Province of New York, 1760–1776.* Madison: University of Wisconsin Press, 1909.

Benton, William A. *Whig-Loyalism: An Aspect of Political Ideology in the American Revolutionary Era.* Teaneck, N.J.: Fairleigh Dickinson University Press, 1969.

Berkin, Carol. *First Generations: Women in Colonial America.* New York: Hill & Wang, 1994.

———. *Jonathan Sewell: Odyssey of an American Loyalist.* New York: Columbia University Press, 1974.

———. *Revolutionary Mothers: Women in the Struggle for America's Independence.* New York: Knopf, 2005.

Billias, George A., ed. *George Washington's Generals.* Westport, Conn.: Greenwood Press, 1967.

———, ed. *George Washington's Opponents.* New York: Morrow, 1969.

Billopp, Charles F. *A History of Thomas and Anne Billopp Farmar, and Some of Their Descendants.* New York: Grafton Press, Genealogical Publishers, 1908.

Bliven, Bruce Jr. *Under the Guns: New York, 1775–1776.* New York: Harper & Row, 1972.

Bodine, Audrey W. *A History of the Bodine Family of Staten Island, New York, from 1680.* La Jolla, Calif.: Published by the author, 1986.

Bonomi, Patricia U. *A Factious People: Politics and Society in Colonial New York.* New York: Columbia University Press, 1971.

———. *Under the Cope of Heaven: Religion, Society, and Politics in Colonial America.* New York: Oxford University Press, 1986.

Bowler, R. Arthur. *Logistics and the Failure of the British Army in America, 1775–1783.* Princeton, N.J.: Princeton University Press, 1975.

Breen, T. H. "Baubles of Britain: The American and British Consumer Revolutions of the Eighteenth Century." *Past and Present* 119 (1988): 73–104.

Bridenbaugh, Carl. *Mitre and Sceptre: Transatlantic Faiths, Ideas, Personalities, and Politics: 1689–1775.* New York: Oxford University Press, 1962.

Brown, Wallace. *The Good Americans.* New York: Morrow, 1969.

———. *The King's Friends: The Composition and Motives of the American Loyalist Claimants.* Providence, R.I.: Brown University Press, 1965.

———. "Negroes and the American Revolution." *History Today* 14 (1964): 556–563.

Brown, Weldon A. *Empire or Independence: A Study in the Failure of Reconciliation, 1774–1783.* Baton Rouge: Louisiana State University Press, 1941.

Bultemann, Walter A. "The S.P.G. and the French Huguenots in Colonial America." *Historical Magazine of the Protestant Episcopal* Church 20 (1951): 156–172.

Burch, Reverend Charles S. "History of Saint Andrew's Church, Richmond, Staten Island." *Grafton Magazine of History and Genealogy* 1 (1908): 1–24.

Burr, Nelson R. "The Episcopal Church and the Dutch in Colonial New York and New Jersey, 1664–1784." *Historical Magazine of the Protestant Episcopal Church* 19 (1950): 90–109.

Burrows, Edwin G., and Michael Wallace. *Gotham: A History of New York City to 1898.* New York: Oxford University Press, 1998.

Bushman, Richard L. "Markets and Composite Farms in Early America." *William and Mary Quarterly*, 3rd series, 55 (1998): 351–374.

————. *The Refinement of America: Persons, Houses, and Cities.* New York: Knopf, 1992.

Butler, Jon. *The Huguenots in America: A Refugee People in New World Society.* Cambridge, Mass.: Harvard University Press, 1983.

Calam, John. *Parsons and Pedagogues: The SPG Adventure in American Education.* New York: Columbia University Press, 1971.

Calhoon, Robert M. *The Loyalist Perception and Other Essays.* Columbia: University of South Carolina Press, 1989.

————. *The Loyalists in Revolutionary America, 1760–1781.* New York: Harcourt Brace Jovanovich, 1973.

Calhoon, Robert M., Timothy M. Barnes, and George A. Rawlyk, eds. *Loyalists and Community in North America.* Westport, Conn.: Greenwood Press, 1994.

Callahan, North. *Royal Raiders: The Tories of the American Revolution.* Indianapolis: Bobbs-Merrill, 1963.

Cashin, Edward J. *The King's Ranger: Thomas Brown and the American Revolution on the Southern Frontier.* New York: Fordham University Press, 1999.

Chadwick, Bruce. *George Washington's War: The Forging of a Revolutionary Leader and the American Presidency.* Naperville, Ill.: Sourcebooks, 2004.

Champagne, Roger J. "Family Politics versus Constitutional Principles: The New York Assembly Elections of 1768 and 1769." *William and Mary Quarterly*, 3rd series, 20 (1963): 57–79.

————. "New York's Radicals and the Coming of Independence." *Journal of American History* 51 (1964): 21–40.

Clark, Jonathan. "The American Revolution: A War of Religion?" *History Today* 39 (1989): 10–16.

Clark, Samuel A. *The History of St. John's Church, Elizabeth Town, New Jersey, from the Year 1703 to the Present Time.* Philadelphia: Lippincott, 1857.

Clute, John J. *Annals of Staten Island: From Its Discovery to the Present Time.* New York: Press of Charles Vogt, 1877.

Coalter, Milton J. Jr. *Gilbert Tennent, Son of Thunder: A Case Study of Conti-*

*nental Pietism's Impact on the First Great Awakening in the Middle Colonies.* Westport, Conn.: Greenwood Press, 1986.

Coles, Roswell S. "Some Effects of Physical Geography on the Culture of Staten Island." *Staten Island Historian*, 1st series, 5 (1942): 6–7, 14.

Conner, Oscar T. *The Genealogy of the Descendants of Richard Conner, Born in Ireland in 1723.* Ridgewood, N.J.: Published by the author, 1987.

Conway, Stephen. "'The Great Mischief Complain'd Of': Reflections on the Misconduct of British Soldiers in the Revolutionary War." *William and Mary Quarterly*, 3rd series, 47 (1990), 370–390.

Cortelyou, John Van Zandt. *The Cortelyou Genealogy: A Record of Jaques Corteljou and Many of His Descendants.* Lincoln, Neb.: Press of Brown Printing Service, 1942.

Corwin, Edward T. *A Manual of the Reformed Church in America: 1628– 1902.* New York: Board of Publication of the Reformed Church in America, 1902.

Countryman, Edward. *A People in Revolution: The American Revolution and Political Society in New York, 1760–1790.* Baltimore: Johns Hopkins University Press, 1981.

Cross, Arthur L. *The Anglican Episcopate and the American Colonies.* Cambridge, Mass.: Harvard University Press, 1902.

Dandridge, Danske, ed. *Historic Shepherdstown.* Charlottesville: University Press of Virginia, 1910.

Davis, William T. *The Conference/Billopp House.* Staten Island, N.Y.: Staten Island Historical Society, 1926.

Decker, Malcolm. *Brink of Revolution: New York in Crisis, 1765–1776.* New York: Argosy Antiquarian LTD., 1964.

De Jong, Gerald F. *The Dutch Reformed Church in the American Colonies.* Grand Rapids, Mich.: Eerdmans, 1978.

De Mond, Robert O. *The Loyalists of North Carolina during the Revolution.* Durham, N.C.: Duke University Press, 1940.

Derry, Ellis L. *Old and Historic Churches of New Jersey.* 2 vols. Medford, N.J.: Plexus Publishing, 1994.

Dix, Morgan. *A History of the Parish of Trinity Church in the City of New York.* 2 vols. New York: Putnam, 1898–1901.

Dongan, Thomas P. *John Dongan of Dublin: An Elizabethan Gentleman and His Family.* Baltimore: Gateway Press, 1996.

Dornfest, Walter T. "Sullivan's Raid on Staten Island, August 22, 1777." *Staten Island Historian*, 1st series, 31 (1972): 97–102.

Dubeau, Sharon. *New Brunswick Loyalists: A Bicentennial Tribute.* Agincourt, Ontario: Generation Press, 1983.

Dubois, Theodora, and Dorothy Valentine Smith. *Staten Island Patroons.* Staten Island, N.Y.: Staten Island Historical Society, 1961.

East, Robert A., and Jacob Judd, eds. *The Loyalist Americans: A Focus on Greater New York.* Tarrytown, N.Y.: Sleepy Hollow Restorations, 1975.

Edgar, Walter. *Partisans and Redcoats: The Southern Conflict That Turned the Tide of the American Revolution.* New York: Morrow, 2001.

Fabend, Firth H. *Zion on the Hudson: Dutch New York and New Jersey in the Age of Revivals.* New Brunswick, N.J.: Rutgers University Press, 2000.

Fellows, Robert. "The Loyalists and Land Settlement in New Brunswick, 1783–90." *Canadian Archivist* 2 (1971): 5–15.

Fenn, Elizabeth A. *Pox Americana: The Great Smallpox Epidemic of 1775–82.* New York: Hill & Wang, 2001.

Ferling, John. *The First of Men: A Life of George Washington.* Knoxville: University of Tennessee Press, 1988.

———. *Setting the World Ablaze: Washington, Adams, Jefferson, and the American Revolution.* New York: Oxford University Press, 2000.

——— ed. *The World Turned Upside Down: The American Victory in the War of Independence.* Westport, Conn.: Greenwood Press, 1988.

Fingerhut, Eugene R. "Uses and Abuses of the American Loyalists' Claims: A Critique of Quantitative Analyses." *William and Mary Quarterly*, 3rd series, 25 (1968): 245–258.

Fischer, David Hackett. *Albion's Seed: Four British Folkways in America.* New York: Oxford University Press, 1989.

———. *Washington's Crossing.* New York: Oxford University Press, 2004.

Fishburn, Janet. "Gilbert Tennent, Established Dissenter." *Church History* 63 (1994): 31–49.

Fleming, Thomas. *The Battle of Springfield.* Trenton: New Jersey Historical Commission, 1975.

———. *1776: Year of Illusions.* New York: Norton, 1975.

Flexner, James Thomas. *States Dyckman: American Loyalist.* Boston: Little, Brown, 1980.

Flick, Alexander C. *Loyalism in New York during the American Revolution.* 1901. Reprint, New York: AMS Press, 1970.

———, ed. *The American Revolution in New York: Its Political, Social, and Economic Significance.* Albany: New York State Department of Education, Division of Archives and History, 1926.

Foner, Philip. *Labor and the American Revolution.* Westport, Conn.: Greenwood Press, 1976.

Foote, Thelma Wills. *Black and White Manhattan: The History of Racial Formation in Colonial New York City.* New York: Oxford University Press, 2004.

Frey, Sylvia R. *The British Soldier in America: A Social History of Military Life in the Revolutionary Period.* Austin: University of Texas Press, 1981.

Gallagher, John J. *The Battle of Brooklyn, 1776.* New York: Da Capo Press, 1995.

Gerlach, Larry R. *Prologue to Independence: New Jersey in the Coming of the American Revolution.* New Brunswick, N.J.: Rutgers University Press, 1976.

Gilje, Paul A. *The Road to Mobocracy: Popular Disorder in New York City, 1763–1834.* Chapel Hill: University of North Carolina Press, 1987.

Gould, Eliga H., and Peter S. Onuf, eds. *Empire and Nation: The American Revolution in the Atlantic World.* Baltimore: Johns Hopkins University Press, 2005.

Gruber, Ira D. *The Howe Brothers and the American Revolution.* New York: Atheneum, 1972.

———. "Lord Howe and Lord George Germain: British Politics and the Winning of American Independence." *William and Mary Quarterly,* 3rd series, 22 (1965): 225–243.

Gunderson, Joan R. *To Be Useful to the World: Women in Revolutionary America, 1740–1790.* New York: Twayne, 1996.

Hageman, Howard G. "Colonial New Jersey's First Domine: Part I." *De Halve Maen* 43 (1969): 9–10.

———. "Colonial New Jersey's First Domine: Part II." *De Halve Maen* 44 (1970): 17–18.

Hall, Timothy D. *Contested Boundaries: Itinerancy and the Reshaping of the Colonial American Religious World.* Durham, N.C.: Duke University Press, 1994.

Hammond, Otis G. *The Tories of New Hampshire.* Concord: New Hampshire Historical Society, 1917.

Hancock, Harold B. *The Delaware Loyalists.* 1940. Reprint, Boston: Gregg Press, 1972.

———. *The Loyalists of Revolutionary Delaware.* Newark: University of Delaware Press, 1977.

Harmelink, Herman III. "Another Look at Frelinghuysen and His 'Awakening.'" *Church History* 37 (1968): 423–438.

Harrell, Isaac S. *Loyalism in Virginia.* Durham, N.C.: Duke University Press, 1926.

Harrington, Virginia D. *The New York Merchant on the Eve of the Revolution.* New York: Columbia University Press, 1935.

Hast, Adele. *Loyalism in Revolutionary Virginia: The Norfolk Area and the Eastern Shore.* Ann Arbor: UMich. Research Press, 1982.

Hatfield, Reverend Edwin F. *History of Elizabeth, New Jersey: Including the Early History of Union County.* New York: Carlton and Lanahan, 1868.

Hawke, David Freeman. *Everyday Life in Early America.* New York: Harper & Row, 1988.

Hibbert, Christopher. *Redcoats and Rebels: The American Revolution through British Eyes*. New York: Norton, 1990.

Higginbotham, Don. *The War of American Independence: Military Attitudes, Policies, and Practice, 1763–1789*. 1971. Reprint, Boston: Northeastern University Press, 1981.

————, ed. *Reconsiderations on the Revolutionary War: Selected Essays*. Westport, Conn.: Greenwood Press, 1978.

————, ed. *War and Society in Revolutionary America*. Columbia: University of South Carolina Press, 1988.

Hix, Charlotte M. *The Crocheron Family of Staten Island, New York*. Garden City, N.Y.: Published by the author, 1979.

Hodges, Graham Russell. *Root and Branch: African Americans in New York and East Jersey, 1613–1863*. Chapel Hill: University of North Carolina Press, 1999.

————. *Slavery and Freedom in the Rural North: African Americans in Monmouth County, New Jersey, 1665–1865*. Madison, Wis.: Madison House, 1997.

————, ed. *The Black Loyalist Directory: African Americans in Exile after the American Revolution*. New York: Garland, 1996.

Hoffman, Ronald, Thad W. Tate, and Peter J. Albert, eds. *An Uncivil War: The Southern Backcountry during the American Revolution*. Charlottesville: University Press of Virginia, 1985.

Horne, Field. *The Conference House Revisited: A History of the Billopp Manor House*. Staten Island, N.Y.: Conference House Association, 1990.

————. *A Social-Historical Context of the Voorlezer's House at Richmond Town, Staten Island, New York: A Guide for Interpretation*. Saratoga Springs, N.Y.: Public History and Museum Services, 1986.

Jackson, Kenneth T., ed. *The Encyclopedia of New York City*. New Haven, Conn.: Yale University Press, 1995.

Jackson, Ronald D. "The Freedom Seekers: Staten Island's Runaway Slaves." *Staten Island Historian*, 2nd series, 14 (1996): 1–12, 16.

Jacobsen, Douglas G. *Unprov'd Experiment: Religious Pluralism in Colonial New Jersey*. Brooklyn, N.Y.: Carlson Publishers, 1991.

Jameson, J. Franklin. *The American Revolution Considered as a Social Movement*. Princeton, N.J.: Princeton University Press, 1926.

Johnson, Marjorie. *Christopher Billopp Family Genealogy: Captain Christopher Billopp (1631–1725) and His Descendants and the Allied Farmar Family*. Staten Island, N.Y.: Conference House Association, 1991.

Johnston, Henry P. *The Campaign of 1776 around New York and Brooklyn*. 1878. Reprint, New York: Da Capo Press, 1971.

Judd, Jacob, and Irwin H. Polishook, eds. *Aspects of Early New York Society and Politics*. Tarrytown, N.Y.: Sleepy Hollow Restorations, 1974.

Kammen, Michael. *Colonial New York: A History*. New York: Oxford University Press, 1975.

Keesey, Ruth M. "Loyalism in Bergen County, New Jersey." *William and Mary Quarterly*, 3rd series, 18 (1961): 558–576.

Kemp, William Webb. *The Support of Schools in Colonial New York by the Society for the Propagation of the Gospel in Foreign Parts*. New York: Columbia University Press, 1913.

Ketchum, Richard M. *Divided Loyalties: How the American Revolution Came to New York*. New York: Henry Holt, 2002.

Kim, Sung Bok. *Landlord and Tenant in Colonial New York: Manorial Society, 1664–1775*. Chapel Hill: University of North Carolina Press, 1978.

Kingdom, Robert M. "Why Did the Huguenot Refugees in the American Colonies Become Episcopalian?" *Historical Magazine of the Protestant Episcopal Church* 49 (1980): 317–335.

Klein, Milton M. "An Experiment That Failed: General James Robertson and Civil Government in British New York, 1779–1783." *New York History* 61 (1980): 229–254.

Kollmer, Burton A. "The Yesterday of the Oysterman." *Staten Island Historian*, 1st series, 3 (1940): 17, 19–24.

Kulikoff, Allan. *The Agrarian Origins of American Capitalism*. Charlottesville: University Press of Virginia, 1992.

———. "The Transition to Capitalism in Rural America." *William and Mary Quarterly*, 3rd series, 46 (1989): 120–144.

Kurtz, Stephen G., and James H. Hutson, eds. *Essays on the American Revolution*. New York: Norton, 1973.

Kwasny, Mark V. *Washington's Partisan War, 1775–1783*. Kent, Ohio: Kent State University Press, 1996.

Labaree, Leonard W. *Conservatism in Early American History*. New York: New York University Press, 1948.

Lambert, Frank. *The Founding Fathers and the Place of Religion in America*. Princeton, N.J.: Princeton University Press, 2003.

———. *Inventing the "Great Awakening."* Princeton, N.J.: Princeton University Press, 1999.

Lambert, Robert S. *South Carolina Loyalists in the American Revolution*. Columbia: University of South Carolina Press, 1987.

Landsman, Ned C. *From Colonials to Provincials: American Thought and Culture, 1680–1760*. Ithaca, N.Y.: Cornell University Press, 1997.

Lawrence, Joseph W. *The Judges of New Brunswick and Their Times*. Edited by Alfred A. Stockton. Saint John, New Brunswick: Acadiensis, 1907.

Lee, Francis B. *New Jersey: As a Colony and as a State*. 5 vols. New York: Publishing Society of New Jersey, 1902.

Lefkowitz, Arthur S. *The Long Retreat: The Calamitous American Defense of New Jersey, 1776*. New Brunswick, N.J.: Rutgers University Press, 1998.

Leiby, Adrian C. "The Coetus-Conferentie Controversy: Part I—Events up to the Time the Conferentie Was Formed, 1755." *De Halve Maen* 38 (1963): 11–13.

———. "The Coetus-Conferentie Controversy: Part II—The Conferentie Faction Is Overthrown, 1771." *De Halve Maen* 39 (1964): 13–14.

———. *The Revolutionary War in the Hackensack Valley: The Jersey Dutch and the Neutral Ground*. New Brunswick, N.J.: Rutgers University Press, 1992.

Leng, Charles W., and William T. Davis. *Staten Island and Its People: A History, 1609–1929*. 3 vols. New York: Lewis Historical Publishing, 1930.

Levitt, James H. *For Want of Trade: Shipping and the New Jersey Ports, 1680–1783*. Newark: New Jersey Historical Society, 1981.

Lundin, Leonard. *Cockpit of the Revolution: The War for Independence in New Jersey*. Princeton, N.J.: Princeton University Press, 1940.

Lydon, James A. "New York and the Slave Trade, 1700 to 1774." *William and Mary Quarterly*, 3rd series, 35 (1978): 375–394.

Lynd, Staughton. *Anti-Federalism in Dutchess County, New York: A Study of Democracy and Class Conflict in the Revolutionary Era*. Chicago: Loyola University Press, 1962.

———. "Who Shall Rule at Home? Dutchess County, New York, in the American Revolution." *William and Mary Quarterly*, 3rd series, 18 (1961): 330–359.

Mackenzie, Clyde L. *The Fisheries of the Raritan Bay*. New Brunswick, N.J.: Rutgers University Press, 1992.

Mackesy, Piers. *The War for America, 1775–1783*. 1964. Reprint, Lincoln: University of Nebraska Press, Bison Books, 1993.

Mackinnon, Neil. *This Unfriendly Soil: The Loyalist Experience in Nova Scotia, 1783–1791*. Kingston, Ont.: McGill–Queen's University Press, 1986.

Maier, Pauline. *From Resistance to Revolution: Colonial Radicals and the Development of American Opposition to Britain, 1765–1776*. New York: Norton, 1972.

Main, Jackson Turner. *The Social Structure of Revolutionary America*. Princeton, N.J.: Princeton University Press, 1965.

Marston, Jerrilyn G. *King and Congress: The Transfer of Political Legitimacy, 1774–1776*. Princeton, N.J.: Princeton University Press, 1987.

Mason, Bernard. *The Road to Independence: The Revolutionary Movement in New York, 1773–1777*. Lexington: University of Kentucky Press, 1966.

Mason, Keith. "Localism, Evangelicalism, and Loyalism: The Sources of Discontent in the Revolutionary Chesapeake." *Journal of Southern History* 56 (1990): 23–54.

Matson, Cathy. *Merchants and Empire: Trading in Colonial New York*. Baltimore: Johns Hopkins University Press, 1998.

Maxson, Charles H. *The Great Awakening in the Middle Colonies*. Chicago: University of Chicago Press, 1920.

McCaughey, Elizabeth P. *From Loyalist to Founding Father: The Political Odyssey of William Samuel Johnson*. New York: Columbia University Press, 1980.

McCay, Bonnie J. "The Pirates of Piscary: Ethnohistory of Illegal Fishing in New Jersey." *Ethnohistory* 31 (1984): 17–37.

McCormick, Richard P. *New Jersey: From Colony to State, 1609–1789*. Newark: New Jersey Historical Society, 1981.

McCullough, David. *John Adams*. New York: Simon & Schuster, 2001.

———. *1776*. New York: Simon & Schuster, 2005.

McDonald, Forrest. *Alexander Hamilton: A Biography*. New York: Norton, 1979.

McGinn, William E. "John Palmer, Thomas Dongan, and the Manor of Cassiltowne." *Staten Island Historian*, 1st series, 29 (1968): 9–13.

McManus, Edgar J. *A History of Negro Slavery in New York*. Syracuse, N.Y.: Syracuse University Press, 1966.

McMillen, Harlow. "Green, and Red, and a Little Blue: The Story of Staten Island in the American Revolution." *Staten Island Historian*, 1st series, 32–33 (1975–1977).

———. *A History of Staten Island, New York, during the American Revolution*. Staten Island, N.Y.: Staten Island Historical Society, 1976.

———. "Richmondtown Prior to 1837—Innkeepers and Merchants, Part I." *Staten Island Historian*, 1st series, 24 (1963): 12–15.

———. "Richmondtown Prior to 1837—Innkeepers and Merchants, Part II." *Staten Island Historian*, 1st series, 25 (1964): 20–23.

———. "Richmondtown: The First 160 Years, Part II: Richmondtown as the County Seat, 1782–1837." *Staten Island Historian*, 1st series, 22 (1961): 13–14.

———. "Richmondtown: The First 160 Years, Part V: The Church of St. Andrew." *Staten Island Historian*, 1st series, 22 (1961): 25–28.

———. "Richmondtown: The First 160 Years, Part VI: The Residents of Richmondtown—The Tradesmen." *Staten Island Historian*, 1st series, 23 (1962): 1–3.

———. "Richmondtown: The First 160 Years, Part VII: The Residents of Richmondtown—The Millers." *Staten Island Historian*, 1st series, 23 (1962): 14–16.

McMillen, Loring. "The Broome Family." *Chronicles of Staten Island* 1 (1990–1991): 194–195, 199–200.

———. "Captain Alexander McDonald: Part I." *Chronicles of Staten Island* 1 (1986): 45–48.

_____. "Captain Alexander McDonald: Part II." *Chronicles of Staten Island* 1 (1986–1987): 49–51.

_____. "David Pietersz de Vries and the First Settlement of Staten Island." *Staten Island Historian*, 1st series, 2 (1939): 25–27.

_____. "Dongan's Mills." *Staten Island Historian*, 1st series, 1 (1938): 25–27, 31.

_____. "The First Presbyterian Church of Staten Island, 1717–1776–1808: Part I." *Chronicles of Staten Island* 1 (1985): 1–7.

_____. "The First Presbyterian Church of Staten Island, 1717–1776–1808: Part II." *Chronicles of Staten Island* 1 (1985–1986): 9, 14–15.

_____. "An Island Saga: The Mersereau Family, Part 1." *Chronicles of Staten Island* 1 (1989): 150–153.

_____. "An Island Saga: The Mersereau Family, Part 2." *Chronicles of Staten Island* 1 (1989–1990): 154, 156–159.

_____. "An Island Saga: The Mersereau Family, Part 3." *Chronicles of Staten Island* 1 (1990): 168–172.

_____. "An Island Saga: The Mersereau Family, Part 4." *Chronicles of Staten Island* 1 (1990): 184–185.

_____. "An Island Saga: The Mersereau Family, Part 5." *Chronicles of Staten Island* 1 (1990–1991): 201–202.

_____. "Old Mills of Staten Island." *Staten Island Historian*, 1st series, 10 (1949): 1–4, 9, 15–16.

_____. "The Voorlezer." *Staten Island Historian*, 1st series, 8 (1946): 17–19, 22.

Merritt, Bruce G. "Loyalism and Social Conflict in Revolutionary Deerfield, Massachusetts." *Journal of American History* 57 (1970): 277–289.

Mettam, Louis. "Louis XIV and the Huguenots." *History Today* 35 (1985): 15–21.

Middlekauff, Robert. *The Glorious Cause: The American Revolution, 1763–1789*. New York: Oxford University Press, 1982.

Monaghan, Charles. *The Murrays of Murray Hill*. Brooklyn, N.Y.: Urban Press, 1998.

Moore, Christopher. *The Loyalists: Revolution, Exile, Settlement*. Toronto: Mc-Clelland and Stewart, 1984.

Morris, Ira K. *Morris's Memorial History of Staten Island, New York*. 2 vols. New York: Memorial Publishing, 1898–1900.

Nadelhaft, Jerome J. *The Disorders of War: The Revolution in South Carolina*. Orono: University of Maine at Orono Press, 1981.

Nash, Gary B. *The Unknown American Revolution: The Unruly Birth of Democracy and the Struggle to Create America*. New York: Viking, 2005.

_____. *The Urban Crucible: The Northern Seaports and the Origins of the American Revolution*. Cambridge, Mass.: Harvard University Press, 1979.

Nelson, Paul D. *William Alexander, Lord Stirling.* Tuscaloosa: University of Alabama Press, 1987.

_____. *William Tryon and the Course of Empire: A Life in British Imperial Service.* Chapel Hill: University of North Carolina Press, 1990.

Nelson, William H. *The American Tory.* Boston: Beacon Press, 1968.

Norton, Mary Beth. *The British Americans: The Loyalist Exiles in England, 1774–1789.* Boston: Little, Brown, 1972.

_____. "The Fate of Some Black Loyalists of the American Revolution." *Journal of Negro History* 58 (1973): 402–426.

_____. *Liberty's Daughters: The Revolutionary Experience of American Women, 1750–1800.* New York: HarperCollins, 1980.

O' Hallaran, John D. "The Patroons of Pavonia and Staten Island." *Staten Island Historian,* 1st series, 14 (1952): 11–12.

Osterhaven, M. Eugene. "The Experimental Theology of Early Dutch Calvinism." *Reformed Review* 27 (1974): 186–192.

Ousterhut, Anne M. *A State Divided: Opposition in Pennsylvania to the American Revolution.* Westport, Conn.: Greenwood Press, 1987.

Palmer, Gregory, ed. *Biographical Sketches of Loyalists of the American Revolution.* Westport, Conn.: Meckler Publishing, 1984.

Pancake, John S. *1777: The Year of the Hangman.* Tuscaloosa: University of Alabama Press, 1977.

_____. *This Destructive War: The British Campaign in the Carolinas, 1780–1782.* Tuscaloosa: University of Alabama Press, 1985.

Pascoe, C. F. *Two Hundred Years of the SPG: A Historical Account of the SPG, 1701–1900.* 2 vols. London: Published by the Society, 1901.

Pomfret, John E. *Colonial New Jersey: A History.* New York: Scribner, 1973.

_____. *The Province of East New Jersey, 1609–1702: The Rebellious Proprietary.* Princeton, N.J.: Princeton University Press, 1962.

Potter, Janice. *The Liberty We Seek: Loyalist Ideology in Colonial New York and Massachusetts.* Cambridge, Mass.: Harvard University Press, 1983.

Pulis, John W., ed. *Moving On: Black Loyalists in the Afro-Atlantic World.* New York: Garland, 1999.

Quarles, Benjamin. *The Negro in the American Revolution.* Chapel Hill: University of North Carolina Press, 1961.

Randall, Willard S. *George Washington: A Life.* New York: Henry Holt, 1997.

Ranlet, Philip. *The New York Loyalists.* Knoxville: University of Tennessee Press, 1986.

Raphael, Ray. *A People's History of the American Revolution: How Common People Shaped the Fight for Independence.* New York: HarperCollins, 2002.

Reed, Herbert B. "The Early Staten Island Roads." *Staten Island Historian,* 1st series, 26 (1965): 17–21.

_____. "The Old Ridgway House." *Staten Island Historian*, 1st series, 25 (1964): 5–6.

Rhoden, Nancy L. *Revolutionary Anglicanism: The Colonial Church of England during the American Revolution*. New York: New York University Press, 1999.

Rose, Alexander. *Washington's Spies: The Story of America's First Spy Ring*. New York: Bantam, 2006.

Rosenfeld, Michael, and Charles La Cerra, eds. *Community, Continuity, and Change: New Perspectives on Staten Island History*. New York: Pace University Press, 1999.

Rosenwaike, Ira. *Population History of New York City*. Syracuse, N.Y.: Syracuse University Press, 1972.

Royster, Charles. *A Revolutionary People at War: The Continental Army and American Character, 1775–1783*. Chapel Hill: University of North Carolina Press, 1979.

Ryan, Dennis P. *New Jersey's Loyalists*. Trenton: New Jersey Historical Commission, 1975.

Sabine, Lorenzo. *Biographical Sketches of Loyalists of the American Revolution with an Historical Essay*. 2 vols. Boston: Little, Brown, 1864.

Sachs, Charles L. *Made on Staten Island: Agriculture, Industry, and Suburban Living in the City*. Staten Island, N.Y.: Staten Island Historical Society, 1988.

_____. "Treasure Chest of Family History." *Seaport* (1992): 48–49.

Sachs, William S., and Ari Hoogenboom. *The Enterprising Colonials: Society on the Eve of the Revolution*. Chicago: Argonaut, 1965.

Schecter, Barnet. *The Battle for New York: The City at the Heart of the American Revolution*. New York: Walker, 2002.

Schimizzi, Ernest, and Gregory Schimizzi. *The Staten Island Peace Conference: September 11, 1776*. Albany: New York State American Revolution Bicentennial Commission, 1976.

Schlesinger, Arthur M. *The Colonial Merchants and the American Revolution, 1763–1776*. New York: Frederick Unger, 1957.

Schrag, F. J. "Theodorus Jacobus Frelinghuysen, The Father of American Pietism." *Church History* 14 (1945): 201–216.

Scott, Kenneth. "The Colonial Ferries of Staten Island." *Proceedings of the Staten Island Institute of Arts and Sciences* 14 (1951): 45–68.

_____. "The Colonial Ferries of Staten Island: Part II." *Proceedings of the Staten Island Institute of Arts and Sciences* 15 (1952): 9–31.

_____. "Cutting of Staten Island Forests during the Revolution." *Proceedings of the Staten Island Institute of Arts and Sciences* 17 (1955): 8–13.

Seaman, Mary T. *The Seaman Family in America as Descended from Captain John Seaman of Hempstead, Long Island*. New York: T. A. Wright, 1928.

Shammas, Carole. *The Pre-Industrial Consumer in England and America.* New York: Oxford University Press, 1990.

Shy, John. *A People Numerous and Armed: Reflections on the Military Struggle for American Independence.* Ann Arbor: University of Michigan Press, 1990.

————. *Toward Lexington: The Role of the British Army in the Coming of the American Revolution.* Princeton, N.J.: Princeton University Press, 1965.

Smith, Dorothy Valentine. *Staten Island: Gateway to New York.* Philadelphia: Chilton Book Company, 1970.

Smith, Paul H. "The American Loyalists: Notes on Their Organization and Numerical Strength." *William and Mary Quarterly*, 3rd series, 25 (1968): 259–277.

————. *Loyalists and Redcoats: A Study in British Revolutionary Policy.* New York: Norton, 1964.

Spencer-Wood, Suzanne M., ed. *Consumer Choice in Historical Archaeology.* New York: Plenum Press, 1987.

Sprague, William B. *Annals of the American Reformed Dutch Pulpit; Or Commemorative Notices of Distinguished Clergymen of That Denomination in the United States from Its Commencement to the Close of the Year Eighteen Hundred and Fifty-five.* New York: Carter, 1869.

St. G. Walker, James W. *The Black Loyalists: The Search for a Promised Land in Nova Scotia and Sierra Leone, 1783–1870.* New York: Africana Publishing, 1976.

Stark, James H. *The Loyalists of Massachusetts and the Other Side of the American Revolution.* Boston: W. B. Clarke, 1907.

Steinmeyer, Henry G. *Staten Island: 1524–1898.* Staten Island, N.Y.: Staten Island Historical Society, 1950.

————. *Staten Island under British Rule, 1776–1783.* Staten Island, N.Y.: Staten Island Historical Society, 1949.

Stocker, Harry E. *A History of the Moravian Church in New York City.* New York: Published by the author, 1922.

Stout, Harry S. *The Divine Dramatist: George Whitefield and the Rise of Modern Evangelicism.* Grand Rapids, Mich.: Eerdmans, 1991.

Syrett, David. *The Royal Navy in American Waters, 1775–1783.* Brookfield, Vt.: Gower, 1989.

Tanis, James. *Dutch Calvinistic Pietism in the Middle Colonies: A Study of the Life and Theology of Theodorus Jacobus Frelinghuysen.* The Hague: Nijhoff, 1967.

————. "The Dutch Reformed Church and the American Revolution: Part I." *De Halve Maen* 52 (summer 1977): 1–2, 15.

————. "The Dutch Reformed Church and the American Revolution: Part II." *De Halve Maen* 52 (fall 1977): 1–2, 12–13, 19.

Taylor, Paul B. *John Belleville, the Huguenot, His Descendants.* Kettering, Ohio: Belleville Family Association, 1973.

*Tercentenary Studies, 1928: Reformed Church in America, A Record of Beginnings.* Compiled by the Tercentenary Committee on Research and Publication. New York: Published by the church, 1928.

Thayer, Theodore. *As We Were: The Story of Old Elizabethtown.* Elizabeth, N.J.: Grassmann, 1964.

———. *Colonial and Revolutionary Morris County.* Morristown, N.J.: Morris County Heritage Commission, 1975.

———. "The War in New Jersey: Battles, Alarums and Men of the Revolution." *Proceedings of the New Jersey Historical Society* 71 (1953): 83–110.

Tiedemann, Joseph S. "Communities in the Midst of the American Revolution: Queen's County, New York, 1774–1775." *Journal of Social History* 18 (1984): 57–78.

———. "Patriots by Default: Queen's County, New York, and the British Army, 1776–1783." *William and Mary Quarterly,* 3rd series, 43 (1986): 35–63.

———. *Reluctant Revolutionaries: New York City and the Road to Independence, 1763–1776.* Ithaca, N.Y.: Cornell University Press, 1997.

———. "A Revolution Foiled: Queens County, New York, 1775–1776." *Journal of American History* 75 (1988): 417–444.

Tillson, Albert H. Jr. "The Localist Roots of Backcountry Loyalism: An Examination of Popular Political Culture in Virginia's New River Valley." *Journal of Southern History* 54 (1988): 387–404.

Tyerman, Luke. *The Life of the Reverend George Whitefield, B.A., of Pembroke College, Oxford.* 2 vols. New York: Anson D. F. Randolph, 1877.

Tyler, Moses C. "The Party of the Loyalists in the American Revolution." *American Historical Review* 1 (1895): 24–45.

Upton, Leslie F. S. *The Loyal-Whig: William Smith of New York and Quebec.* Toronto: University of Toronto Press, 1969.

Valentine, Alan. *Lord Stirling.* New York: Oxford University Press, 1969.

Van Buskirk, Judith L. *Generous Enemies: Patriots and Loyalists in Revolutionary New York.* Philadelphia: University of Pennsylvania Press, 2002.

Vander Naald, Cornelius. "History of the Reformed Church on Staten Island." *Staten Island Historian,* 1st series, 16 (1955): 1–5.

Van Tuyl, R. L., and Jan N. A. Groenendijk. *A Van Tuyl Chronicle: 650 Years in the History of a Dutch-American Family.* Decorah, Ia.: Anundsen Publishing, 1996.

Van Tyne, Claude H. *The Loyalists in the American Revolution.* New York: Macmillan, 1902.

Van Winkle, Daniel. *Old Bergen: History and Reminiscences.* Jersey City, N.J.: J. W. Harrison, 1902.

Venables, Robert W. "A Historical Overview of Staten Island's Trade Networks." *Proceedings of the Staten Island Institute of Arts and Sciences* 34 (1989): 1–24.

Wagman, Morton. "Staten Island Roots: The Dutch Heritage." *Staten Island Historian*, 2nd series, 3 (1985): 10–12.

Waldman, John. *Heartbeats in the Muck: A Dramatic Look at the History, Sea Life, and Environment of New York Harbor.* New York: Lyons Press, 1999.

Ward, Christopher. *The War of the Revolution.* Edited by John R. Alden. 2 vols. New York: Macmillan, 1952.

Ward, Harry M. *Between the Lines: Banditti of the American Revolution.* Westport, Conn.: Praeger, 2002.

Warren, Mercy Otis. *The History of the Rise, Progress, and Termination of the American Revolution.* 2 vols. Boston: Manning and Loring, 1805.

Weintraub, Stanley. *Iron Tears: America's Battle for Independence, Britain's Quagmire: 1775–1783.* New York: Free Press, 2005.

Weis, Frederick L. *The Colonial Clergy of the Middle Colonies: New York, New Jersey, and Pennsylvania, 1628–1776.* Worcester, Mass.: American Antiquarian Society, 1957.

Wells, Robert V. *The Population of the British Colonies in America before 1776: A Survey of Census Data.* Princeton, N.J.: Princeton University Press, 1975.

Whitehead, William A. *Contributions to the Early History of Perth Amboy and Adjoining Country.* New York: D. Appleton, 1856.

Whittemore, Charles P. *A General of the Revolution: John Sullivan of New Hampshire.* New York: Columbia University Press, 1961.

Wood, Gordon S. *The Radicalism of the American Revolution.* New York: Knopf, 1992.

Wright, Esmond, ed. *Red, White, and True Blue: The Loyalists in the Revolution.* New York: AMS Press, 1976.

Wright, Esther C. *The Loyalists of New Brunswick.* 5th ed. Yarmouth, Nova Scotia: Sentinel Printing, Ltd., 1985.

Yoshpe, Harry B. *The Disposition of Loyalist Estates in the Southern District of the State of New York.* 1939. Reprint, New York: AMS Press, 1967.

Young, Alfred F., ed. *The American Revolution: Explorations in the History of American Radicalism.* DeKalb: Northern Illinois University Press, 1976.

Zeichner, Oscar. "The Loyalist Problem in New York after the Revolution." *New York History* 21 (1940): 284–302.

DOCTORAL DISSERTATIONS

Ashton, Rick J. "The Loyalist Experience: New York, 1763–1789." PhD diss., Northwestern University, 1973.

Barnwell, Robert W. "Loyalism in South Carolina, 1765–1785." PhD diss., Duke University, 1941.

Baugher-Perlin, Sherene. "The Prall Site: A Case Study in Historical Archaeology." PhD diss., State University of New York at Stony Brook, 1978.

Bernstein, David A. "New Jersey in the American Revolution: The Establishment of a Government amid Civil and Military Disorder, 1770–1781." PhD diss., Rutgers University, 1970.

Howard, Ronald W. "Education and Ethnicity in Colonial New York, 1664–1763: A Study in the Transmission of Culture in Early America." PhD diss., University of Tennessee, 1978.

Jordan, Jean P. "The Anglican Establishment in Colonial New York, 1693–1783." PhD diss., Columbia University, 1971.

Kruger, Vivienne L. "Born to Run: The Slave Family in Early New York, 1626 to 1827." PhD diss., Columbia University, 1985.

Lender, Mark E. "The Enlisted Line: The Continental Soldiers of New Jersey." PhD diss., Rutgers University, 1975.

Lodge, Martin E. "The Great Awakening in the Middle Colonies." PhD diss., University of California, Berkeley, 1964.

Tiedemann, Joseph S. "Response to Revolution: Queens County, New York, during the Era of the American Revolution." PhD diss., City University of New York, 1977.

# Index

Adams, John, 16nh, 82, 141n4
African Americans: in British military,
   72–74, 77, 97, 139n67; population
   of, on Staten Island, 109, *111–12*,
   149n121; slaves, 14, 19, 72–74,
   77, 83
Alexander, William (Lord Stirling),
   49; correspondence with Tucker,
   51; correspondence with Washington, 54; New York City and,
   48–51, 53–57, 59; promotion to
   brigadier general, 130n27; as replacement for Lee, C., 48–50;
   Staten Island attack by, 89–90, 96;
   Thompson as replacement for, 54
Alsop, John, 27, 127n64
American Revolution: Billopp, C.,
   after, 108, 109, 148n118; challenges of, 7; as civil war, 2, 5, 7,
   81; effects of, 2; military lines
   crossed during, 101–2; revisionist
   historiography of Loyalism and, 2;
   Seaman after, 109, 149n118
*The American Tory* (Nelson), 3–4
Amherst, Sir Jeffrey, 65, 94
Anglican culture hearth, 2, 6
Anglicanism: American bishop appointment and, 23, 121n56; dissenters to, 21–26; Ministry Act of
   1693 and, 118n28; politics and,
   23–26, 109; on Staten Island, 2, 6,

7–8, 19–26, 109. *See also* St. An-
   drew's parish
Anne, Queen (of England), 19
Arnold, Benedict, 58
Arnold, Jonathan, 22–23
Arthur Kill (Staten Island Sound), 9,
   11–12
Artisans, absence of, 14, 26
Ashton, Rick J., 5
*Asia* (British warship), 36–38, 60, 73
Association for Retaliation, 97–98
Awakeners, 21–24

Bailyn, Bernard, 4
Ball, Stephen, 95, 144n52
Bancker, Abraham, 67, 70, 106, 109
Bancker, Adrian, 39, 46, 69–70, 70nb,
   109
Baptists, 23
Barnes, George, 34
Barnet, Ichabod, 29, 123n10
Battery Park, 34na
Battles: of Bunker Hill, 51, 53, 65; of
   Long Island, 82, 94, 141n3; of
   Monmouth, 97
Becker, Carl L., 2
Bedell, John, 84
Bentley Manor, 13, 16, 16nh, *17*, 82,
   84, 116n15, 141n4
Bergen Point, 14
*Beulah* (merchant ship), 29

# About the Author

Phillip Papas is a native Staten Islander. He received his BA and MA degrees in history from Hunter College (CUNY) and his PhD in history from the City University of New York Graduate Center. He is currently an assistant professor of history at Union County College in Cranford, New Jersey.